Annual Editions:
Criminal Justice
38/e

Edited by Joanne Naughton

http://create.mcgraw-hill.com

ISBN-10: 1259171396   ISBN-13: 9781259171390

Contents

Preface

In publishing ANNUAL EDITIONS we recognize the enormous role played by the magazines, newspapers, and journals of the public press in providing current, first-rate educational information in a broad spectrum of interest areas. Many of these articles are appropriate for students, researchers, and professionals seeking accurate, current material to help bridge the gap between principles and theories and the real world. These articles, however, become more useful for study when those of lasting value are carefully collected, organized, indexed, and reproduced in a low-cost format, which provides easy and permanent access when the material is needed. That is the role played by ANNUAL EDITIONS.

During the 1970s, Criminal Justice emerged as an appealing, vital, and unique academic discipline. It emphasizes the professional development of students who plan careers in the field, and attracts those who want to know more about a complex social problem and how this country deals with it. Criminal Justice incorporates a vast range of knowledge from a number of specialties, including law, history, and the behavioral and social sciences. Each specialty contributes to our fuller understanding of criminal behavior and of society's attitudes toward deviance.

In view of the fact that the criminal justice system is in a constant state of flux, and because the study of criminal justice covers such a broad spectrum, today's students must be aware of a variety of subjects and topics. Standard textbooks and traditional anthologies cannot keep pace with the changes as quickly as they occur. In fact, many such sources are already out of date the day they are published. *Annual Editions: Criminal Justice, 38/e* strives to maintain currency in matters of concern by providing up-to-date commentaries, articles, reports, and statistics from the most recent literature in the criminal justice field.

This volume contains units concerning crime and justice in America, victimology, the police, the judicial system, juvenile justice, and punishment and corrections. The articles in these units were selected because they are informative, as well as provocative. The selections are timely and useful in their treatment of ethics, punishment, juveniles, courts and other related topics.

Included in this volume are a number of features designed to be useful to students, researchers, and professionals in the criminal justice field. These include the table of contents, which summarizes each article; a *topic guide* for locating articles on specific subjects; and *Learning Outcomes, Critical Thinking* questions, and *Internet References* for each article. In addition, each unit is preceded by an *overview* that provides a background for informed reading of the articles, and emphasizes critical issues to consider.

Editor

Joanne Naughton

Joanne Naughton is a former member of the NYPD, where she encountered most aspects of police work as a police officer, detective, sergeant, and lieutenant. She is also a former staff attorney with The Legal Aid Society, where she represented indigent criminal defendants. In addition to her hands-on experience in criminal justice, she was an adjunct professor at John Jay College of Criminal Justice and has retired from Mercy College where she was an assistant professor. She received her BA and JD at Fordham University.

Academic Advisory Board

Members of the Academic Advisory Board are instrumental in the final selection of articles for Annual Editions books and ExpressBooks. Their review of the articles for content, level, and appropriateness provides critical direction to the editor(s) and staff. We think that you will find their careful consideration reflected here.

Harry N. Babb
Farmingdale State University of New York

Richard Baranzini
Liberty University

Joseph A. Bobak IV
Mount Aloysius College

Alton Braddock
University of Louisiana - Monroe

Frank Butler
La Salle University

James Byrne
University of Massachusetts, Lowell

Kelli Callahan
Park University

Terry Campbell
Kaplan University

Peter D. Chimbos
Brescia College at The University of Western Ontario

David Coffey
Thomas Nelson Community College

Bernard Cohen
Queens College

James Cunningham
State Fair Community College

Roger Cunningham
Eastern Illinois University

Michael T. Eskey
Park University

Bonnie Fisher
University of Cincinnati

David Forristal
Brown Mackie College

Paul Frankenhauser
Allied American University

Bernard Frye
University of Texas, Arlington

Paul Fuller
Knoxville College

Peter Galante
Farmingdale State College

Alan Garcia
Bristol Community College

Arnett Gaston
University of Maryland

Barry Goodson
Columbia Southern University

Ken Haas
University of Delaware

Julia Hall
Drexel University

Bridget A. Hepner-Williamson
Sam Houston State University

Rick Herbert
South Plains College

Rosalee Hodges
Glendale Community College

Michael K. Hooper
Sonoma State University

Richard Hough
University of West Florida

Amanda Humphrey
Mount Mercy College

Larry Jablecki
Rice University

Gayle Jentz
North Hennepin Community College

Jennelle London Joset
Sanford-Brown College

Rachel Jung
Mesa Community College

Kim Kamins
Brown Mackie College

Scott Kelly
Penn State Altoona

William E. Kelly
Auburn University

Chandrika Kelso
National University

Steven Kempisty
Bryant & Stratton College

Lloyd Klein
St. Francis College/Hostos Community College

Kevin Kolbe
Solano Junior College

Jordan Land
Southwest Florida College

Michael A. Langer
Loyola University - Chicago

Barney Ledford
Mid-Michigan Community College

Matthew C. Leone
University of Nevada

Xiangdong Li
New York City College of Technology

Celia Lo
University of Alabama

Mark Marsolais
Northern Kentucky University

Vertel Martin
Northampton Community College

Jon Maskaly
University of South Florida, Tampa

Suzanne Montiel
Nash Community College

James Murphy
College of Western Idaho

Bonnie O. Neher
Harrisburg Area Community College

Gary Neumeyer
Arizona Western College, Yuma

Michael Palmiotto
Wichita State University

Gary Prawel
Keuka College

Jeffrey Ian Ross
University of Baltimore

Michael P. Roy
Alpena Community College

Vincent M. Russo
Richard J. Daley College

Leslie Samuelson
University of Saskatchewan

Clifford L. Sanders Jr.
Clayton State University

Robin Sawyer
University of Maryland, College Park

Gary A. Sokolow
College of the Redwoods

Joseph A. Spadaro
Goodwin College

Michael Such
Hudson Valley Community College

Candace Tabenanika
Sam Houston State University

Amy Thistlethwaite
Northern Kentucky University

Al Trego
McCann School

Joseph L. Victor
Mercy College

Jason Weber
Rasmussen College, Bloomington

Lisa Grey Whitaker
Arizona State University

Larry Woods
Tennessee State University

Laura Woods Fidelie
Midwestern State University

Correlation Guide

The *Annual Editions* series provides students with convenient, inexpensive access to current, carefully selected articles from the public press. **Annual Editions: Criminal Justice, 38/e** is an easy-to-use reader that presents articles on important topics such as *victimology, policing, the judicial system, juvenile justice, punishment and corrections,* and many more. For more information on *Annual Editions* and other *McGraw-Hill Create™* titles, visit www.mcgrawhillcreate.com.

This convenient guide matches the articles in **Annual Editions: Criminal Justice, 38/e** with **Introduction to Criminal Justice, 8/e** by Bohm/Haley

Introduction to Criminal Justice, 8/e	Annual Editions: Criminal Justice, 38/e
Chapter 1: Crime and Justice in the United States	An About-Face on Crime The Cyber Terror Bogeyman Maze of Gun Laws in U.S. Hurts Gun Control Efforts Our Dangerous Devotion to Eyewitness Testimony What Is the Sequence of Events in the Criminal Justice System?
Chapter 2: Crime and Its Consequences	22 Years of Promises California Accuses JPMorgan Chase of Unlawful Debt Collection Practices Human Sex Trafficking Telling the Truth about Damned Lies and Statistics University of Montana Rape Reports Botched, U.S. Finds
Chapter 3: Explaining Crime	
Chapter 4: The Rule of Law	
Chapter 5: History and Structure of American Law Enforcement	An About-Face on Crime Cameras on Cops: Stop-and-Frisk Ruling's NYPD Accountability Plan Worked in California The Changing Environment for Policing, 1985–2008 The Cyber Terror Bogeyman Dog Sniff Unconstitutional? Supreme Court Rules Drug Dog Sniffs Constitute Illegal Search Judge Rejects New York's Stop-and-Frisk Policy Maze of Gun Laws in U.S. Hurts Gun Control Efforts Our Dangerous Devotion to Eyewitness Testimony Understanding the Psychology of Police Misconduct What Is the Sequence of Events in the Criminal Justice System?
Chapter 6: Policing: Roles, Styles, and Functions	Cameras on Cops: Stop-and-Frisk Ruling's NYPD Accountability Plan Worked in California The Changing Environment for Policing, 1985–2008 Dog Sniff Unconstitutional? Supreme Court Rules Drug Dog Sniffs Constitute Illegal Search Judge Rejects New York's Stop-and-Frisk Policy Understanding the Psychology of Police Misconduct
Chapter 7: Policing America: Issues and Ethics	An About-Face on Crime Cameras on Cops: Stop-and-Frisk Ruling's NYPD Accountability Plan Worked in California The Changing Environment for Policing, 1985–2008 The Cyber Terror Bogeyman Dog Sniff Unconstitutional? Supreme Court Rules Drug Dog Sniffs Constitute Illegal Search Judge Rejects New York's Stop-and-Frisk Policy Maze of Gun Laws in U.S. Hurts Gun Control Efforts Our Dangerous Devotion to Eyewitness Testimony Understanding the Psychology of Police Misconduct What Is the Sequence of Events in the Criminal Justice System?
Chapter 8: The Administration of Justice	Freed Amid Scandal, They Soon Found Trouble Again "I Did It": Why Do People Confess to Crimes They Didn't Commit? In Miranda Case, Supreme Court Rules on the Limits of Silence Lasting Damage: A Rogue Prosecutor's Final Case Neuroscience in the Courtroom Torturer's Apprentice U.S. Reviewing 27 Death Penalty Convictions for FBI Forensic Testimony Errors
Chapter 9: Sentencing, Appeals, and the Death Penalty	Freed Amid Scandal, They Soon Found Trouble Again "I Did It": Why Do People Confess to Crimes They Didn't Commit? In Miranda Case, Supreme Court Rules on the Limits of Silence Lasting Damage: A Rogue Prosecutor's Final Case Neuroscience in the Courtroom Torturer's Apprentice U.S. Reviewing 27 Death Penalty Convictions for FBI Forensic Testimony Errors

Chapter 10: Institutional Corrections	Addressing Gender Issues among Staff in Community Corrections Bring Back the Lash: Why Flogging Is More Humane than Prison The F.B.I. Deemed Agents Faultless in 150 Shootings Gaming the System: How the Political Strategies of Private Prison Companies Promote Ineffective Incarceration Policies Prison Re-entry Programs Help Inmates Leave the Criminal Mindset Behind, but Few Have Access to the Classes The Torture of Solitary War on Drugs Failure Gives Way to Treatment in States, Cities
Chapter 11: Prison Life, Inmate Rights, Release, and Recidivism	
Chapter 12: Community Corrections	Addressing Gender Issues among Staff in Community Corrections Preventing Future Crime with Cognitive Behavioral Therapy Prison Re-entry Programs Help Inmates Leave the Criminal Mindset Behind, but Few Have Access to the Classes War on Drugs Failure Gives Way to Treatment in States, Cities
Chapter 13: Juvenile Justice	Calculating "Return On Mission": Music as Medicine for Imprisoned Boys Juvenile Confinement in Context Juvenile Recidivism—Measuring Success or Failure: Is There a Difference? No Remorse Preventing Future Crime with Cognitive Behavioral Therapy Violence in Adolescent Dating Relationships Whither Young Offenders? The Debate Has Begun Why Jonathan McClard Still Matters
Chapter 14: The Future of Criminal Justice in the United States	

This convenient guide matches the articles in **Annual Editions: Criminal Justice, 38/e** with **CJ: Realities and Challenges, 2/e** by Masters et al.

CJ: Realities and Challenges, 2/e	Annual Editions: Criminal Justice, 38/e
Chapter 1: What is the Criminal Justice System?	An About-Face on Crime The Cyber Terror Bogeyman Maze of Gun Laws in U.S. Hurts Gun Control Efforts Our Dangerous Devotion to Eyewitness Testimony What Is the Sequence of Events in the Criminal Justice System?
Chapter 2: Types of Crime	
Chapter 3: Causes of Crime	Freed Amid Scandal, They Soon Found Trouble Again Neuroscience in the Courtroom
Chapter 4: Criminal Law and Defenses	22 Years of Promises California Accuses JPMorgan Chase of Unlawful Debt Collection Practices Human Sex Trafficking Telling the Truth about Damned Lies and Statistics University of Montana Rape Reports Botched, U.S. Finds
Chapter 5: Overview of Policing	Cameras on Cops: Stop-and-Frisk Ruling's NYPD Accountability Plan Worked in California The Changing Environment for Policing, 1985–2008 Dog Sniff Unconstitutional? Supreme Court Rules Drug Dog Sniffs Constitute Illegal Search Judge Rejects New York's Stop-and-Frisk Policy Understanding the Psychology of Police Misconduct
Chapter 6: Policing Operations	Cameras on Cops: Stop-and-Frisk Ruling's NYPD Accountability Plan Worked in California The Changing Environment for Policing, 1985–2008 Dog Sniff Unconstitutional? Supreme Court Rules Drug Dog Sniffs Constitute Illegal Search Judge Rejects New York's Stop-and-Frisk Policy Understanding the Psychology of Police Misconduct
Chapter 7: Legal and Special Issues in Policing	Cameras on Cops: Stop-and-Frisk Ruling's NYPD Accountability Plan Worked in California The Changing Environment for Policing, 1985–2008 Dog Sniff Unconstitutional? Supreme Court Rules Drug Dog Sniffs Constitute Illegal Search Judge Rejects New York's Stop-and-Frisk Policy Understanding the Psychology of Police Misconduct
Chapter 8: The Courts	Freed Amid Scandal, They Soon Found Trouble Again "I Did It": Why Do People Confess to Crimes They Didn't Commit? In Miranda Case, Supreme Court Rules on the Limits of Silence Lasting Damage: A Rogue Prosecutor's Final Case Neuroscience in the Courtroom Torturer's Apprentice U.S. Reviewing 27 Death Penalty Convictions for FBI Forensic Testimony Errors

Topic Guide

Unit 1

UNIT

Prepared by: Joanne Naughton

Crime and Justice in America

Crime continues to be a major problem in the United States. Court dockets are full, our prisons are overcrowded, probation and parole caseloads are overwhelming, and our police are being urged to do more. The bulging prison population places a heavy strain on the economy of the country. Clearly, crime is a complex problem that defies simple explanations or solutions. While the more familiar crimes of murder, rape, assault, and drug law violations are still with us, international terrorism has become a pressing worry. The debate also continues about how best to handle juvenile offenders, sex offenders, and those who commit acts of domestic violence. Crime committed using computers and the Internet also demands attention from the criminal justice system.

Focuses on criminal justice in America highlight the three traditional components of the criminal justice system: police, the courts, and corrections. In addition, special attention to crime victims, and juveniles also serve as a foundation for exploring criminal justice.

Article   Prepared by: Joanne Naughton

What Is the Sequence of Events in the Criminal Justice System?

Learning Outcomes

After reading this article, you will be able to:

- Name the agencies that make up the criminal justice system.
- State the various steps from the time someone is arrested for a crime.

The Private Sector Initiates the Response to Crime

This first response may come from individuals, families, neighborhood associations, business, industry, agriculture, educational institutions, the news media, or any other private service to the public.

It involves crime prevention as well as participation in the criminal justice process once a crime has been committed. Private crime prevention is more than providing private security or burglar alarms or participating in neighborhood watch. It also includes a commitment to stop criminal behavior by not engaging in it or condoning it when it is committed by others.

Citizens take part directly in the criminal justice process by reporting crime to the police, by being a reliable participant (for example, a witness or a juror) in a criminal proceeding and by accepting the disposition of the system as just or reasonable. As voters and taxpayers, citizens also participate in criminal justice through the policymaking process that affects how the criminal justice process operates, the resources available to it, and its goals and objectives. At every stage of the process from the original formulation of objectives to the decision about where to locate jails and prisons to the reintegration of inmates into society, the private sector has a role to play. Without such involvement, the criminal justice process cannot serve the citizens it is intended to protect.

The Response to Crime and Public Safety Involves Many Agencies and Services

Many of the services needed to prevent crime and make neighborhoods safe are supplied by noncriminal justice agencies, including agencies with primary concern for public health, education, welfare, public works, and housing. Individual citizens as well as public and private sector organizations have joined with criminal justice agencies to prevent crime and make neighborhoods safe.

Criminal Cases Are Brought by the Government Through the Criminal Justice System

We apprehend, try, and punish offenders by means of a loose confederation of agencies at all levels of government. Our American system of justice has evolved from the English common law into a complex series of procedures and decisions. Founded on the concept that crimes against an individual are crimes against the State, our justice system prosecutes individuals as though they victimized all of society. However, crime victims are involved throughout the process and many justice agencies have programs that focus on helping victims.

There is no single criminal justice system in this country. We have many similar systems that are individually unique. Criminal cases may be handled differently in different jurisdictions, but court decisions based on the due process guarantees of the U.S. Constitution require that specific steps be taken in the administration of criminal justice so that the individual will be protected from undue intervention from the State.

The description of the criminal and juvenile justice systems that follows portrays the most common sequence of events in response to serious criminal behavior.

Entry into the System

The justice system does not respond to most crime because so much crime is not discovered or reported to the police. Law enforcement agencies learn about crime from the reports of victims or other citizens, from discovery by a police officer in the field, from informants, or from investigative and intelligence work.

Once a law enforcement agency has established that a crime has been committed, a suspect must be identified and apprehended for the case to proceed through the system. Sometimes, a suspect is apprehended at the scene; however, identification of a suspect sometimes requires an extensive investigation. Often, no one is identified or apprehended. In some instances, a suspect is arrested and later the police determine that no crime was committed and the suspect is released.

Prosecution and Pretrial Services

After an arrest, law enforcement agencies present information about the case and about the accused to the prosecutor, who will decide if formal charges will be filed with the court. If no charges are filed, the accused must be released. The prosecutor can also drop charges after making efforts to prosecute (*nolle prosequi*).

A suspect charged with a crime must be taken before a judge or magistrate without unnecessary delay. At the initial appearance, the judge or magistrate informs the accused of the charges and decides whether there is probable cause to detain the accused person. If the offense is not very serious, the determination of guilt and assessment of a penalty may also occur at this stage.

Often, the defense counsel is also assigned at the initial appearance. All suspects prosecuted for serious crimes have a right to be represented by an attorney. If the court determines the suspect is indigent and cannot afford such representation, the court will assign counsel at the public's expense.

A pretrial-release decision may be made at the initial appearance, but may occur at other hearings or may be changed at another time during the process. Pretrial release and bail were traditionally intended to ensure appearance at trial. However, many jurisdictions permit pretrial detention of defendants accused of serious offenses and deemed to be dangerous to prevent them from committing crimes prior to trial.

The court often bases its pretrial decision on information about the defendant's drug use, as well as residence, employment, and family ties. The court may decide to release the accused on his/her own recognizance or into the custody of a third party after the posting of a financial bond or on the promise of satisfying certain conditions such as taking periodic drug tests to ensure drug abstinence.

In many jurisdictions, the initial appearance may be followed by a preliminary hearing. The main function of this hearing is to discover if there is probable cause to believe that the accused committed a known crime within the jurisdiction of the court. If the judge does not find probable cause, the case is dismissed; however, if the judge or magistrate finds probable cause for such a belief, or the accused waives his or her right to a preliminary hearing, the case may be bound over to a grand jury.

A grand jury hears evidence against the accused presented by the prosecutor and decides if there is sufficient evidence to cause the accused to be brought to trial. If the grand jury finds sufficient evidence, it submits to the court an indictment, a written statement of the essential facts of the offense charged against the accused.

Where the grand jury system is used, the grand jury may also investigate criminal activity generally and issue indictments called grand jury originals that initiate criminal cases. These investigations and indictments are often used in drug and conspiracy cases that involve complex organizations. After such an indictment, law enforcement tries to apprehend and arrest the suspects named in the indictment.

Misdemeanor cases and some felony cases proceed by the issuance of an information, a formal, written accusation submitted to the court by a prosecutor. In some jurisdictions, indictments may be required in felony cases. However, the accused may choose to waive a grand jury indictment and, instead, accept service of an information for the crime.

In some jurisdictions, defendants, often those without prior criminal records, may be eligible for diversion from prosecution subject to the completion of specific conditions such as drug treatment. Successful completion of the conditions may result in the dropping of charges or the expunging of the criminal record where the defendant is required to plead guilty prior to the diversion.

Adjudication

Once an indictment or information has been filed with the trial court, the accused is scheduled for arraignment. At the arraignment, the accused is informed of the charges, advised of the rights of criminal defendants, and asked to enter a plea to the charges. Sometimes, a plea of guilty is the result of negotiations between the prosecutor and the defendant.

If the accused pleads guilty or pleads *nolo contendere* (accepts penalty without admitting guilt), the judge may accept or reject the plea. If the plea is accepted, no trial is held and the offender is sentenced at this proceeding or at a later date. The plea may be rejected and proceed to trial if, for example, the judge believes that the accused may have been coerced.

If the accused pleads not guilty or not guilty by reason of insanity, a date is set for the trial. A person accused of a serious crime is guaranteed a trial by jury. However, the accused may ask for a bench trial where the judge, rather than a jury, serves as the finder of fact. In both instances the prosecution and defense present evidence by questioning witnesses while the judge decides on issues of law. The trial results in acquittal or conviction on the original charges or on lesser included offenses.

After the trial a defendant may request appellate review of the conviction or sentence. In some cases, appeals of convictions are a matter of right; all States with the death penalty provide for automatic appeal of cases involving a death sentence. Appeals may be subject to the discretion of the appellate court and may be granted only on acceptance of a defendant's petition for a *writ of certiorari*. Prisoners may also appeal their sentences through civil rights petitions and *writs of habeas corpus* where they claim unlawful detention.

Sentencing and Sanctions

After a conviction, sentence is imposed. In most cases the judge decides on the sentence, but in some jurisdictions the sentence is decided by the jury, particularly for capital offenses.

In arriving at an appropriate sentence, a sentencing hearing may be held at which evidence of aggravating or mitigating circumstances is considered. In assessing the circumstances surrounding a convicted person's criminal behavior, courts often rely on presentence investigations by probation agencies or other designated authorities. Courts may also consider victim impact statements.

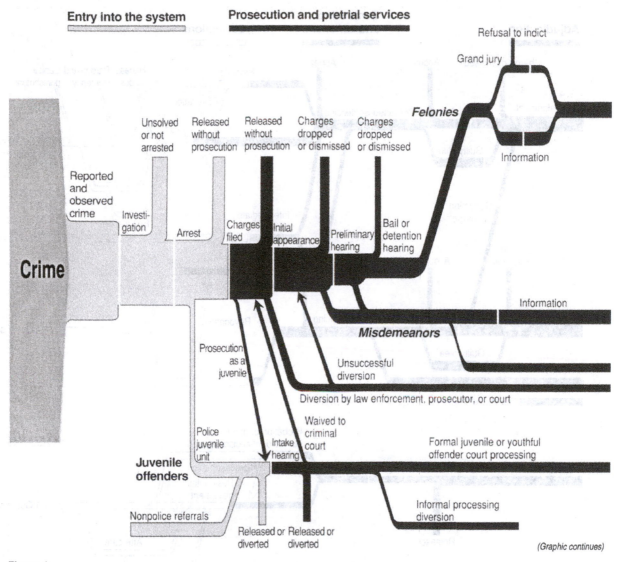

Figure 1

Note: This chart gives a simplified view of caseflow through the criminal justice system. Procedures vary among jurisdictions. The weights of the lines are not intended to show the actual size of caseloads.

The sentencing choices that may be available to judges and juries include one or more of the following:

- the death penalty
- incarceration in a prison, jail, or other confinement facility
- probation—allowing the convicted person to remain at liberty but subject to certain conditions and restrictions such as drug testing or drug restrictions such as drug testing or drug treatment
- fines—primarily applied as penalties in minor offenses
- restitution—requiring the offender to pay compensation to the victim. In some jurisdictions, offenders may be

sentenced to alternatives to incarceration that are considered more severe than straight probation but less severe than a prison term. Examples of such sanctions include boot camps, intense supervision often with drug treatment and testing, house arrest and electronic monitoring, denial of Federal benefits, and community service.

In many jurisdictions, the law mandates that persons convicted of certain types of offenses serve a prison term. Most jurisdictions permit the judge to set the sentence length within certain limits, but some have determinate sentencing laws that stipulate a specific sentence length that must be served and cannot be altered by a parole board.

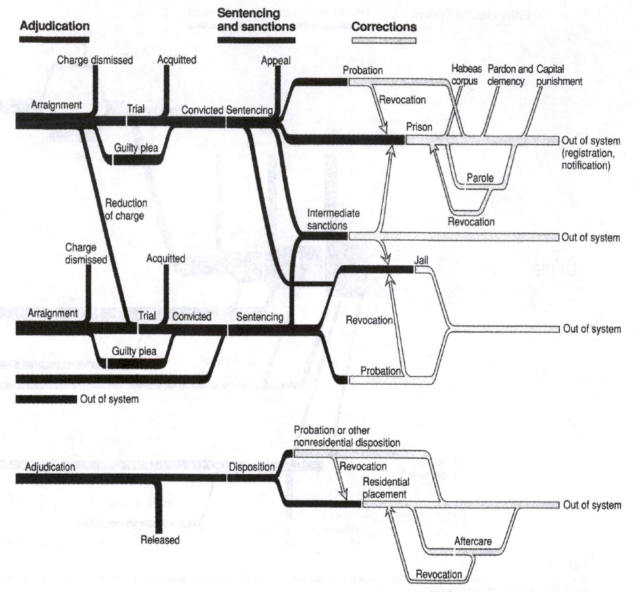

Figure 1 *(continued)*

Source: Adapted from *The challenge of crime in a free society*. President's Commission on Law Enforcement and Administration of Justice, 1967. This revision, a result of the Symposium on the 30th Anniversary of the President's Commission, was prepared by the Bureau of Justice Statistics in 1997.

Corrections

Offenders sentenced to incarceration usually serve time in a local jail or a State prison. Offenders sentenced to less than 1 year generally go to jail; those sentenced to more than 1 year go to prison. Persons admitted to the Federal system or a State prison system may be held in prison with varying levels of custody or in a community correctional facility.

A prisoner may become eligible for parole after serving a specific part of his or her sentence. Parole is the conditional release of a prisoner before the prisoner's full sentence has been served. The decision to grant parole is made by an authority such as a parole board, which has power to grant or revoke parole or to discharge a parolee altogether. The way parole decisions are made varies widely among jurisdictions.

Offenders may also be required to serve out their full sentences prior to release (expiration of term). Those sentenced under determinate sentencing laws can be released only after they have served their full sentence (mandatory release) less any "goodtime" received while in prison. Inmates get goodtime

Discretion Is Exercised throughout the Criminal Justice System

Discretion is "an authority conferred by law to act in certain conditions or situations in accordance with an official's or an official agency's own considered judgment and conscience."[1] Discretion is exercised throughout the government. It is a part of decision making in all government systems from mental health to education, as well as criminal justice. The limits of discretion vary from jurisdiction to jurisdiction.

Concerning crime and justice, legislative bodies have recognized that they cannot anticipate the range of circumstances surrounding each crime, anticipate local mores, and enact laws that clearly encompass all conduct that is criminal and all that is not.[2]

Therefore, persons charged with the day-to-day response to crime are expected to exercise their own judgment within limits set by law. Basically, they must decide—

- whether to take action
- where the situation fits in the scheme of law, rules, and precedent
- which official response is appropriate.[3]

To ensure that discretion is exercised responsibly, government authority is often delegated to professionals. Professionalism requires a minimum level of training and orientation, which guide officials in making decisions. The professionalism of policing is due largely to the desire to ensure the proper exercise of police discretion.

The limits of discretion vary from State to State and locality to locality. For example, some State judges have wide discretion in the type of sentence they may impose. In recent years, other states have sought to limit the judge's discretion in sentencing by passing mandatory sentencing laws that require prison sentences for certain offenses.

Notes

1. Roscoe Pound, "Discretion, dispensation and mitigation: The problem of the individual special case," *New York University Law Review* (1960) 35:925, 926.
2. Wayne R. LaFave, *Arrest: The decision to take a suspect into custody* (Boston: Little, Brown & Co., 1964), pp. 63–184.
3. Memorandum of June 21, 1977, from Mark Moore to James Vorenberg, "Some abstract notes on the issue of discretion."

Bureau of Justice Statistics (www.ojp.usdoj.gov/bjs/). January 1998. NCJ 167894. To order: 1-800-732-3277.

Who Exercises Discretion?

These criminal justice officials . . .	must often decide whether or not or how to—
Police	Enforce specific laws Investigate specific crimes; Search people
Prosecutors	File charges or petitions for adjudication Seek indictments Drop cases Reduce charges
Judges or magistrates	Set bail or conditions for release Accept pleas Determine delinquency Dismiss charges Impose sentence Revoke probation
Correctional officials	Assign to type of correctional facility Award privileges Punish for disciplinary infractions
Paroling authorities	Determine date and conditions of parole Revoke parole

credits against their sentences automatically or by earning them through participation in programs.

If released by a parole board decision or by mandatory release, the releasee will be under the supervision of a parole officer in the community for the balance of his or her unexpired sentence. This supervision is governed by specific conditions of release, and the releasee may be returned to prison for violations of such conditions.

Recidivism

Once the suspects, defendants, or offenders are released from the jurisdiction of a criminal justice agency, they may be processed through the criminal justice system again for a new crime. Long term studies show that many suspects who are arrested have prior criminal histories and those with a greater number of prior arrests were more likely to be arrested again. As the courts take prior criminal history into account at sentencing, most prison inmates have a prior criminal history and many have been incarcerated before. Nationally, about half the inmates released from State prison will return to prison.

The Juvenile Justice System

Juvenile courts usually have jurisdiction over matters concerning children, including delinquency, neglect, and adoption. They also handle "status offenses" such as truancy and running away, which are not applicable to adults. State statutes define which persons are under the original jurisdiction of the juvenile court. The upper age of juvenile court jurisdiction in delinquency matters is 17 in most States.

The processing of juvenile offenders is not entirely dissimilar to adult criminal processing, but there are crucial differences. Many juveniles are referred to juvenile courts by law enforcement officers, but many others are referred by school officials, social services agencies, neighbors, and even parents, for behavior or conditions that are determined to require intervention by the formal system for social control.

At arrest, a decision is made either to send the matter further into the justice system or to divert the case out of the system, often to alternative programs. Examples of alternative programs include drug treatment, individual or group counseling, or referral to educational and recreational programs.

When juveniles are referred to the juvenile courts, the court's intake department or the prosecuting attorney determines whether sufficient grounds exist to warrant filing a petition that requests an adjudicatory hearing or a request to transfer jurisdiction to criminal court. At this point, many juveniles are released or diverted to alternative programs.

All States allow juveniles to be tried as adults in criminal court under certain circumstances. In many States, the legislature *statutorily excludes* certain (usually serious) offenses from the jurisdiction of the juvenile court regardless of the age of the accused. In some States and at the Federal level under certain circumstances, prosecutors have the *discretion* to either file criminal charges against juveniles directly in criminal courts or proceed through the juvenile justice process. The juvenile court's intake department or the prosecutor may petition the juvenile court to *waive* jurisdiction to criminal court. The juvenile court also may order *referral* to criminal court for trial as adults. In some jurisdictions, juveniles processed as adults may upon conviction be sentenced to either an adult or a juvenile facility.

In those cases where the juvenile court retains jurisdiction, the case may be handled formally by filing a delinquency petition or informally by diverting the juvenile to other agencies or programs in lieu of further court processing.

If a petition for an adjudicatory hearing is accepted, the juvenile may be brought before a court quite unlike the court with jurisdiction over adult offenders. Despite the considerable discretion associated with juvenile court proceedings, juveniles are afforded many of the due-process safeguards associated with adult criminal trials. Several States permit the use of juries in juvenile courts; however, in light of the U.S. Supreme Court holding that juries are not essential to juvenile hearings, most States do not make provisions for juries in juvenile courts.

In disposing of cases, juvenile courts usually have far more discretion than adult courts. In addition to such options as probation, commitment to a residential facility, restitution, or fines, State laws grant juvenile courts the power to order removal of children from their homes to foster homes or treatment facilities. Juvenile courts also may order participation in special programs aimed at shoplifting prevention, drug counseling, or driver education.

Once a juvenile is under juvenile court disposition, the court may retain jurisdiction until the juvenile legally becomes an adult (at age 21 in most States). In some jurisdictions, juvenile offenders may be classified as youthful offenders, which can lead to extended sentences.

Following release from an institution, juveniles are often ordered to a period of aftercare that is similar to parole supervision for adult offenders. Juvenile offenders who violate the conditions of aftercare may have their aftercare revoked, resulting in being recommitted to a facility. Juveniles who are classified as youthful offenders and violate the conditions of aftercare may be subject to adult sanctions.

The Governmental Response to Crime Is Founded in the Intergovernmental Structure of the United States

Under our form of government, each State and the Federal Government has its own criminal justice system. All systems must respect the rights of individuals set forth in court interpretation of the U.S. Constitution and defined in case law.

State constitutions and laws define the criminal justice system within each State and delegate the authority and responsibility for criminal justice to various jurisdictions, officials, and institutions. State laws also define criminal behavior and groups of children or acts under jurisdiction of the juvenile courts.

Municipalities and counties further define their criminal justice systems through local ordinances that proscribe the local agencies responsible for criminal justice processing that were not established by the State.

Congress has also established a criminal justice system at the Federal level to respond to Federal crimes such as bank robbery, kidnaping, and transporting stolen goods across State lines.

The Response to Crime Is Mainly a State and Local Function

Very few crimes are under exclusive Federal jurisdiction. The responsibility to respond to most crime rests with State and local governments. Police protection is primarily a function of cities and towns. Corrections is primarily a function of State governments. Most justice personnel are employed at the local level.

Critical Thinking

1. Explain discretion and how it is exercised in the criminal justice system.
2. What are the steps that follow once a suspect is arrested by police and charged with a crime?
3. How are young people who violate the law treated?

Create Central

www.mhhe.com/createcentral

Internet References

Bureau of Justice Statistics
www.bjs.gov/content/justsys.cfm

The National Center for Victims of Crime
www.victimsofcrime.org/help-for-crime-victims/get-help-bulletins-for-crime-victims/the-criminal-justice-system

U.S. Department of Justice, 1998.

Article   Prepared by: Joanne Naughton

Our Dangerous Devotion to Eyewitness Testimony

PATRICIA J. WILLIAMS

Learning Outcomes

After reading this article, you will be able to:

- Understand the problems associated with eyewitness testimony.
- Show the effect of *Perry v. New Hampshire* on the issue of requiring pretrial hearings in order to test eyewitness evidence for reliability.

"We see what we want to see," my grandmother used to say. This insight visited me recently after I ran across the mall chasing a woman I thought was my cousin. It wasn't, as it turned out, but I didn't realize that until after I had puffed up behind her, bopped her amiably on the shoulder and cried out, "Boo!"

How was it possible, I thought in retrospective embarrassment, to so wrongly misidentify someone I know so well? Empirically my experience was all too common. I'd been thinking about my cousin a few moments before and saw the woman through the lens of those thoughts. We often project our life's associations onto the faces of strangers. Constantly—if mostly unconsciously—we familiarize them with learned stereotypes. If we are wise, we learn to take caution with our assumptions. We recognize this innate fallibility, and most of the time it doesn't matter very much.

Oddly enough, however, we reverse that supposition in the one context where fallibility matters most: in criminal cases, eyewitness testimony is viewed as the *ne plus ultra* for the prosecution, despite a century's worth of psychological and sociological studies revealing that, from Sacco and Vanzetti to Troy Davis, witnesses misperceive a startling percentage of the time. "Human beings are not very good at identifying people they saw only once for a relatively short period of time," writes Cornell law professor Michael Dorf. "The studies reveal error rates of as high as fifty percent—a frightening statistic given that many convictions may be based largely or solely on such testimony. These studies show further that the ability to identify a stranger is diminished by stress (and what crime situation is not intensely stressful?), that cross-racial identifications are especially unreliable, and that contrary to what one might think, those witnesses who claim to be 'certain' of their identifications are no better at it than everyone else, just more confident."

The costs of this phenomenon are perhaps best revealed in data compiled by the Innocence Project, which has concluded that out of 281 postconviction exonerations secured through DNA in the United States, eyewitness misidentification "was a factor in 75 percent . . . making it the leading cause of these wrongful convictions." Luckily, there are substantiated ways to guard against such error. Experts have cited two main types of variables that can adversely affect eyewitness identification: "estimator variables," the hardest to control for, which include things like the degree of lighting, distance or speed within a given crime scene, as well as the level of trauma to the witness; and "system variables," defined as "those that the criminal justice system can and should control," which include law enforcement tools like lineups and photo arrays. A number of reforms involving the latter have the proven capacity to boost the accuracy of witness IDs. These include "blind administration," where an officer conducting a lineup is not aware of who the suspect is (and thus not capable of revealing his or her identity via gestures, vocal inflections or body language); "non-suggestive" lineups, made up of people who generally resemble a witness's description, so that the suspect does not stand out; allowing witnesses to sign a statement indicating their level of confidence in their choice; and presenting members of a lineup sequentially rather than simultaneously (to mitigate the pressure to choose any kind of close-looking one when we are presented with a bunch of faces at once). Such remedial safeguards have so reduced the error rate—and so indisputably—that a number of local jurisdictions and eleven states thus far have adopted some or all of them as standard operating procedure.

It would seem logical, then, to implement these reforms universally, and for courts to screen eyewitness evidence for those basics of procedural reliability before such testimony is heard by a jury. But on January 11, in *Perry v. New Hampshire*, the Supreme Court rejected that notion, ruling that such a pretrial inquiry is not a requirement of due process "when the identification was not procured under unnecessarily suggestive circumstances arranged by law enforcement." This is subtle language: it's not the same as what we think of as police corruption, as in overt suppression of evidence. Rather, it relates to the kinds of situations at stake in *Perry:* Was the suspect the only black man in a lineup? Was he handcuffed and flanked by police? Was his image shown in photo array after photo array until he began to look familiar? If the chief investigator was the one administering a lineup, was his belief in the suspect's guilt communicated to the witness via subtle coaching? All such factors may be highly suggestive, triggering the irrelevant associations and false memories that can lead to inaccurate results.

Perry does two unfortunate things. It undercuts pretrial examination of virtually all "estimator variables," no matter how problematic, since those are less likely to directly involve police. And by drawing the line at "unnecessarily suggestive" actions by state actors, the ruling sets a very high bar for challenging eyewitness evidence, ignoring the hefty empirical proof that misidentification is a pervasive fact of life. Justice Sonia Sotomayor, the lone dissenter in *Perry,* wrote that this ruling invites arbitrary results by making "police arrangement" the "inflexible step zero." The concerns of due process ought to be based on the actual likelihood of misidentification, said Sotomayor, "not predicated on the source of suggestiveness." Reiterating that any preventable misidentification is a miscarriage

of justice—not merely where the police are setting the stage—she underscored the Innocence Project's concern that inaccurate eyewitness testimony is the leading cause of wrongful convictions in US courts. DNA has exonerated eight misidentified inmates on death row. If we have at our disposal simple reforms that have been proven to guard against such tragic mistakes, why on earth should we not implement them universally?

Critical Thinking

1. What steps can courts take to guard against eyewitness misidentification?
2. What did Justice Sotomayor mean about the concerns of due process?

Create Central

www.mhhe.com/createcentral

Internet References

Innocence Project
www.innocenceproject.org/understand/Eyewitness-Misidentification.php
Livescience
www.livescience.com/16194-crime-eyewitnesses-mistakes.html

Article   Prepared by: Joanne Naughton

Maze of Gun Laws in U.S. Hurts Gun Control Efforts

EILEEN SULLIVAN

Learning Outcomes

After reading this article, you will be able to:

- Appreciate the difficulty of regulating guns in the United States.
- Describe the roadblock created by Congressional opposition to new gun laws.

There is a legal avenue to try to get any gun you want somewhere in the U.S., thanks to the maze of gun statutes across the country and the lack of certain federal laws.

That undermines gun-control efforts in communities with tougher gun laws—and pushes advocates of tighter controls to seek a federal standard. Gun rights proponents say enforcing all existing laws makes more sense than passing new ones.

An Associated Press analysis found that there are thousands of laws, rules and regulations at the local, county, state and federal levels. The laws and rules vary by state, and even within states, according to a 2011 compilation of state gun laws by the Bureau of Alcohol, Tobacco, Firearms and Explosives.

These laws and regulations govern who can carry a firearm, what kind of firearm is legal, the size of ammunition magazines, and more. In some places, a person can buy as many guns as desired.

Not only can people acquire military-style assault weapons, they can also get gangster-style Tommy guns, World War II-era bazookas and even sawed-off shotguns.

"If you regulate something on the local or state level, you are still a victim to guns coming into other localities or states," said Laura Cutilletta, a senior staff attorney at the California-based Law Center to Prevent Gun Violence.

In California, most guns come from Nevada, where there is almost no regulation of firearms, Cutilletta said, and in Arizona, gun owners don't need a permit.

President Barack Obama earlier this month announced a $500 million plan to tighten federal gun laws. The December shooting massacre in Newtown, Conn., that killed 20 children and six adults at an elementary school launched the issue of gun control policy to a national focus not seen in decades.

Obama is urging Congress to pass new laws, some of which would set a minimum standard for the types of firearms and ammunition that are commercially available. Sen. Dianne Feinstein, D-Calif., on Thursday said she was introducing a new assault weapons ban.

The powerful gun lobby says the problem lies in enforcement of existing laws.

"Which begs the question: Why are we putting more laws on the books if we're not enforcing the laws we already have on the books?" said Andrew Arulanandam, spokesman for the National Rifle Association.

New gun laws will face tough opposition in Congress, particularly from members who rely on the NRA during election campaigns. The NRA contributed more than $700,000 to members of Congress during the 2012 election cycle, according to the Center for Responsive Politics.

Recognizing the opposition in Congress, states already are passing their own new gun laws while officials from some states are promising to ignore any new federal mandates. As the national debate on gun control and Second Amendment rights escalates, the terms being used won't mean the same thing everywhere, due to the thousands of laws, rules and regulations across the country.

"The patchwork of laws in many ways means that the laws are only as effective as the weakest law there is," said Gene Voegtlin of the International Association of Chiefs of Police. "Those that are trying to acquire firearms and may not be able to do that by walking into their local gun shop will try to find a way to do that. This patchwork of laws allows them to seek out the weak links and acquire weapons."

Obama wants to address this, in part, by passing federal gun-trafficking laws that carry heavy penalties. It's difficult to crack down on trafficking because the penalties are too low to serve as a deterrent, and federal prosecutors decline many cases because of a lack of evidence. For instance, in order to charge someone with willfully participating in a business of selling firearms without a license, the ATF needs to prove that the guns were not sold out of the suspect's private collection, the Justice Department inspector general has said.

Obama has also called for a new federal law banning magazines that carry more than 10 rounds of ammunition—a measure that was in effect during the previous assault weapons ban, between 1994 and 2004. High-capacity magazines have been used in recent deadly mass shootings, including those in Newtown, and in the suburban Denver movie theater attack last summer.

A high-capacity ammunition magazine means different things in different places.

In California, considered by many to have some of the strongest gun laws in the country, a large-capacity magazine is one that holds more than 10 rounds. In Illinois there is no state law regarding magazines. Yet, there are laws regarding magazines in Chicago where the threshold is more than 12 rounds. But about 40 miles away in Aurora, Ill., this type of magazine is called a large-capacity ammunition feeding device and means anything more than 15 rounds.

In 44 states, including Arizona, Colorado, Connecticut, Texas and Virginia where these magazines have been used in deadly mass shootings, there are no laws against using them, according to a 2012 analysis by the Law Center to Prevent Gun Violence. If a federal law banned magazines that hold more than 10 rounds, it would become the minimum standard.

The definition of "assault weapon" also varies. There is no federal definition of an assault weapon, and the meaning of the term is inconsistent even within the gun industry. California defines an assault weapon as a "firearm (that) has such a high rate of fire and capacity for fire-power that its function as a legitimate sports or recreational firearm is substantially outweighed by the danger that it can be used to kill and injure human beings." The law specifically lists 60 rifles, 14 pistols and five shotguns. Neighboring states Nevada and Arizona have no assault weapon restrictions.

Federal law does not prohibit the ownership of any weapon, said Ginger Colbrun, a Bureau of Alcohol, Tobacco, Firearms and Explosives spokeswoman in Washington. In order to buy or own certain firearms, including automatic weapons, machine guns and bazookas, people do have to apply for permission from the federal government. But as long as the application for a restricted firearm is approved, and there is no state law barring ownership of that type of gun, it's legal.

"There is such a variation in the number of laws that regulate the distribution of guns that there is no adequate minimum standard," said Richard Aborn, president of the New York-based Citizens Crime Commission. "The federal government has an obligation to establish at least minimum standards that have to be complied with before a gun can be sold anywhere in America."

Critical Thinking

1. What kind of gun laws would be most effective at controlling gun violence?

2. Would federal definitions be beneficial?

Create Central

www.mhhe.com/createcentral

Internet References

Bureau of Alcohol, Tobacco, Firearms and Explorsives
   www.atf.gov
Law Center to Prevent Gun Violence
   http://smartgunlaws.org

Article   Prepared by: Joanne Naughton

The Cyber Terror Bogeyman

Peter W. Singer

Learning Outcomes

After reading this article, you will be able to:

- Discuss some of the problems involved when dealing with cyber terrorism.
- Show how the language used in describing cyber terrorism can be confusing.

We have let our fears obscure how terrorists really use the Internet.

About 31,300. That is roughly the number of magazine and journal articles written so far that discuss the phenomenon of cyber terrorism.

Zero. That is the number of people that have been hurt or killed by cyber terrorism at the time this went to press.

In many ways, cyber terrorism is like the Discovery Channel's "Shark Week," when we obsess about shark attacks despite the fact that you are roughly 15,000 times more likely to be hurt or killed in an accident involving a toilet. But by looking at how terror groups actually use the Internet, rather than fixating on nightmare scenarios, we can properly prioritize and focus our efforts.

Part of the problem is the way we talk about the issue. The FBI defines cyber terrorism as a "premeditated, politically motivated attack against information, computer systems, computer programs and data which results in violence against non-combatant targets by subnational groups or clandestine agents." A key word there is "violence," yet many discussions sweep all sorts of nonviolent online mischief into the "terror" bin. Various reports lump together everything from Defense Secretary Leon Panetta's recent statements that a terror group might launch a "digital Pearl Harbor" to Stuxnet-like sabotage (ahem, committed by state forces) to hacktivism, WikiLeaks and credit card fraud. As one congressional staffer put it, the way we use a term like cyber terrorism "has as much clarity as cybersecurity—that is, none at all."

Another part of the problem is that we often mix up our fears with the actual state of affairs. Last year, Deputy Defense Secretary William Lynn, the Pentagon's lead official for cybersecurity, spoke to the top experts in the field at the RSA Conference in San Francisco. "It is possible for a terrorist group to develop cyber-attack tools on their own or to buy them on the black market," Lynn warned. "A couple dozen talented programmers wearing flip-flops and drinking Red Bull can do a lot of damage."

The deputy defense secretary was conflating fear and reality, not just about what stimulant-drinking programmers are actually hired to do, but also what is needed to pull off an attack that causes meaningful violence. The requirements go well beyond finding top cyber experts. Taking down hydroelectric generators, or designing malware like Stuxnet that causes nuclear centrifuges to spin out of sequence doesn't just require the skills and means to get into a computer system. It's also knowing what to do once you are in. To cause true damage requires an understanding of the devices themselves and how they run, the engineering and physics behind the target.

The Stuxnet case, for example, involved not just cyber experts well beyond a few wearing flip-flops, but also experts in areas that ranged from intelligence and surveillance to nuclear physics to the engineering of a specific kind of Siemens-brand industrial equipment. It also required expensive tests, not only of the software, but on working versions of the target hardware as well.

As George R. Lucas Jr., a professor at the U.S. Naval Academy, put it, conducting a truly mass-scale action using cyber means "simply outstrips the intellectual, organizational and personnel capacities of even the most well-funded and well-organized terrorist organization, as well as those of even the most sophisticated international criminal enterprises."

Lucas said the threat of cyber terrorism has been vastly overblown.

"To be blunt, neither the 14-year-old hacker in your next-door neighbor's upstairs bedroom, nor the two- or three-person al-Qaida cell holed up in some apartment in Hamburg are going to bring down the Glen Canyon and Hoover dams," he said.

We should be crystal clear: This is not to say that terrorist groups are uninterested in using the technology of cyber-space to carry out acts of violence. In 2001, al-Qaida computers seized in Afghanistan were found to contain models of a dam, plus engineering software that simulated the catastrophic failure of controls. Five years later, jihadist websites were urging cyber attacks on the U.S. financial industry to retaliate for abuses at Guantanamo Bay.

Nor does it mean that cyber terrorism, particularly attacks on critical infrastructure, is of no concern. In 2007, Idaho National Lab researchers experimented with cyber attacks on their own facility; they learned that remotely changing the operating cycle of a power generator could make it catch fire. Four years later, the *Los Angeles Times* reported that white-hat hackers hired by a water provider in California broke into the system in less than a week. Policymakers must worry that real-world versions of such attacks might have a ripple effect that could, for example, knock out parts of the national power grid or shut down a municipal or even regional water supply.

> *But so far, what terrorists have accomplished in the cyber realm doesn't match our fears, their dreams or even what they have managed through traditional means.*

But so far, what terrorists have accomplished in the cyber realm doesn't match our fears, their dreams or even what they have managed through traditional means.

The only publicly documented case of an actual al-Qaida attempt at a cyber attack wouldn't have even met the FBI definition. Under questioning at Guantanamo Bay, Mohmedou Ould Slahi confessed to trying to knock offline the Israeli prime minister's public website. The same goes for the September denial-of-service attacks on five U.S. banking firms, for which the Islamist group "Izz ad-Din al-Qassam Cyber Fighters" claimed responsibility. (Some experts believe the group was merely stealing credit for someone else's work.) The attacks, which prevented customers from accessing the sites for a few hours, were the equivalent of a crowd standing in your lobby blocking access or a gang of neighborhood kids constantly doing "ring and runs" at your front doorbell. It's annoying, to be sure, but nothing that would make the terrorism threat matrix if you removed the word "cyber." And while it may make for good headlines, it is certainly not in the vein of a "cyber 9/11" or "digital Pearl Harbor."

Even the 2007 cyber attacks on Estonia, the most-discussed incident of its kind, had little impact on the daily life of the average Estonian and certainly no long-term effect. Allegedly assisted by the Russian government, and hence well beyond the capacity of most terror organizations, the attacks merely disrupted public-facing government websites for a few days. Compare that with the impact of planes crashing into the center of the U.S. financial system, the London subway attacks or the thousands of homemade bomb attacks that happen around the world each year.

Even when you move into the "what if" side the damage potential of cyber terror still pales compared with other types of potential terror attacks. A disruption of the power grid for a few days would certainly be catastrophic (though it's something that Washington, D.C., residents have lived through in the last year. Does the Pepco power company qualify as a cyber threat?). But, again, in strategic planning, we have to put threats into context. The explosion of just one nuclear bomb, even a jury-rigged radiological "dirty bomb," could irradiate an American city for centuries. Similarly, while a computer virus could wreak havoc in the economy, a biological attack could change our very patterns of life forever. As one cyber expert said, "There are [cyber] threats out there, but there are no threats that threaten our fundamental way of life."

Terrorists Online

Better than fixating on an unlikely hack that opens the floodgates of Hoover Dam, in assessing cyber terrorism we should look at how terror groups actually use the Internet. The answer turns out to be: pretty much how everyone else uses it. Yes, the Internet is becoming a place of growing danger and new digital weaponry is being developed. We must be mindful of forces that would use malware against us, much as we have used it in offensive operations against Iran. But the Internet's main function remains to gather and share information across great distances with instant ease.

For instance, online dating sites and terror groups alike use the Internet to connect people of similar interests and beliefs who otherwise wouldn't normally meet. Similarly, online voices—be they restaurant bloggers or radical imams—are magnified, reaching more people than ever. (Indeed, the Internet seems to reward the more extreme with more attention.) Al-Qaida, denied safe havens by U.S. military operations after 9/11, spent the next decade shifting its propaganda distribution from hand-carried cassette tapes to vastly superior online methods. The last video that Osama bin Laden issued before his death was simultaneously uploaded onto five sites. Counterterrorism groups rushed to take them down, but within one hour, the video had been captured and copied to more than 600 sites. Within a day, the number of sites hosting the video had doubled again, each watchable by thousands.

Beyond propaganda, cyberspace allows groups to spread particular knowledge in new and innovative ways. The same kinds of tools that allow positive organizations such as the Khan Academy to help kids around the world learn math and science has given terrorist groups unprecedented ways to discuss and disseminate tactics, techniques and procedures. The recipes for explosives are readily available on the Internet, while terror groups have used the Internet to share designs for IEDs instantly across conflict zones from Iraq to Afghanistan.

Online sharing has helped such groups continue their work even as drone strikes and other global counterterror efforts deprive them of geographic spaces to teach and train. And what terror groups value from the Internet is the same as the rest of us—reliable service, easy terms and virtual anonymity—which complicates the old way of thinking about the locale of threats. The Taliban, for example, ran a website for more than a year that released propaganda and kept a running tally of suicide bombings, rocket attacks and raids against U.S. troops in Afghanistan. And yet the host for the website was a Texas company called The Planet, which rented out websites for $70 a month, payable by credit card. The company, which hosted some 16 million accounts, wasn't aware that one of them was a Taliban information clearinghouse until it was contacted by U.S. authorities and shut the site down.

This gaining of knowledge is not just about the "how" of a terror attack, but even the "who" and the "where" on the targeting side. Groups have used cyberspace as a low-cost, low-risk means to gather intelligence in ways they could only dream about a generation ago. For example, no terrorist group has the financial resources to afford a spy satellite to scope out targets from above with pinpoint precision, let alone the capability to build and launch it. Yet, Google Earth filled in just as effectively for Lashkar-e-Taiba, a Pakistan-based terror group, when it was planning the 2008 Mumbai attacks, and for the Taliban team that planned the raid earlier this year on Camp Bastion in Afghanistan.

What this means when it comes to terrorism is that, much like in other areas of cybersecurity, we have to be aware of our own habits and uses of the Internet and how bad actors might take advantage. In 2007, when U.S. Army helicopters landed at a base in Iraq, soldiers reportedly used their smartphones to snap photos and upload them to the Internet. The geotags embedded in the photos allowed insurgents to pinpoint and destroy four of the helicopters in a mortar attack. The incident has become a standard part of experts' warnings. "Is a badge on Foursquare worth your life?" asks Brittany Brown, the social media manager at Fort Benning, GA.

A growing worry here is that groups might use social networking and Kevin Mitnick-style "social engineering" to seek information not just about hard targets, but human ones. After the bin Laden raid in 2011, an American cybersecurity analyst wondered what he could find out about the supposedly super-secret unit that carried it out. He was able to find 12 current or former members' names, their families' names and their home addresses. This information was acquired not as the result of leaks to the press, but rather through the use of social networking tricks (for instance, tracking people and their network of friends and family by their appearances in pictures wearing T-shirts with unit logos or through websites that mention BUDS training classes). In similar experiments, he uncovered the names of FBI undercover agents and, in one particularly saucy example, a pair of senior U.S. government officials who opened themselves up to potential blackmail by participating in a swinger site. The analyst uses the results of such exercises to warn his "targets" that there was more about them on the Internet than they realized—a useful reminder for us all.

Ultimately, in making a global risk assessment, we have to weigh an imagined future, in which terror groups unleash a cataclysm via computer virus, against the present reality, in which they use information flows to inform and improve their actions in the physical world.

So what does that suggest for cyber counterterror efforts?

A Double-Edged Sword

"It seems that someone is using my account and is somehow sending messages with my name," emailed one person who fell for an online trick. "The dangerous thing in the matter is that they [his contacts replying to what they thought was a genuine email] say that I had sent them a message including a link for download, which they downloaded."

We can all empathize with this fellow, whose story was captured by *Wired* magazine's Danger Room blog. Many of us have gone through the same experience or received similar warnings from friends or family that someone's hacked their account and to be aware of suspicious messages. The difference is that the person complaining about being hacked in this case was "Yaman Mukhadab," a prominent poster inside what was supposed to be an elite password-protected forum for radicals, called Shumukh. Before he sent out his warning to the forum, the group had been engaged in such activities as assembling a "wish list" of American security industry leaders, defense officials and other public figures for terrorists to target and kill.

Mukhadab's cyber hardships—induced, of course, by counterterrorism agencies—illustrate how technology remains a double-edged sword. The realm of the Internet is supposed to be a fearful place, perfect for terrorists, and yet it can also work for us. Some counterterror experts argue that instead of playing a never-ending game of Whac-a-Mole—trying to track and then shut down all terrorist use of the Internet—it might be better to take advantage of their presence online. "You can learn a lot from the enemy by watching them chat online," Martin Libicki, a senior policy analyst at the Rand Corp., told the *Washington Post*.

While the cyber era allows terror groups to easily distribute the playbook of potential terrorist tactics, techniques and procedures, it also reveals to defenders which ones are popular and spreading. If individuals and groups can link up as never before, so too do intelligence analysts have unprecedented abilities to track them and map out social networks. This applies both to identifying would-be cyber terrorists designing malware as well as those still using the bombs and guns of the present world.

In 2008 and 2009, U.S. intelligence agencies reportedly tried to attack and shut down the top terrorist propaganda websites on the anniversary of 9/11, to try to delay the release of a bin Laden video celebrating the attacks. In 2010, however, they took a different tack. As *Wired* magazine reported, "The user account for al-Qaida's al-Fajr media distribution network was hacked and used to encourage forum members to sign up for Ekhlaas, a forum which had closed a year before and mysteriously resurfaced." The new forum was a fake, the equivalent of an online spider web, stickily entangling would-be terrorists and their fans.

The following year, a similar thing happened to the Global Islamic Media Front, a network for producing and distributing radical propaganda online. GIMF was forced to warn its members that the group's own encryption program, "Mujahideen Secrets 2.0," shouldn't be downloaded because it had been compromised. More amusing was the 2010 episode in which al-Qaida in the Arabian Peninsula posted the first issue of *Inspire,* an English-language online magazine designed to draw in recruits and spread terror tactics. Excited terrorist readers instead found the pages replaced by a PDF for a cupcake recipe, reportedly put there by hackers for British intelligence agencies. One can imagine deadlier forms of information corruption, such as changing the online recipes of how to make a bomb, so that a would-be bombmaker blows himself up during assembly.

We can look at the digital world with only fear or we can recognize that every new technology brings promise and peril. The advent of reliable post in the 1800s allowed the most dangerous terrorists of that time, anarchist groups, to correspond across state borders, recruiting and coordinating in a way previously not possible, and even to deploy a new weapon: letter bombs. But it also allowed police to read their letters and crack down on them. So, too, today with the digital post. When it comes to cyber terrorism versus the terrorist use of cyberspace, we must balance chasing the chimeras of our fevered imaginations with watching the information flows where the real action is taking place.

Critical Thinking

1. What was wrong with Secretary Lynn's statement at the RSA Conference?

2. How does that compare with what Professor Lucas had to say?

3. How do terror groups actually use the Internet?

Create Central

www.mhhe.com/createcentral

Internet References

Cyberterrorism Defense Analysis Center
www.cyberterrorismcenter.org
United States Institute of Peace
www.usip.org

PETER W. SINGER Director, 21st Century Defense Initiative Senior Fellow, Foreign Policy @peterwsinger.

Article   Prepared by: Joanne Naughton

An About-Face on Crime

CHARLIE SAVAGE AND ERICA GOODE

Learning Outcomes

After reading this article, you will be able to:

- Explain how fear of crime has caused some policing tactics to go too far.
- Show how mandatory minimum sentence laws came about.

Two decisions Monday, one by a federal judge in New York and the other by Attorney General Eric H. Holder Jr., were powerful signals that the pendulum has swung away from the tough-on-crime policies of a generation ago. Those policies have been denounced as discriminatory and responsible for explosive growth in the prison population.

Critics have long contended that draconian mandatory minimum sentence laws for low-level drug offenses, as well as stop-and-frisk police policies that target higher-crime and minority neighborhoods, have a disproportionate impact on members of minority groups. On Monday, Mr. Holder announced that federal prosecutors would no longer invoke the sentencing laws, and a judge found that stop-and-frisk practices in New York were unconstitutional racial profiling.

While the timing was a coincidence, Barbara Arnwine, the president of the Lawyers Committee for Civil Rights Under Law, said that the effect was "historic, groundbreaking, and potentially game-changing."

"I thought that the most important significance of both events was the sense of enough is enough," said Ms. Arnwine, who attended the speech in San Francisco where Mr. Holder unveiled the new Justice Department policy. "It's a feeling that this is the moment to make needed change. This just can't continue, this level of extreme heightened injustice in our policing, our law enforcement and our criminal justice system."

A generation ago, amid a crack epidemic, state and federal lawmakers enacted a wave of tough-on-crime measures that resulted in an 800 percent increase in the number of prisoners in the United States, even as the population grew by only a third. The spike in prisoners centered on an increase in the number of African-American and Hispanic men convicted of drug crimes; blacks are about six times as likely as whites to be incarcerated.

But the crack wave has long since passed and violent crime rates have plummeted to four-decade lows, in the process reducing crime as a salient political issue. Traditionally conservative states, driven by a need to save money on building and maintaining prisons, have taken the lead in scaling back policies of mass incarceration. Against that backdrop, the move away from mandatory sentences and Judge Shira A. Scheindlin's ruling on stop-and-frisk practices signaled that a course correction on two big criminal justice issues that disproportionately affect minorities has finally been made, according to the advocates who have pushed for those changes.

"I think that there is a sea change now of thinking around the impact of over-incarceration and selective enforcement in our criminal justice system on racial minorities," said Vanita Gupta of the American Civil Liberties Union. "These are hugely significant and symbolic events, because we would not have either of these even five years ago."

Michelle Alexander, an Ohio State University law professor who wrote "The New Jim Crow: Mass Incarceration in the Age of Colorblindness," an influential 2010 book about the racial impact of policies like stop-and-frisk and mandatory minimum drug sentences, said the two developments gave her a sense of "cautious optimism."

"For those of us who have become increasingly alarmed over the years at the millions of lives that have been wasted due to the drug war and the types of police tactics that have been deployed in the get-tough-on-crime movement, today's announcements give us fresh hope that there is, in fact, a growing public consensus that the path that we, the nation, have been on for the past 40 years has been deeply misguided and has caused far more harm and suffering than it has prevented," she said.

But not everyone was celebrating. William G. Otis, a former federal prosecutor and an adjunct professor at Georgetown Law School, described Mr. Holder's move as a victory for drug dealers that would incentivize greater sales of addictive contraband, and he suggested that the stop-and-frisk ruling could be overturned on appeal.

Mr. Otis also warned that society was becoming "complacent" and forgetting that the drug and sentencing policies enacted over the last three decades had contributed to the falling crime rates.

Yet Chuck Wexler, executive director of the Police Executive Research Forum, a Washington-based research group, said many police chiefs agreed that it was time to rethink mandatory sentencing for low-level drug offenses. And he said departments across the country would examine the stop-and-frisk ruling in New York "to see if their practices pass muster."

But he added: "You can't get away from the fact that in most large cities, crime is concentrated in poor areas which are predominantly minority. The question becomes, what tactics are acceptable in those communities to reduce crime? And there is a trade-off between the tactics that may be used and the issue of fairness."

David Rudovsky, a civil rights lawyer in Philadelphia who has been involved in a lawsuit over stop-and-frisk in that city, said both Holder's announcement and the ruling were "part of a national re-examination of criminal justice policy that has been spurred for the last 40 years by a fear of crime."

As that fear has lessened, he added, there has been more room to be heard for critics who say that some policies have gone too far and may be counterproductive. Those critics cite the low rate of finding guns with stop-and-frisk actions, and say that the experience of being searched—and the consequences if drugs are discovered—alienate people in targeted communities, making them less willing to give the police information about more serious violent crimes.

"There was the thought that if we stop, frisk, arrest and incarcerate huge numbers of people, that will reduce crime," Rudovsky said. "But while that may have had some effect on crime, the negative parts outweighed the positive parts."

Critics have argued that aggressive policing in minority neighborhoods can distort overall crime statistics. Federal data show, for example, that black Americans were nearly four times as likely as whites to be arrested on charges of marijuana possession in 2010, even though the two groups used the drug at similar rates.

"There is just as much drugs going on in the Upper East Side of New York or Cleveland Park in D.C.," said Jamie Fellner, a specialist on race and criminal drug law enforcement for Human Rights Watch, citing predominantly affluent and white neighborhoods. "But that is not where police are doing their searches for drugs."

Alfred Blumstein, a Carnegie Mellon professor who has studied race and incarceration issues, said Mr. Holder's speech and Judge Scheindlin's stop-and-frisk ruling both addressed policies that "were attempts to stop crime, but they weren't terribly effective."

Together, he said, the events indicated that society was "trying to become more effective and more targeted and, in the process, to reduce the heavy impact on particularly African-Americans."

Critical Thinking

1. What's wrong with the tough-on-crime policies of a generation ago?

2. Do you believe William Otis's warning is valid?

Create Central

www.mhhe.com/createcentral

Internet References

Drug War Facts
www.drugwarfacts.org/cms/Mandatory_Minimum_Sentencing#sthash.Jl4rCKxz.dpbs

The Sentencing Project
www.sentencingproject.org/detail/news.cfm?news_id=1659

Unit 2

UNIT

Prepared by: Joanne Naughton

Victimology

For many years, crime victims were not considered an important topic for criminological study. Now, however, criminologists consider that focusing on victims and victimization is essential to understanding the phenomenon of crime. The popularity of this area of study can be attributed to the early work of Hans Von Hentig and the later work of Stephen Schafer. These writers were the first to assert that crime victims play an integral role in the criminal event, that their actions may actually precipitate crime, and that unless the victim's role is considered, the study of crime is not complete.

In recent years, a growing number of criminologists have devoted increasing attention to the victim's role in the criminal justice process. Generally, areas of particular interest include establishing probabilities of victimization risks, studying victim precipitation of crime and culpability, and designing services expressly for victims of crime. As more criminologists focus their attention on the victim's role in the criminal process, victimology will take on even greater importance.

Article   Prepared by: Joanne Naughton

Telling the Truth about Damned Lies and Statistics

JOEL BEST

Learning Outcomes

After reading this article, you will be able to:

- Evaluate statistics more critically.
- Understand how statistics can be misinterpreted.

The dissertation prospectus began by quoting a statistic—a "grabber" meant to capture the reader's attention. The graduate student who wrote this prospectus undoubtedly wanted to seem scholarly to the professors who would read it; they would be supervising the proposed research. And what could be more scholarly than a nice, authoritative statistic, quoted from a professional journal in the student's field?

So the prospectus began with this (carefully footnoted) quotation: "Every year since 1950, the number of American children gunned down has doubled." I had been invited to serve on the student's dissertation committee. When I read the quotation, I assumed the student had made an error in copying it. I went to the library and looked up the article the student had cited. There, in the journal's 1995 volume, was exactly the same sentence: "Every year since 1950, the number of American children gunned down has doubled."

This quotation is my nomination for a dubious distinction: I think it may be the worst—that is, the most inaccurate—social statistic ever.

What makes this statistic so bad? Just for the sake of argument, let's assume that "the number of American children gunned down" in 1950 was one. If the number doubled each year, there must have been two children gunned down in 1951, four in 1952, eight in 1953, and so on. By 1960, the number would have been 1,024. By 1965, it would have been 32,768 (in 1965, the F.B.I. identified only 9,960 criminal homicides in the entire country, including adult as well as child victims). By 1970, the number would have passed one million; by 1980, one billion (more than four times the total U.S. population in that year). Only three years later, in 1983, the number of American children gunned down would have been 8.6 billion (nearly twice the earth's population at the time). Another milestone would have been passed in 1987, when the number of gunned-down

American children (137 billion) would have surpassed the best estimates for the total human population throughout history (110 billion). By 1995, when the article was published, the annual number of victims would have been over 35 trillion—a really big number, of a magnitude you rarely encounter outside economics or astronomy.

Thus my nomination: estimating the number of American child gunshot victims in 1995 at 35 trillion must be as far off—as hilariously, wildly wrong—as a social statistic can be. (If anyone spots a more inaccurate social statistic, I'd love to hear about it.)

Where did the article's author get this statistic? I wrote the author, who responded that the statistic came from the Children's Defense Fund, a well-known advocacy group for children. The C.D.F.'s *The State of America's Children Yearbook 1994* does state: "The number of American children killed each year by guns has doubled since 1950." Note the difference in the wording—the C.D.F. claimed there were twice as many deaths in 1994 as in 1950; the article's author reworded that claim and created a very different meaning.

It is worth examining the history of this statistic. It began with the C.D.F. noting that child gunshot deaths had doubled from 1950 to 1994. This is not quite as dramatic an increase as it might seem. Remember that the U.S. population also rose throughout this period; in fact, it grew about 73 percent—or nearly double. Therefore, we might expect all sorts of things—including the number of child gunshot deaths—to increase, to nearly double, just because the population grew. Before we can decide whether twice as many deaths indicate that things are getting worse, we'd have to know more. The C.D.F. statistic raises other issues as well: Where did the statistic come from? Who counts child gunshot deaths, and how? What is meant by a "child" (some C.D.F. statistics about violence include everyone under age 25)? What is meant by "killed by guns" (gunshot-death statistics often include suicides and accidents, as well as homicides)? But people rarely ask questions of this sort when they encounter statistics. Most of the time, most people simply accept statistics without question.

Certainly, the article's author didn't ask many probing, critical questions about the C.D.F.'s claim. Impressed by the statistic, the author repeated it—well, meant to repeat it. Instead, by rewording the C.D.F.'s claim, the author created a mutant statistic, one garbled almost beyond recognition.

But people treat mutant statistics just as they do other statistics—that is, they usually accept even the most implausible claims without question. For example, the journal editor who accepted the author's article for publication did not bother to consider the implications of child victims doubling each year. And people repeat bad statistics: The graduate student copied the garbled statistic and inserted it into the dissertation prospectus. Who knows whether still other readers were impressed by the author's statistic and remembered it or repeated it? The article remains on the shelf in hundreds of libraries, available to anyone who needs a dramatic quote. The lesson should be clear: Bad statistics live on; they take on lives of their own.

Some statistics are born bad—they aren't much good from the start, because they are based on nothing more than guesses or dubious data. Other statistics mutate; they become bad after being mangled (as in the case of the author's creative rewording). Either way, bad statistics are potentially important: They can be used to stir up public outrage or fear; they can distort our understanding of our world; and they can lead us to make poor policy choices.

The notion that we need to watch out for bad statistics isn't new. We've all heard people say, "You can prove anything with statistics." The title of my book, *Damned Lies and Statistics*, comes from a famous aphorism (usually attributed to Mark Twain or Benjamin Disraeli): "There are three kinds of lies: lies, damned lies, and statistics." There is even a useful little book, still in print after more than 40 years, called *How to Lie With Statistics*.

We shouldn't ignore all statistics, or assume that every number is false. Some statistics are bad, but others are pretty good. And we need good statistics to talk sensibly about social problems.

Statistics, then, have a bad reputation. We suspect that statistics may be wrong, that people who use statistics may be "lying"—trying to manipulate us by using numbers to somehow distort the truth. Yet, at the same time, we need statistics; we depend upon them to summarize and clarify the nature of our complex society. This is particularly true when we talk about social problems. Debates about social problems routinely raise questions that demand statistical answers: Is the problem widespread? How many people—and which people—does it affect? Is it getting worse? What does it cost society? What will it cost to deal with it? Convincing answers to such questions demand evidence, and that usually means numbers, measurements, statistics.

But can't you prove anything with statistics? It depends on what "prove" means. If we want to know, say, how many children are "gunned down" each year, we can't simply guess—pluck a number from thin air: 100, 1,000, 10,000, 35 trillion,

whatever. Obviously, there's no reason to consider an arbitrary guess "proof" of anything. However, it might be possible for someone—using records kept by police departments or hospital emergency rooms or coroners—to keep track of children who have been shot; compiling careful, complete records might give us a fairly accurate idea of the number of gunned-down children. If that number seems accurate enough, we might consider it very strong evidence—or proof.

The solution to the problem of bad statistics is not to ignore all statistics, or to assume that every number is false. Some statistics are bad, but others are pretty good, and we need statistics—good statistics—to talk sensibly about social problems. The solution, then, is not to give up on statistics, but to become better judges of the numbers we encounter. We need to think critically about statistics—at least critically enough to suspect that the number of children gunned down hasn't been doubling each year since 1950.

A few years ago, the mathematician John Allen Paulos wrote *Innumeracy*, a short, readable book about "mathematical illiteracy." Too few people, he argued, are comfortable with basic mathematical principles, and this makes them poor judges of the numbers they encounter. No doubt this is one reason we have so many bad statistics. But there are other reasons, as well.

Social statistics describe society, but they are also products of our social arrangements. The people who bring social statistics to our attention have reasons for doing so; they inevitably want something, just as reporters and the other media figures who repeat and publicize statistics have their own goals. Statistics are tools, used for particular purposes. Thinking critically about statistics requires understanding their place in society.

While we may be more suspicious of statistics presented by people with whom we disagree—people who favor different political parties or have different beliefs—bad statistics are used to promote all sorts of causes. Bad statistics come from conservatives on the political right and liberals on the left, from wealthy corporations and powerful government agencies, and from advocates of the poor and the powerless.

In order to interpret statistics, we need more than a checklist of common errors. We need a general approach, an orientation, a mind-set that we can use to think about new statistics that we encounter. We ought to approach statistics thoughtfully. This can be hard to do, precisely because so many people in our society treat statistics as fetishes. We might call this the mind-set of the awestruck—the people who don't think critically, who act as though statistics have magical powers. The awestruck know they don't always understand the statistics they hear, but this doesn't bother them. After all, who can expect to understand magical numbers? The reverential fatalism of the awestruck is not thoughtful—it is a way of avoiding thought. We need a different approach.

One choice is to approach statistics critically. Being critical does not mean being negative or hostile—it is not cynicism. The critical approach statistics thoughtfully; they avoid the extremes of both naïve acceptance and cynical rejection of the numbers they encounter. Instead, the critical attempt to evaluate numbers, to distinguish between good statistics and bad statistics.

The critical understand that, while some social statistics may be pretty good, they are never perfect. Every statistic is a way of summarizing complex information into relatively simple numbers. Inevitably, some information, some of the complexity, is lost whenever we use statistics. The critical recognize that this is an inevitable limitation of statistics. Moreover, they realize that every statistic is the product of choices—the choice between defining a category broadly or narrowly, the choice of one measurement over another, the choice of a sample. People choose definitions, measurements, and samples for all sorts of reasons: Perhaps they want to emphasize some aspect of a problem; perhaps it is easier or cheaper to gather data in a particular way—many considerations can come into play. Every statistic is a compromise among choices. This means that every definition—and every measurement and every sample—probably has limitations and can be criticized.

Being critical means more than simply pointing to the flaws in a statistic. Again, every statistic has flaws. The issue is whether a particular statistic's flaws are severe enough to damage its usefulness. Is the definition so broad that it encompasses too many false positives (or so narrow that it excludes too many false negatives)? How would changing the definition alter the statistic? Similarly, how do the choices of measurements and samples affect the statistic? What would happen if different measures or samples were chosen? And how is the statistic used? Is it being interpreted appropriately, or has its meaning been mangled to create a mutant statistic? Are the comparisons that are being made appropriate, or are apples being confused with oranges? How do different choices produce the conflicting numbers found in stat wars? These are the sorts of questions the critical ask.

As a practical matter, it is virtually impossible for citizens in contemporary society to avoid statistics about social problems. Statistics arise in all sorts of ways, and in almost every case the people promoting statistics want to persuade us. Activists use statistics to convince us that social problems are serious and deserve our attention and concern. Charities use statistics to encourage donations. Politicians use statistics to persuade us that they understand society's problems and that they deserve our support. The media use statistics to make their reporting more dramatic, more convincing, more compelling. Corporations use statistics to promote and improve their products. Researchers use statistics to document their findings and support their conclusions. Those with whom we agree use statistics to reassure us that we're on the right side, while our opponents use statistics to try and convince us that we are wrong. Statistics are one of the standard types of evidence used by people in our society.

It is not possible simply to ignore statistics, to pretend they don't exist. That sort of head-in-the-sand approach would be too costly. Without statistics, we limit our ability to think thoughtfully about our society; without statistics, we have no accurate ways of judging how big a problem may be, whether it is getting worse, or how well the policies designed to address

that problem actually work. And awestruck or naïve attitudes toward statistics are no better than ignoring statistics; statistics have no magical properties, and it is foolish to assume that all statistics are equally valid. Nor is a cynical approach the answer; statistics are too widespread and too useful to be automatically discounted.

It would be nice to have a checklist, a set of items we could consider in evaluating any statistic. The list might detail potential problems with definitions, measurements, sampling, mutation, and so on. These are, in fact, common sorts of flaws found in many statistics, but they should not be considered a formal, complete checklist. It is probably impossible to produce a complete list of statistical flaws—no matter how long the list, there will be other possible problems that could affect statistics.

The goal is not to memorize a list, but to develop a thoughtful approach. Becoming critical about statistics requires being prepared to ask questions about numbers. When encountering a new statistic in, say, a news report, the critical try to assess it. What might be the sources for this number? How could one go about producing the figure? Who produced the number, and what interests might they have? What are the different ways key terms might have been defined, and which definitions have been chosen? How might the phenomena be measured, and which measurement choices have been made? What sort of sample was gathered, and how might that sample affect the result? Is the statistic being properly interpreted? Are comparisons being made, and if so, are the comparisons appropriate? Are there competing statistics? If so, what stakes do the opponents have in the issue, and how are those stakes likely to affect their use of statistics? And is it possible to figure out why the statistics seem to disagree, what the differences are in the ways the competing sides are using figures?

At first, this list of questions may seem overwhelming. How can an ordinary person—someone who reads a statistic in a magazine article or hears it on a news broadcast—determine the answers to such questions? Certainly news reports rarely give detailed information on the processes by which statistics are created. And few of us have time to drop everything and investigate the background of some new number we encounter. Being critical, it seems, involves an impossible amount of work.

In practice, however, the critical need not investigate the origin of every statistic. Rather, being critical means appreciating the inevitable limitations that affect all statistics, rather than being awestruck in the presence of numbers. It means not being too credulous, not accepting every statistic at face value. But it also means appreciating that statistics, while always imperfect, can be useful. Instead of automatically discounting every statistic, the critical reserve judgment. When confronted with an interesting number, they may try to learn more, to evaluate, to weigh the figure's strengths and weaknesses.

Of course, this critical approach need not—and should not—be limited to statistics. It ought to apply to all the evidence we encounter when we scan a news report, or listen to a speech—whenever we learn about social problems.

Claims about social problems often feature dramatic, compelling examples; the critical might ask whether an example is likely to be a typical case or an extreme, exceptional instance. Claims about social problems often include quotations from different sources, and the critical might wonder why those sources have spoken and why they have been quoted: Do they have particular expertise? Do they stand to benefit if they influence others? Claims about social problems usually involve arguments about the problem's causes and potential solutions. The critical might ask whether these arguments are convincing. Are they logical? Does the proposed solution seem feasible and appropriate? And so on. Being critical—adopting a skeptical, analytical stance when confronted with claims—is an approach that goes far beyond simply dealing with statistics.

Statistics are not magical. Nor are they always true—or always false. Nor need they be incomprehensible. Adopting a critical approach offers an effective way of responding to the numbers we are sure to encounter. Being critical requires more thought, but failing to adopt a critical mind-set makes us powerless to evaluate what others tell us. When we fail to think critically, the statistics we hear might just as well be magical.

Critical Thinking

1. Why are there bad statistics?

2. How can one approach statistics critically?

3. What was wrong with the following statement made in 1995: "Every year since 1950 the number of American children gunned down has doubled"?

Create Central

www.mhhe.com/createcentral

Internet References

Bureau of Justice Statistics
www.bjs.gov

Federal Bureau of Investigation (F.B.I.)
www.fbi.gov/about-us/cjis/ucr/ucr-statistics-their-proper-use

---

JOEL BEST is a professor of sociology and criminal justice at the University of Delaware. This essay is excerpted from *Damned Lies and Statistics: Untangling Numbers from the Media, Politicians, and Activists*, published by the University of California Press and reprinted by permission. Copyright © 2001 by the Regents of the University of California.

Article Prepared by: Joanne Naughton

California Accuses JPMorgan Chase of Unlawful Debt Collection Practices

DON THOMPSON

Learning Outcomes

After reading this article, you will be able to:

- Describe the allegedly illegal tactics used by JPMorgan Chase & Co. to collect debts from credit card holders.

- State some of the rights bank customers are entitled to.

California's attorney general sued one of the nation's largest banks Thursday, alleging that JPMorgan Chase & Co. used illegal tactics in its efforts to collect debts from more than 100,000 credit card holders.

The lawsuit filed in Los Angeles Superior Court says the company filed thousands of debt collection lawsuits each month between 2008 and April 2011 using improper practices that shortcut procedures required by California law.

JPMorgan Chase spokesman Paul Hartwick said the company had no comment.

"At nearly every stage of the collection process, defendants cut corners in the name of speed, cost savings, and their own convenience, providing only the thinnest veneer of legitimacy to their lawsuits," the complaint says. It alleges the company sued borrowers "based on patently insufficient evidence—betting that borrowers would lack the resources or legal sophistication to call defendants' bluff."

Attorney General Kamala Harris' office said the company's methods included "robo-signing" legal documents, a practice that was widely used in mortgage foreclosures until it was outlawed. JPMorgan Chase is one of five major banks that settled with California and other states after the housing market meltdown.

The lawsuit contends that in filing the debt-collection lawsuits, company officials similarly signed legal documents, including sworn declarations, without reviewing the related files and bank records or even reading the documents.

That and other practices let the company file 469 debt-recovery lawsuits in one day alone, according to the lawsuit.

The company's in-house lawyers filed an average of 100 lawsuits a day for each day the courts were open, the state says, while its outside counsel filed another 20,000 lawsuits.

The lawsuit says the company also failed to properly notify its customers that the lawsuits had been filed, even though it represented that they had been served with court papers as required by law.

The company also did a poor job of drafting the legal filings, including failing to remove consumers' personal information from the public records, according to the lawsuit. That makes the customers vulnerable to identity theft and violates state law, the state says.

Company officials also routinely swore that its customers were not on active military duty, without actually checking if that was true. The omission deprived members of the military of proper legal protections, the complaint says.

The lawsuit also names the affiliated Chase Bank USA and Chase Bankcard Services Inc.

Harris is seeking a permanent ban on the allegedly illegal practices as well as damages for borrowers who were harmed as the company rushed to obtain court judgments and wage garnishment orders. The lawsuit says the company also should be fined $2,500 for each violation of state law, and an additional $2,500 for each violation that involves a senior citizen or disabled person.

"Chase abused the judicial process and engaged in serious misconduct against California credit card borrowers," Harris said in a statement.

Critical Thinking

1. What's wrong with "robo-signing" legal documents?
2. Don't banks have a right to do what is necessary to collect their debts from customers?

Create Central

www.mhhe.com/createcentral

Internet References

Bureau of Consumer Protection - Business Center
www.business.ftc.gov/documents/fair-debt-collection-practices-act

Federal Deposit Insurance Corporation (FDIC)
www.fdic.gov/bank/individual/failed/pls

Article

Prepared by: Joanne Naughton

22 Years of Promises

Military leaders have promised in recent months that they are taking sexual assault seriously and doing everything they can to combat it. But haven't they been saying the same thing for two decades?

NANCY MONTGOMERY

Learning Outcomes

After reading this article, you will be able to:

* Recount the problems faced by victims of sexual assault in the military.

* Report whether the military has taken steps to abate the problem of sexual assault.

The nation's top military officers told Congress last month that the chain of command was crucial to curbing sexual assault in the services. The message is not a new one; they have been saying the same thing for nearly two decades—sometimes using remarkably similar language.

"The success of our missions depends in large measure on the degree of trust and understanding that exists among the people in our units," then Air Force Secretary Sheila Widnall told the Senate Armed Services Committee in 1997 in a hearing on sexual harassment. "Anything that might erode that trust is just not tolerable. We will maintain it, and we will enforce it. We will ensure that our people are treated with the human respect and dignity that they deserve."

Sixteen years later, Army Chief of Staff Ray Odierno seemed to be reading from the same set of notes.

"Our profession is built on the bedrock of trust—the trust that must inherently exist among soldiers, and between soldiers and their leaders to accomplish their mission," Odierno said at a June 4 hearing on sexual assault. "These acts . . . will not be tolerated. This is about inculcating a culture that is in line with our values, specifically treating all with dignity and respect."

In 1997, Widnall told the senators that commanders were key in ending sexual harassment.

"The most effective way of ensuring accountability in military organizations is to give commanders the direct responsibility . . . ," she said. "Commanders' demonstrated leadership and personal commitment . . . must be visible and unequivocal."

Odierno agreed in his testimony in June.

"Command authority is the most critical mechanism for ensuring discipline and accountability, cohesion and the integrity of the force," Odierno told the committee. "It is imperative

that we keep the chain of command fully engaged and at the center of any solution."

Critics say that the current rash of military sexual assaults, following a half-dozen national scandals, shows that the military is unwilling or incapable of dealing with the issue.

"They're stuck in denial. They still think they can fix things by themselves," said Rep. Jackie Speier, D-Calif., who has introduced legislation for the past two years to remove sexual assault prosecutions from command purview and give it to a new office of civilian and military experts.

"They shrug it off, as they have for two and a half decades. But the chain of command is the problem. A fallen house doesn't magically rebuild itself."

Critics say that after each sexual abuse scandal, military officials have resisted reforms, insisted they knew best how to fix things, then done little, proclaimed victory and waited for public attention to move elsewhere.

"This epidemic has persisted for at least 20 years and probably four decades," said Nancy Parrish, president of Protect Our Defenders, an advocacy group for military sexual assault victims. "Nothing has changed."

Until the 1991 Tailhook Convention, there was little public awareness that military women could be at risk from their brothers in arms.

At a reunion of retired and active-duty Navy aviators at a Las Vegas hotel, scores of women were assaulted. Some victims were passed through a hallway gauntlet of men who ripped off their clothes and groped them, with the Navy's top brass doing nothing to stop them.

The initial Navy investigation blamed a few lower-ranking men, and the rear admiral in charge of the investigation said he believed that many female Navy pilots were "go-go dancers, topless dancers or hookers," according to a Pentagon report.

He was the first of numerous high-ranking Navy officers forced to resign after the Pentagon investigation.

"We get it," then Acting Navy Secretary Sean O'Keefe said in 1992. "We know that the larger issue is a cultural problem which has allowed demeaning behavior and attitudes towards women to exist within the Navy Department," O'Keefe said in the *Los Angeles Times*. "Our senior leadership is totally committed to confronting this problem and demonstrating that sexual harassment will not be tolerated. Those who don't get the message will be driven from our ranks."

O'Keefe's remarks were echoed at the SASC hearing in June.

"The Joint Chiefs and our senior enlisted leaders are committed to correcting this crisis," said Chairman of the Joint Chiefs of Staff Gen. Martin Dempsey. "We are acting swiftly and deliberately to change a culture that has become too complacent."

Victims' advocates have for years called for changes in the way military sexual assault is handled. They have called for allowing victims to sue the services for damages and for changes to the Uniform Code of Military Justice, which gives commanders unfettered discretion in prosecution and sentencing, a situation that they say is rife with conflict of interest and bias. Most victims don't report their assaults, advocates say, because they don't trust the chain of command will believe them or hold perpetrators accountable and that they'll be scapegoated.

The Pentagon estimates that sexual abuse throughout the services increased from 19,000 incidents in 2010 to 26,000 last year, although only a fraction were reported through the chain of command. But the disposition in the case of Air Force fighter pilot Lt. Col. James Wilkerson galvanized a number of senators, all women, to consider making changes to the Uniform Code of Military Justice.

Wilkerson was convicted in November at an Aviano Air Base court-martial of sexually assaulting a sleeping houseguest after an impromptu party.

Three months later, Third Air Force commander Lt. Gen. Craig Franklin overturned the verdict, explaining that it was "incongruent" that a family man like Wilkerson would assault a woman in his own home and that he was perplexed about why the woman had been sleeping there.

As a result of Franklin's action, Congress is widely expected to pass legislation as part of the National Defense Authorization Act to strip commanders of discretion to overturn guilty verdicts. Such a measure has received the support of Defense Secretary Chuck Hagel and, after initial resistance, the service chiefs.

More sweeping legislation introduced by Sen. Kirsten Gillebrand, D-N.Y., to make military prosecutors the disposition authority in sexual assault cases, removing the chain of command from the process, failed to pass the committee.

Gillibrand vowed to offer her amendment again when the full Senate takes up the defense authorization act.

"I am deeply disappointed the voices of the victims of sexual assault have been drowned out by the military leaders who have failed to combat this crisis," she said in a statement.

In 2003, six years after Widnall said that sexual abuse would not be tolerated in the Air Force—that command climate assessments would hold accountable and weed out bad commanders—the Air Force Academy was beset with accusations that male cadets had been assaulting female cadets.

Air Force Secretary James Roche said the service would "learn about the problem and deal with it ourselves rather than turning to some outsiders who may not understand the culture as well," the *Los Angeles Times* reported.

"We still believe this is one of the finest institutions in the world. It stumbled, and now it's got to get fixed," Roche said.

An investigatory civilian panel, ordered by Congress and headed by former Florida Republican congresswoman Tillie Fowler, reached a bleaker conclusion.

A "deep chasm" in leadership, the 2003 report said, had "helped create an environment in which sexual assault became a part of life at the Academy."

The panel found that sexual assaults had likely occurred and gone unpunished since the academy began admitting women in 1976. "The highest levels of Air Force leadership have known of serious sexual misconduct problems" for at least a decade, the report said, and done little about it.

Female cadets had suffered, the report said, noting that no one had been prosecuted and "sexual offenders may have been commissioned as Air Force officers."

The academies, which educate a potential select group of future commanders, have continued to struggle with reports of sexual assault and misogyny.

Eighty cases of sexual assault were reported by cadets and midshipmen during the last academic year, up from 65 the previous year, according to a Pentagon report.

The Naval Academy is investigating a report that three members of its football team raped a fellow midshipman at a party as she lay unconscious, passed out from drinking alcohol.

The entire men's rugby team at the U.S. Military Academy was temporarily disbanded shortly before graduation this year after cadets routinely forwarded emails that a West Point spokesman described as "locker room trash" that degraded women.

At the Senate hearing, the service chiefs said sexual assault had not been the top priority in a decade of war, but that it was now.

They were making progress, they said.

"There is more work to do, much more work, but we are seeing indicators that tell us we are on the right track," said Gen. James Amos, Marine Corps commandant. "I believe we have momentum on our side."

Critical Thinking

1. What does Rep. Speier mean when she says the military is "stuck in denial"?

2. What has the military done about the problem of sexual abuse?

3. Have the military's efforts to combat sexual abuse been effective?

Create Central

www.mhhe.com/createcentral

Internet References

Democracy Now
    www.democracynow.org/2013/11/14/senate_faces_historic_vote_on_handling

United States Department of Defense - Sexual Assault Prevention and Response
    www.sapr.mil/index.php/annual-reports

Article   Prepared by: Joanne Naughton

University of Montana Rape Reports Botched, U.S. Finds

RYAN J. REILLY

Learning Outcomes

After reading this article, you will be able to:

- Understand that victims do not always appear visibly upset when reporting that they have been the victim of a violent crime.

- Appreciate the importance of not treating victims of sexual assault with disrespect or indifference.

Members of the University of Montana football team were treated as "gods" and were "allowed to get away with anything," including sexual assault, members of the university community told federal officials, according to a report released Thursday.

The University of Montana cooperated with probes by the Justice Department's Civil Rights Division and the Department of Education's Office of Civil Rights starting in May 2012. Two agreements with the university require the campus police force, found to have discriminated against women students, to work with an independent monitor to ensure proper responses to rape and sexual harassment allegations in the future, and order university officials to revise policies.

The investigation found that six football players were accused of aiding, attempting or committing sexual assault from spring 2009 to spring 2012 and that three of the players weren't prosecuted through the campus judicial system for more than a year after their coach was notified that the victim had filed a complaint with the Missoula Police Department. Former Montana quarterback Jordan Johnson was acquitted of rape earlier this year.

A campus police officer reported that one woman who said she was physically and sexually assaulted "did not appear visibly upset" and wrote that she did "appear somewhat angry and agitated," according to the Justice Department report. Further, the campus officer failed to note any of the woman's physical injuries, only her alcohol-scented breath. The Justice Department said the officer appeared to have relied on "unwarranted gender-based assumptions and stereotypes."

Two campus police officers responding to a different sexual assault report used the term "regretted sex," according to the report. Students and community activists described the officers' responses as "incompetent" and said they were "not well-trained," the report said.

Women reporting sexual assault were exposed to initial police interviews that could "discourage women from reporting sexual assaults," the Justice Department found.

"Women reported to us that being interviewed by [campus police] officers was emotionally difficult because they were simultaneously interviewed by multiple officers, because they were asked very personal questions without warning and without explanation of the questions' relevance to the investigation, and because the officers' emphasis on the personal burdens involved in seeking criminal justice heightened their fears," the report said. One advocate said the process was "painful" for victims.

The head of campus security told federal officials that his officers tried to assess whether an offense is "provable" and whether it seemed "credible" during their initial contact with a victim. The Justice Department said that was "in direct contradiction" to what the role of a first responder should be.

"The problems we found at the University of Montana were real and significant," Roy L. Austin of the Justice Department Civil Rights Division said in a statement. "These concerns, however, are not unique to this campus. The women who are subject to sexual harassment and assault know that without support the devastating consequences for them, their classmates and their community are made all the worse. Institutions of higher learning across the country must be absolutely tireless in their determination to fully and effectively respond to reports of sexual assault and sexual harassment on their campuses involving their students."

Critical Thinking

1. When taking a report about sexual assault from the victim, how important is it for campus security officers to assess whether the allegation is provable?

2. Should a campus security officer make a determination about whether a victim's report is credible?

Create Central

www.mhhe.com/createcentral

Internet References

Not in Our Town
www.niot.org/action-hub/local-lessons/not-our-campus-5-ways-move-action?gclid=COCjsIzmlrsCFUsV7AodgCgA2g

The Center for Public Integrity
www.publicintegrity.org/accountability/education/sexual-assault-campus

Article

Prepared by: Joanne Naughton

Human Sex Trafficking

AMANDA WALKER-RODRIGUEZ AND RODNEY HILL

Learning Outcomes

After reading this article, you will be able to:

- Outline the scope of human sex trafficking.
- Describe how victims are recruited into the business of human sex trafficking.

Human sex trafficking is the most common form of modern-day slavery. Estimates place the number of its domestic and international victims in the millions, mostly females and children enslaved in the commercial sex industry for little or no money.[1] The terms *human trafficking* and *sex slavery* usually conjure up images of young girls beaten and abused in faraway places, like Eastern Europe, Asia, or Africa. Actually, human sex trafficking and sex slavery happen locally in cities and towns, both large and small, throughout the United States, right in citizens' backyards.

Appreciating the magnitude of the problem requires first understanding what the issue is and what it is not. Additionally, people must be able to identify the victim in common trafficking situations.

Human Sex Trafficking

Many people probably remember popular movies and television shows depicting pimps as dressing flashy and driving large fancy cars. More important, the women—adults—consensually and voluntarily engaged in the business of prostitution without complaint. This characterization is extremely inaccurate, nothing more than fiction. In reality, the pimp *traffics* young women (and sometimes men) completely against their will by force or threat of force; this is human sex trafficking.

The Scope

Not only is human sex trafficking slavery but it is big business. It is the fastest-growing business of organized crime and the third-largest criminal enterprise in the world.[2] The majority of sex trafficking is international, with victims taken from such places as South and Southeast Asia, the former Soviet Union, Central and South America, and other less developed areas and moved to more developed ones, including Asia, the Middle East, Western Europe, and North America.[3]

Unfortunately, however, sex trafficking also occurs domestically.[4] The United States not only faces an influx of international victims but also has its own homegrown problem of interstate sex trafficking of minors.[5]

The United States not only faces an influx of international victims but also has its own homegrown problem of interstate sex trafficking of minors.

Although comprehensive research to document the number of children engaged in prostitution in the United States is lacking, an estimated 293,000 American youths currently are at risk of becoming victims of commercial sexual exploitation.[6] The majority of these victims are runaway or thrown-away youths who live on the streets and become victims of prostitution.[7] These children generally come from homes where they have been abused or from families who have abandoned them. Often, they become involved in prostitution to support themselves financially or to get the things they feel they need or want (like drugs).

Other young people are recruited into prostitution through forced abduction, pressure from parents, or through deceptive agreements between parents and traffickers. Once these children become involved in prostitution, they often are forced to travel far from their homes and, as a result, are isolated from their friends and family. Few children in this situation can develop new relationships with peers or adults other than the person victimizing them. The lifestyle of such youths revolves around violence, forced drug use, and constant threats.[8]

Among children and teens living on the streets in the United States, involvement in commercial sex activity is a problem of epidemic proportion. Many girls living on the street engage in formal prostitution, and some become entangled in nationwide organized crime networks where they are trafficked nationally. Criminal networks transport these children around the United States by a variety of means—cars, buses, vans, trucks, or planes—and often provide them counterfeit identification to use in the event of arrest. The average age at which girls first become victims of prostitution is 12 to 14. It is not only the girls on the streets who are affected; boys and transgender youth enter into prostitution between the ages of 11 and 13 on average.[9]

The Operation

Today, the business of human sex trafficking is much more organized and violent. These women and young girls are sold to traffickers, locked up in rooms or brothels for weeks or months, drugged, terrorized, and raped repeatedly.[10] These continual abuses make it easier for the traffickers to control their victims. The captives are so afraid and intimidated that they rarely speak out against their traffickers, even when faced with an opportunity to escape.

> **Today, the business of human sex trafficking is much more organized and violent.**

Generally, the traffickers are very organized. Many have a hierarchy system similar to that of other criminal organizations. Traffickers who have more than one victim often have a "bottom," who sits atop the hierarchy of prostitutes. The bottom, a victim herself, has been with the trafficker the longest and has earned his trust. Bottoms collect the money from the other girls, discipline them, seduce unwitting youths into trafficking, and handle the day-to-day business for the trafficker.

Traffickers represent every social, ethnic, and racial group. Various organizational types exist in trafficking. Some perpetrators are involved with local street and motorcycle gangs, others are members of larger nationwide gangs and criminal organizations, and some have no affiliation with any one group or organization. Traffickers are not only men—women run many established rings.

> **Traffickers represent every social, ethnic, and racial group.**

Traffickers use force, drugs, emotional tactics, and financial methods to control their victims. They have an especially easy time establishing a strong bond with young girls. These perpetrators may promise marriage and a lifestyle the youths often did not have in their previous familial relationships. They claim they "love" and "need" the victim and that any sex acts are for their future together. In cases where the children have few or no positive male role models in their lives, the traffickers take advantage of this fact and, in many cases, demand that the victims refer to them as "daddy," making it tougher for the youths to break the hold the perpetrator has on them.

Sometimes, the traffickers use violence, such as gang rape and other forms of abuse, to force the youths to work for them and remain under their control. One victim, a runaway from Baltimore County, Maryland, was gang raped by a group of men associated with the trafficker, who subsequently staged a "rescue." He then demanded that she repay him by working for him as one of his prostitutes. In many cases, however, the victims simply are beaten until they submit to the trafficker's demands.

In some situations, the youths have become addicted to drugs. The traffickers simply can use their ability to supply them with drugs as a means of control.

Traffickers often take their victims' identity forms, including birth certificates, passports, and drivers' licenses. In these cases, even if youths do leave they would have no ability to support themselves and often will return to the trafficker.

These abusive methods of control impact the victims both physically and mentally. Similar to cases involving Stockholm Syndrome, these victims, who have been abused over an extended period of time, begin to feel an attachment to the perpetrator.[11] This paradoxical psychological phenomenon makes it difficult for law enforcement to breach the bond of control, albeit abusive, the trafficker holds over the victim.

National Problem with Local Ties

The Federal Level

In 2000, Congress passed the Trafficking Victims Protection Act (TVPA), which created the first comprehensive federal law to address trafficking, with a significant focus on the international dimension of the problem. The law provides a three-pronged approach: *prevention* through public awareness programs overseas and a State Department-led monitoring and sanctions program; *protection* through a new T Visa and services for foreign national victims; and *prosecution* through new federal crimes and severe penalties.[12]

As a result of the passing of the TVPA, the Office to Monitor and Combat Trafficking in Persons was established in October 2001. This enabling legislation led to the creation of a bureau within the State Department to specifically address human trafficking and exploitation on all levels and to take legal action against perpetrators.[13] Additionally, this act was designed to enforce all laws within the 13th Amendment to the U.S. Constitution that apply.[14]

U.S. Immigration and Customs Enforcement (ICE) is one of the lead federal agencies charged with enforcing the TVPA. Human trafficking represents significant risks to homeland security. Would-be terrorists and criminals often can access the same routes and use the same methods as human traffickers. ICE's Human Smuggling and Trafficking Unit works to identify criminals and organizations involved in these illicit activities.

The FBI also enforces the TVPA. In June 2003, the FBI, in conjunction with the Department of Justice Child Exploitation and Obscenity Section and the National Center for Missing and Exploited Children, launched the Innocence Lost National Initiative. The agencies' combined efforts address the growing problem of domestic sex trafficking of children in the United States. To date, these groups have worked successfully to rescue nearly 900 children. Investigations successfully have led to the conviction of more than 500 pimps, madams, and their associates who exploit children through prostitution. These convictions have resulted in lengthy sentences, including multiple 25-year-to-life sentences and the seizure of real property, vehicles, and monetary assets.[15]

Both ICE and the FBI, along with other local, state, and federal law enforcement agencies and national victim-based advocacy groups in joint task forces, have combined resources and expertise on the issue. Today, the FBI participates in approximately 30 law enforcement task forces and about 42 Bureau of Justice Assistance (BJA)-sponsored task forces around the nation.[16]

In July 2004, the Human Smuggling Trafficking Center (HSTC) was created. The HSTC serves as a fusion center for information on human smuggling and trafficking, bringing together analysts, officers, and investigators from such agencies as the CIA, FBI, ICE, Department of State, and Department of Homeland Security.

The Local Level

With DOJ funding assistance, many jurisdictions have created human trafficking task forces to combat the problem. BJA's 42 such task forces can be demonstrated by several examples.[17]

- In 2004, the FBI's Washington field office and the D.C. Metropolitan Police Department joined with a variety of nongovernment organizations and service providers to combat the growing problem of human trafficking within Washington, D.C.
- In January 2005, the Massachusetts Human Trafficking Task Force was formed, with the Boston Police Department serving as the lead law enforcement entity. It uses a two-pronged approach, addressing investigations focusing on international victims and those focusing on the commercial sexual exploitation of children.
- The New Jersey Human Trafficking Task Force attacks the problem by training law enforcement in the methods of identifying victims and signs of trafficking, coordinating statewide efforts in the identification and provision of services to victims of human trafficking, and increasing the successful interdiction and prosecution of trafficking of human persons.
- Since 2006, the Louisiana Human Trafficking Task Force, which has law enforcement, training, and victim services components, has focused its law enforcement and victim rescue efforts on the Interstate 10 corridor from the Texas border on the west to the Mississippi border on the east. This corridor, the basic northern border of the hurricane-ravaged areas of Louisiana, long has served as a major avenue of illegal immigration efforts. The I-10 corridor also is the main avenue for individuals participating in human trafficking to supply the labor needs in the hurricane-damaged areas of the state.
- In 2007, the Maryland Human Trafficking Task Force was formed. It aims to create a heightened law enforcement and victim service presence in the community. Its law enforcement efforts include establishing roving operations to identify victims and traffickers, deputizing local law enforcement to assist in federal human trafficking investigations, and providing training for law enforcement officers.

Anytown, USA

In December 2008, Corey Davis, the ringleader of a sex-trafficking ring that spanned at least three states, was sentenced in federal court in Bridgeport, Connecticut, on federal civil rights charges for organizing and leading the sex-trafficking operation that exploited as many as 20 females, including minors. Davis received a sentence of 293 months in prison followed by a lifetime term of supervised release. He pleaded guilty to multiple sex-trafficking charges, including recruiting a girl under the age of 18 to engage in prostitution. Davis admitted that he recruited a minor to engage in prostitution; that he was the organizer of a sex-trafficking venture; and that he used force, fraud, and coercion to compel the victim to commit commercial sex acts from which he obtained the proceeds.

According to the indictment, Davis lured victims to his operation with promises of modeling contracts and a glamorous lifestyle. He then forced them into a grueling schedule of dancing and performing at strip clubs in Connecticut, New York, and New Jersey. When the clubs closed, Davis forced the victims to walk the streets until 4 or 5 A.M. propositioning customers. The indictment also alleged that he beat many of the victims to force them to work for him and that he also used physical abuse as punishment for disobeying the stringent rules he imposed to isolate and control them.[18]

As this and other examples show, human trafficking cases happen all over the United States. A few instances would represent just the "tip of the iceberg" in a growing criminal enterprise. Local and state criminal justice officials must understand that these cases are not isolated incidents that occur infrequently. They must remain alert for signs of trafficking in their jurisdictions and aggressively follow through on the smallest clue. Numerous websites openly (though they try to mask their actions) advertise for prostitution. Many of these sites involve young girls victimized by sex trafficking. Many of the pictures are altered to give the impression of older girls engaged in this activity freely and voluntarily. However, as prosecutors, the authors both have encountered numerous cases of suspected human trafficking involving underage girls.

> **Local and state criminal justice officials must understand that these cases are not isolated incidents that occur infrequently.**

The article "The Girls Next Door" describes a conventional midcentury home in Plainfield, New Jersey, that sat in a nice middle-class neighborhood. Unbeknownst to the neighbors, the house was part of a network of stash houses in the New York area where underage girls and young women from dozens of countries were trafficked and held captive. Acting on a tip, police raided the house in February 2002, expecting to find an underground brothel. Instead, they found four girls between the ages of 14 and 17, all Mexican nationals without documentation.

However, they were not prostitutes; they were sex slaves. These girls did not work for profit or a paycheck. They were captives to the traffickers and keepers who controlled their every move. The police found a squalid, land-based equivalent of a 19th-century slave ship. They encountered rancid, doorless bathrooms; bare, putrid mattresses; and a stash of penicillin, "morning after" pills, and an antiulcer medication that can induce abortion. The girls were pale, exhausted, and malnourished.[19]

Human sex trafficking warning signs include, among other indicators, streetwalkers and strip clubs. However, a jurisdiction's lack of streetwalkers or strip clubs does not mean that it is immune to the problem of trafficking. Because human trafficking involves big money, if money can be made, sex slaves can be sold. Sex trafficking can happen anywhere, however unlikely a place. Investigators should be attuned to reading the signs of trafficking and looking closely for them.

Investigation of Human Sex Trafficking

ICE aggressively targets the global criminal infrastructure, including the people, money, and materials that support human trafficking networks. The agency strives to prevent human trafficking in the United States by prosecuting the traffickers and rescuing and protecting the victims. However, most human trafficking cases start at the local level.

Strategies

Local and state law enforcement officers may unknowingly encounter sex trafficking when they deal with homeless and runaway juveniles; criminal gang activity; crimes involving immigrant children who have no guardians; domestic violence calls; and investigations at truck stops, motels, massage parlors, spas, and strip clubs. To this end, the authors offer various suggestions and indicators to help patrol officers identify victims of sex trafficking, as well as tips for detectives who investigate these crimes.

Patrol Officers

- Document suspicious calls and complaints on a police information report, even if the details seem trivial.
- Be aware of trafficking when responding to certain call types, such as reports of foot traffic in and out of a house. Consider situations that seem similar to drug complaints.
- Look closely at calls for assaults, domestic situations, verbal disputes, or thefts. These could involve a trafficking victim being abused and disciplined by a trafficker, a customer having a dispute with a victim, or a client who had money taken during a sex act.
- Locations, such as truck stops, strip clubs, massage parlors, and cheap motels, are havens for prostitutes forced into sex trafficking. Many massage parlors and strip clubs that engage in sex trafficking will have cramped living quarters where the victims are forced to stay.
- When encountering prostitutes and other victims of trafficking, do not display judgment or talk down to them. Understand the violent nature in how they are forced into trafficking, which explains their lack of cooperation. Speak with them in a location completely safe and away from other people, including potential victims.

- Check for identification. Traffickers take the victims' identification and, in cases of foreign nationals, their travel information. The lack of either item should raise concern.

Detectives/Investigators

- Monitor websites that advertise for dating and hooking up. Most vice units are familiar with the common sites used by sex traffickers as a means of advertisement.
- Conduct surveillance at motels, truck stops, strip clubs, and massage parlors. Look to see if the girls arrive alone or with someone else. Girls being transported to these locations should raise concerns of trafficking.
- Upon an arrest, check cell phone records, motel receipts, computer printouts of advertisements, and tollbooth receipts. Look for phone calls from the jailed prostitute to the pimp. Check surveillance cameras at motels and toll facilities as evidence to indicate the trafficking of the victim.
- Obtain written statements from the customers; get them to work for you.
- Seek assistance from nongovernmental organizations involved in fighting sex trafficking. Many of these entities have workers who will interview these victims on behalf of the police.
- After executing a search warrant, photograph everything. Remember that in court, a picture may be worth a thousand words: nothing else can more effectively describe a cramped living quarter a victim is forced to reside in.
- Look for advertisements in local newspapers, specifically the sports sections, that advertise massage parlors. These businesses should be checked out to ensure they are legitimate and not fronts for trafficking.
- Contact your local U.S. Attorney's Office, FBI field office, or ICE for assistance. Explore what federal resources exist to help address this problem.

Other Considerations

Patrol officers and investigators can look for many other human trafficking indicators as well.[20] These certainly warrant closer attention.

General Indicators

- People who live on or near work premises
- Individuals with restricted or controlled communication and transportation
- Persons frequently moved by traffickers
- A living space with a large number of occupants
- People lacking private space, personal possessions, or financial records
- Someone with limited knowledge about how to get around in a community

Physical Indicators

- Injuries from beatings or weapons
- Signs of torture (e.g., cigarette burns)
- Brands or scarring, indicating ownership
- Signs of malnourishment

Financial/Legal Indicators

- Someone else has possession of an individual's legal/travel documents
- Existing debt issues
- One attorney claiming to represent multiple illegal aliens detained at different locations
- Third party who insists on interpreting. Did the victim sign a contract?

Brothel Indicators

- Large amounts of cash and condoms
- Customer logbook or receipt book ("trick book")
- Sparse rooms
- Men come and go frequently

Conclusion

This form of cruel modern-day slavery occurs more often than many people might think. And, it is not just an international or a national problem—it also is a local one. It is big business, and it involves a lot of perpetrators and victims.

Agencies at all levels must remain alert to this issue and address it vigilantly. Even local officers must understand the problem and know how to recognize it in their jurisdictions. Coordinated and aggressive efforts from all law enforcement organizations can put an end to these perpetrators' operations and free the victims.

Notes

1. www.routledgesociology.com/books/Human-Sex-Trafficking-isbn9780415576789 (accessed July 19, 2010).
2. www.unodc.org/unodc/en/human-trafficking/what-is-human-trafficking.html (accessed July 19, 2010).
3. www.justice.gov/criminal/ceos/trafficking.html (accessed July 19, 2010).
4. Ibid.
5. www.justice.gov/criminal/ceos/prostitution.html (accessed July 19, 2010).
6. Richard J. Estes and Neil Alan Weiner, *Commercial Sexual Exploitation of Children in the U.S., Canada, and Mexico* (University of Pennsylvania, Executive Summary, 2001).
7. Ibid.
8. http://fpc.state.gov/documents/organization/9107.pdf (accessed July 19, 2010).
9. Estes and Weiner.
10. www.womenshealth.gov/violence/types/human-trafficking.cfm (accessed July 19, 2010).
11. For additional information, see Nathalie De Fabrique, Stephen J. Romano, Gregory M. Vecchi, and Vincent B. Van Hasselt, "Understanding Stockholm Syndrome," *FBI Law Enforcement Bulletin,* July 2007, 10–15.
12. Trafficking Victims Protection Act, Pub. L. No. 106–386 (2000), codified at 22 U.S.C. § 7101, et seq.
13. Ibid.
14. U.S. CONST. amend. XIII, § 1: "Neither slavery nor involuntary servitude, except as a punishment for crime whereof the party shall have been duly convicted, shall exist within the United States, or any place subject to their jurisdiction."
15. U.S. Department of Justice, "U.S. Army Soldier Sentenced to Over 17 Years in Prison for Operating a Brothel from Millersville Apartment and to Drug Trafficking," www.justice.gov/usao/md/Public-Affairs/press_releases/press10a.htm (accessed September 30, 2010).
16. www.fbi.gov/hq/cid/civilrights/trafficking_initiatives.htm (accessed September 30, 2010).
17. www.ojp.usdoj.gov/BJA/grant/42HTTF.pdf (accessed September 30, 2010).
18. http://actioncenter.polarisproject.org/the-frontlines/recent-federal-cases/435-leader-of-expansive-multi-state-sex-trafficking-ring-sentenced (accessed July 19, 2010).
19. www.nytimes.com/2004/01/25/magazine/25SEXTRAFFIC.html (accessed July 19, 2010).
20. http://httf.wordpress.com/indicators/ (accessed July 19, 2010).

Critical Thinking

1. Do you believe prostitutes are victims of human sex traffickers?
2. How can sex traffickers compel anyone to become a sex worker against his or her will?
3. What laws have been enacted to deal with sex trafficking?

Create Central

www.mhhe.com/createcentral

Internet References

Polaris Project
    www.polarisproject.org/human-trafficking/sex-trafficking-in-the-us
Science Daily
    www.sciencedaily.com/releases/2013/09/130925132333.htm

From *FBI Law Enforcement Bulletin* by Amanda Walker-Rodriguez and Rodney Hill, March 2011. Published by Federal Bureau of Investigation. www.fbi.gov.

Unit 3

UNIT

Prepared by: Joanne Naughton

The Police

Police officers are the guardians of our rights under the Constitution and the law, and as such they have an awesome task. They are asked to prevent crime, protect citizens, arrest wrongdoers, preserve the peace, aid the sick, control juveniles, control traffic, and provide emergency services on a moment's notice. They are also asked to be ready to lay down their lives, if necessary.

In recent years, the job of the police officer has become even more complex and dangerous. Illegal drug use and trafficking are still major problems; racial tensions are explosive; and terrorism is now an alarming reality. As our population grows more numerous and diverse, the role of the police in America becomes ever more challenging, requiring skills that can only be obtained by greater training and professionalism.

Article   Prepared by: Joanne Naughton

The Changing Environment for Policing, 1985–2008

DAVID H. BAYLEY AND CHRISTINE NIXON

Learning Outcomes

After reading this article, you will be able to:

- State the differences between the policing environments in 1985 and 2008.

- Relate some of the challenges facing police executives today.

- Show how the growth of private security affects policing.

Introduction

In 1967, the President's Commission on Law Enforcement and the Administration of Justice published *The Challenge of Crime in a Free Society*. This publication is generally regarded as inaugurating the scientific study of the police in America in particular but also in other countries. Almost 20 years later, the John F. Kennedy School of Government, Harvard University, convened an Executive Session on the police (1985–1991) to examine the state of policing and to make recommendations for its improvement. Its approximately 30 participants were police executives and academic experts. Now, 20 years further on, the Kennedy School has again organized an Executive Session. Its purpose, like the first, is to combine professional with scholarly appraisals of the police and their contribution to public safety.

So the question naturally arises, what are the differences in the environment for policing between these two time periods? Are the problems as well as the institution of the police similar or different from one period to the next? Our thesis is that policing in the mid-1980s was perceived to be in crisis and there was a strong sense that fundamental changes were needed in the way it was delivered. In contrast, police are considered to be performing well 20 years later by both practitioners and outside observers. Crime has been falling for almost 18 years and any new challenges, including terrorism, appear to be manageable without the invention of new strategies for the delivery of police services. Past experience contains the lessons needed for the future. In our view, this assessment may be mistaken, not because existing policies are defective in controlling crime but because the institutions that provide public safety are changing in profound ways that are not being recognized.

The Policing Environment in 1985

Policing in the United States was under siege in the 1980s for two reasons: (1) crime had been rising from the early 1960s, and (2) research had shown that the traditional strategies of the police were ineffective at coping with it. In 1960, the serious crime rate was 1,887 per 100,000 people. In 1985 it was 5,224, almost a threefold increase. This trend peaked in 1990 at 5,803. Violent crime (i.e., murder, rape, robbery and aggravated assault) rose from 161 per 100,000 people in 1960 to 558 in 1985, on the way to quadrupling by 1991 (Maguire and Pastore, 2007). Crime was, understandably, a big issue, feeding what could properly be called a moral panic.

Prompted by the President's Commission on Law Enforcement and the Administration of Justice in 1967, researchers in universities and private think-tanks began to study the effectiveness of standard police strategies. In the ensuing two decades, studies were published showing that crime rates were not affected by:

- Hiring more police (Loftin and McDowell, 1982; Krahn and Kennedy, 1985; Koenig, 1991; Laurie, 1970; Gurr, 1979; Emsley, 1983; Silberman, 1978; Reiner, 1985; Lane, 1980).

- Random motorized patrolling (Kelling et al., 1974; Kelling, 1985; Morris and Heal, 1981).

- Foot patrols (Police Foundation, 1981).

- Rapid response to calls for service (Tien, Simon and Larson, 1978; Bieck and Kessler, 1977; Spelman and Brown, 1981).

- Routine criminal investigation (Laurie, 1970; Burrows, 1986; Greenwood, Petersilia and Chaiken, 1977; Eck, 1982; Royal Commission on Criminal Procedure, 1981).

These conclusions, despite challenges to some of them on methodological grounds, were considered authoritative. They were so well accepted, in fact, that Bayley could say in 1994 that "one of the best kept secrets of modern life" was that the police do not prevent crime. "Experts know it, the police know it, and the public does not know it" (Bayley, 1994:3).

No wonder, then, that the first Executive Session concluded that fundamental changes were needed in police strategies. The Session took the lead in developing and legitimating a new model for the delivery of police services—community policing. The key recommendation was that police needed to be reconnected to the public in order both to enhance their crime-control effectiveness and to increase public respect. The strategy for doing this was community policing, including problem-oriented policing (Trojanowicz and Bucqueroux, 1990; Goldstein, 1990). Of the 17 studies published by the first Executive Session as *Perspectives on Policing,* eight featured "community" or "community policing" in the title, and several others discussed the importance of community. George Kelling and Mark Moore, members of the session, argued that the evolution of American policing could be described as movement from a politicized system to professionalism, then to constitutionalism, and ultimately to community policing (Kelling and Moore, 1988).

The first Executive Session also encouraged a new management style for policing, namely, one based on the analysis of crime and disorder problems and the evaluation of remediation programs. This process of description and analysis was to be carried out jointly by police and outside experts, such as academic scholars and management consultants.

The Policing Environment in 2008

When the second Executive Session met in January 2008, crime in the United States had declined dramatically since 1990. The serious crime rate (Part I crimes) had fallen to 3,808 per 100,000 people by 2006, a decline of 34 percent (Maguire and Pastore, 2007).[1] Even though the violent crime rate was still three times higher in 2006 than in 1960 (474 versus 161 per 100,000 people), it had declined by 37.5 percent since its peak in 1991, a huge change for the better. The police, in particular, feel that the decline vindicates their crime-control efforts, notably the strategy attributed to Bill Bratton of New York City, of the strict enforcement of laws against disorder and the management technique known as *zero tolerance,* managed through COMPSTAT (Bratton and Knobler, 1998; Eck and Maguire, 2000).

The decline has been so dramatic that it offset the continued questioning by analysts of the importance of police action in controlling crime (Eck and Maguire, 2000). Furthermore, there are now positive findings about the efficacy of certain police strategies. The most authoritative summary of this research comes from a panel of the National Research Council (Skogan and Frydl, 2004).

Reviewing all research conducted since the President's Commission (1967) and available in English, the panel reaffirmed the findings of the 1970s and 1980s that the standard practices of policing—employing more sworn officers, random motorized patrolling, rapid response and criminal investigation—failed to reduce crime when applied generally throughout a jurisdiction. It should be noted that most of the research on these topics, except for analysis of the effect of the number of

police employees on crime, dated from the earlier period. At the same time, the panel found that police could reduce crime when they focused operations on particular problems or places and when they supplemented law enforcement with other regulatory and abatement activities.

The strongest evidence for effectiveness was some form of problem solving, especially when focused on "hot spots," that is, locations accounting for a high volume of repeat calls for police service. Nonenforcement options included changing the physical design of buildings and public spaces, enforcing fire and safety codes, providing social services to dysfunctional families, reducing truancy and providing after-school programs for latch-key children.

By 2008, police executives could feel much happier about their efforts to control crime than they had 20 years before. Scholars, too, agreed that strategies used since the 1980s were efficacious, by and large.

This is not to say that police leaders currently feel that they can rest on their laurels nor that the environment for policing is entirely benign. Police executives understand that they are confronting several challenges, some new and some old:

- **Declining budgets and the rising cost of sworn police officers.** The cost of policing has quadrupled between 1985 and 2005, according to the Bureau of Justice Statistics (Gascón and Foglesong, 2009). The causes are rising labor costs for both sworn officers and civilian personnel, increased demand for police services and the growing complexity of police work. As a result, police budgets are increasingly at risk, with some cities reducing the number of police officers per capita.

- **Terrorism.** The primary impact of the Sept. 11 terrorist attack on state and local policing in the United States has been to improve their capacity for risk assessment of local vulnerabilities and first-responding in the event of terrorist incidents (Bayley and Weisburd, 2009). Although threat assessment and first-responding are understood to be core responsibilities of local police, their role with respect to counterterrorism intelligence gathering and analysis is more problematic. At the moment, most intelligence about terrorism comes from federal sources. Some observers take the view that local law enforcement, especially in the United States with its radically decentralized police system, does not have the personnel or skills to collect operational intelligence in a cost-effective way. Others argue, however, that local general-duties police who work among the population are essential for detecting precursor terrorist activities and building cooperative relations with the communities in which terrorists live (Bayley and Weisburd, 2009). Many police executives are critical of the federal government, therefore, for downgrading its law enforcement attention from nonterrorist crime and for reducing its support for local community-responsive and crime-prevention activities.

- **New immigrants, both legal and illegal.** Until recently, most American police departments took the view that enforcing immigration was a federal rather than a local responsibility. They took this view, in part, because they wanted illegal immigrants to feel free to approach police when they were victims of crime, particularly when they were exploited by employers. Police executives felt that even people who were in the country illegally deserved protection under the law. Recently, however, driven by growing anti-illegal immigration feelings in their jurisdictions, some police departments have begun to enforce immigration regulations. As anticipated, this has alienated these communities at the very moment when the importance of connecting with immigrants—legal as well as illegal—has become imperative as a response to terrorism. Not only may foreign terrorists take cover in immigrant communities but these communities, especially if they are disadvantaged and marginalized, may produce their own home-grown perpetrators. Great Britain and France have both experienced this phenomenon. Thus, the threat of terrorism raises difficult questions about the scope, intensity and methods of law enforcement in immigrant communities.

- **Racial discrimination.** Charges of unequal treatment on the basis of race have been a continual problem for police since the rise of civil rights consciousness in the 1960s. Concerns raised about the substantial amount of discretion possessed by frontline police was one of the first issues taken up by police researchers more than 40 years ago. Various aspects of policing have been implicated—arrests, use of force, shootings, street stops, search and seizure, offense charging and equality of coverage (Fridell et al., 2001; Skolnick and Fyfe, 1993; Walker, 2003). Not only is racial discrimination an enduring issue for police executives to manage but its potential for destroying the reputation of police agencies and the careers of officers is hard to exaggerate. It is the allegation that every police chief dreads.

- **Intensified accountability.** Oversight of police performance, with regard to effectiveness in controlling both crime and personal behavior, has grown steadily in the past few years. The monitoring of institutional performance has been part of a governmentwide movement to specify measurable performance indicators. External oversight of individual behavior has involved complaints commissions, citizen review panels and ombudsmen. Many would argue that the quality of policing with respect to crime control and personal behavior has improved over the last half of the 20th century as a result of these developments. The public, however, seems more skeptical, especially with respect to the behavior of individual officers. At least that would be a fair reading of the fact that in the United States as well as other English-speaking countries, the demand for greater oversight of police behavior continues to grow, fed by the media's insatiable appetite for stories about police misdeeds.

There are two aspects to what is being asked for: (1) holding the police to account for performing the services for which they were created—crime prevention and criminal investigation and (2) disciplining officers who behave improperly in the course of their duties.

Today, more than 100 of America's largest cities have some sort of civilian oversight of police behavior compared with only a handful in the early 1990s (Walker, 2003). Independent civilian review of complaints against the police has been established in the last three decades in Great Britain, New Zealand, Australia and Canada. But this is only the most visible tip of a larger iceberg. Oversight has also intensified in the form of tighter financial auditing, performance indicators mandated by governmental and quasi-governmental bodies, enactment of more stringent legal standards and federal consent decrees. This is in addition to what seems to police to be an unappeasable media appetite for revelations about police, and even ex-police, misbehavior.

- **Police unions.** While acknowledging the reasons that led to the growth of police unions, police executives complain about its impact on management. In particular, they criticize the reflexive defense of work rules that inhibit strategic innovation and organizational change, the elaborate procedures required to discipline poorly performing officers, and the inculcation of an occupational culture preoccupied with tangible rewards.

Although all of these current challenges certainly complicate their work, police executives do not view them as a crisis for policing as was the case in the mid-1980s. These challenges are complex and difficult but manageable within the competence of experienced executives. With the arguable exception of terrorism, they do not require a shift in the strategies of policing.

Embedded in this sense of achievement among police professionals is frustration with the gap between objective measures of public safety and public perceptions. Although crime may have declined, the public's fear has not. Police commonly attribute this discrepancy to the exaggeration of crime by the media and the failure to give credit where credit is due.

The Looming Watershed

We believe that policing may be approaching, if not well into, a period of change that will significantly affect what police do and how they do it. It may be as significant as the period after 1829 when Sir Robert Peel created the London Metropolitan Police. The choice of 1829 as the reference point is not rhetorical. This year marked the beginning of the gradual monopolization of the police function by government. Starting in 1829, governments in Anglo-Saxon countries, much earlier in Europe, assumed responsibility for policing—for hiring, paying, training and supervising. What is happening now is the reverse of that: nation-states are losing their monopoly on policing.

The pressures eroding the monopoly of governments within national boundaries to create and manage policing come from three directions:

- The internationalization of policing.
- The devolution of policing to communities.
- The growth of private policing.

In short, policing is being pushed up, down and sideways from its traditional mooring in government.

The Internationalization of Policing

Policing has shifted away from national governments because of the development of a genuinely international police capacity and increased international collaboration in law enforcement. The United Nations now has more than 11,000 police recruited from about 118 countries and deployed in 13 missions. The United States currently contributes 268 police to UNPOL (formerly CIVPOL). Although UNPOL's primary mission is "to build institutional police capacity in post-conflict environments" (Kroeker, 2007), its officers have been armed in Kosovo, Timor-Leste and Haiti and enforce laws alongside the local police. It is worth mentioning that this is part of a broader development of international institutions of justice, including the development of a portable international criminal code, courts and tribunals authorized to try individuals, and prisons for persons both convicted and under trial.

The United States now collaborates widely with law enforcement agencies abroad. As of February 2010, the FBI has offices in 70 cities overseas and the DEA has offices in almost 90 (see FBI and DEA home pages). The United States trains more than 10,000 police a year at its four International Law Enforcement Training Academies (located in Budapest, Bangkok, Gaborone and San Salvador) and brings many more trainees to the United States. The United States also participates in a host of international task forces and ad hoc law enforcement operations that focus on drugs, terrorism, trafficking in people and, more recently, cyber-crime, including pornography. The United States has also encouraged—some would say "pressured"—countries to bring their laws into conformity with American practice, for example, with respect to wiretapping, the use of informants, asset forfeiture, and the Racketeer Influenced and Corrupt Organizations Act (Nadelman, 1997; Snow, 1997). American influence, direct and indirect, has been so powerful that Chris Stone says there has been an "Americanization of global law enforcement" (Stone, 2003). The United States, furthermore, has begun to create a reserve force of police and other criminal justice experts that can be deployed at short notice to countries emerging from conflict.

If policing is a fundamental attribute of government, along with external defense, then the world has begun to create a world government of sorts. Although seeds of this movement preceded the first Executive Session, a major impetus was the fall of the Berlin Wall in 1989 and the subsequent implosion of the Soviet Union (Bayley, 2006).

The Devolution of Policing to Communities

The attitude of police generally in the Western world, but especially in its English-speaking democracies, toward collaborating with members of the public who act voluntarily to improve public security has undergone a major change since the 1980s. No longer viewed as nuisances or dangerous vigilantes, these people are now seen as "co-producers" of public safety. This transformation of view is attributable in large part to the acceptance of community policing, which the first Executive Session was instrumental in promoting. Police in

democratic countries now actively encourage citizen participation by sharing information, training volunteers, consulting the public about priorities, mobilizing collaborative crime-prevention programs, enlisting the public as informants in problem solving, and soliciting help from city planners, architects and the designers of products to minimize criminal opportunities. Neighborhood Watch is probably the best known police-citizen partnership. Others include Business Improvement Districts, mobile CB-radio patrols, and private-sector programs for providing equipment and professional skills to police departments.

It has become axiomatic in policing that the public should be encouraged to take responsibility for enhancing public safety. As police themselves now recognize, they cannot do the job alone. Public participation is seen by police and academics alike as a critical contributor to police effectiveness and thus to public safety.

The Growth of Private Policing

Policing is being pushed sideways by the growth in the private security industry. Estimates of its strength are not exact because "private security" covers a wide range of activities— e.g., guarding, transporting valuables, investigating, installing protective technology and responding to alarms—and is supplied by companies commercially to others as well as by businesses to themselves. The U.S. Department of Labor estimated that there were slightly more than 1 million private security guards in 2005 (U.S. Bureau of Labor Statistics, 2005). That would be 49 percent more than the number of full-time sworn police officers in the same year (673,146). A report issued by the International Association of Chiefs of Police (IACP) and the Community Oriented Police Services (COPS) Office estimated, however, that in 2004, the number was about 2 million (IACP, 2005). If that were true, there would be almost three times as many private security personnel as full-time police officers. The discrepancy between figures of the Department of Labor and those of IACP-COPS may have arisen because the larger estimate includes in-house security provided by private organizations, whereas the Department of Labor figures only include the personnel of companies providing security services commercially. The larger figure is the one most often cited in commentaries on private policing (Cunningham and Taylor, 1985; Singer, 2003).

The growth of private security appears to be a phenomenon of the last quarter of the 20th century (Nalla and Newman, 1991). It was first documented in *The Hallcrest Report: Private Security and Police in America* (Cunningham and Taylor, 1985), which estimated the number at 1.5 million. This was more than twice the number of public police at that time. Although the use of private security was certainly visible to police officials in the 1980s, the number of *commercial* private security personnel has grown by as much as two-thirds. Their number rose sharply immediately after the Sept. 11 attack, fell in 2003 (although not to pre-Sept. 11 levels) and has continued to increase (U.S. Bureau of Labor Statistics, 2007). It is reasonable to assume that the number of *in-house* private security personnel has also increased, though perhaps not as much.

Worldwide, there are now more private police than government-run police: 348 versus 318 per 100,000, according to a survey by Jan Van Dijk (2008). The highest rates are in the United States, Canada and central Europe. Britain and Australia also have slightly more private security personnel than public police (Australian Bureau of Statistics, 2006; European Union, 2004). In the European Union, only Britain and Ireland have more private than public police (European Union, 2004). Statistics are not available for Latin America, Africa, and South and Southeast Asia, but private security is certainly very visible there.

The point to underscore is that worldwide, and dramatically in the United States, there has been a steady growth in the number of private "police." If visible guardians are a deterrent to crime, as the routine-activities theory of crime asserts and as police themselves strongly believe, then one reason for the decline in crime in the United States since the early 1990s might be the growth in private security. As far as we are aware, analyses of the crime drop in the United States have not tested for this possibility.

The effect of these three changes in the environment for policing is to diversify the providers of public safety. Governments, especially country-based governments, no longer direct or provide public safety exclusively. The domestic security function has spread to new levels of government but, more important, to nonstate actors, volunteers and commercial providers. The police role is now shared. This is not simply saying that there are now both public and private police. Public and private policing have blended and are often hard to distinguish. Governments hire private police to supplement their own police; private entrepreneurs hire public police. We are in an era of what Les Johnston refers to as hybrid policing (Johnston, 1992).

Until now, assessments of the police have focused on two questions: How can they be made more effective, and how can the behavior of individual officers be improved? Now, we suggest, a third question has arisen: Who is responsible for policing?

Changes within Public Policing

Not only are changes occurring in the environment that may affect the structure of policing but police themselves are in the process of changing the way they work. The factors driving this are (1) the threat of terrorism, (2) intelligence-led policing and (3) DNA analysis. Each of these developments transfers initiative in directing operations to specialists who collect and analyze information and away from both general-duties police and the public. Ironically, these changes could undo the signature contribution of the 1980s—community policing.

The Threat of Terrorism

Although many anti-terrorism experts understand the importance of working with communities, especially immigrant ones, counterterrorism centralizes decision making, shifting it upward in police organizations and making it less transparent. In the aftermath of Sept. 11, a new emphasis has been placed on the development of covert intelligence gathering, penetration and disruption. In the United States, the development of covert counterterrorism capacity has been unequally distributed, being more pronounced in larger police forces. Where it occurs, important questions arise about legal accountability as well as operational payoff. These issues are familiar to police, having arisen before in efforts to control illegal narcotics and organized crime.

Intelligence-Led Policing

Intelligence-led policing[2] utilizes crime mapping, data mining and the widespread use of closed-circuit television monitoring, which all rely on analysis based on information collected from impersonal sources. It thereby empowers senior commanders to develop their own agendas for law enforcement rather than consulting with affected communities.

DNA Analysis

DNA analysis allows crimes to be solved without witnesses or confessions. Research in the 1970s showed that the identification of suspects by victims and witnesses was essential to the solving of most crimes (Greenwood, Petersilia and Chaiken, 1977). Detectives, contrary to their fictional portrayals, work from the identification of suspects by the public back to the collection of evidence to prove guilt. DNA changes that, emphasizing forensic evidence over human testimony, promising a technological solution to criminal identification.

The effect of these developments—the threat of terrorism, intelligence-led policing and DNA analysis—impels the police to rely more on their own intellectual and physical resources and on centralized decision making for agendas and strategies. It lessens the importance of consulting with and mobilizing the disaggregate resources of communities. It also favors enforcement as the tool of choice over preventive strategies of regulation and abatement. These changes in orientation may be necessary and may raise police effectiveness, but they also represent a return to the sort of insular professionalism that characterized policing before the 1980s.

The Challenges of Change

The changes described both inside and outside the established police structures and functions create issues that will have to be confronted. With the expansion of private policing, public safety may become more inequitably distributed on the basis of economic class. The affluent sectors of society, especially its commercial interests, may be more protected, and the poor sectors less protected (Bayley and Shearing, 2001). This trend could be exacerbated if the tax-paying public at the same time withdraws its support from the public police in favor of private security. There are indications that this has already occurred in public education, where people with the means to pay for private schools are increasingly reluctant to support public education. If this should occur in policing, a dualistic system could evolve—responsive private policing for the affluent, and increasingly underfunded public policing for the poor (Bayley and Shearing, 2001). The political consequences of this could be calamitous.

Furthermore, who is to hold private policing to legal and moral account? Public police in the United States and other democracies have been made accountable in many ways.

Public police executives themselves often argue that they are too accountable, meaning they are scrutinized too closely, too mechanically and at a substantial cost in reporting. Private policing, however, is imperfectly regulated and it is unclear whether existing law provides sufficient leverage (Joh, 2004; Prenzler and Sarre, 2006).

So, an ironic question arises: Is there a continuing role for government in ensuring an equitable and lawful distribution of security at the very time that government is losing its monopoly control? Should it accomplish by regulation what it no longer can by ownership? If so, how should this be done? In particular, what agency of government would be responsible for it?

The internationalization of policing also raises issues of control and legitimacy. Simply put, whose interests will be served by policing under international auspices? Will it be collective interests articulated by constituent states and powerful organized interests, or by the needs of disaggregate populations represented through participative institutions? Democratic nation-states emphasize the needs of individuals in directing police. It is not at all clear that international institutions will do the same, although they have taken impressive steps on paper to articulate comprehensive standards of police conduct (U.N. High Commissioner for Human Rights, 1996).

Finally, we submit that policing may be facing a clash of cultures as the public increasingly demands participation in the direction and operation of policing while at the same time police agencies become more self-directing and self-sufficient in their use of intelligence resources. This issue is not new. It is the same issue that policing faced in the 1980s and that was tackled in the first Executive Session. How important is public legitimacy for police effectiveness and public safety? How can the support of the public be maintained while police take advantage of powerful new technologies that may decrease interaction with them?

Conclusion

In the United States and other developed democracies, changes are occurring that may undermine the monopoly of state-based policing as well as its community-based paradigm. In pointing out these changes between 1985 and 2008, we are not making value judgments about them. These changes may have made the police more effective at providing public safety without infringing human rights in unacceptable ways. We call attention to these changes because their potential effects are enormous and largely unappreciated. They constitute an invisible agenda as consequential as the problems discussed in the 1980s.

Twenty years ago, policing was in the throes of what is now regarded as a revolution in its operating approach. It shifted from a philosophy of "give us the resources and we can do the job" to realizing the importance of enlisting the public in the coproduction of public safety. Policing today faces much less obvious challenges. Current strategies and technologies seem to be sufficient to deal with foreseeable threats to public safety, with the possible exception of terrorism. If this is so, then policing will develop in an evolutionary way, fine-tuning operational techniques according to experience, particularly the findings of evidence-based evaluations. If, however, changes in the environment are reshaping the structure and hence the governance of policing, and adaptations within the police are weakening the connection between police and public, then we may be entering a period of evolutionary discontinuity that could be greater than that of the 1980s, perhaps even of 1829. Both the role of police in relation to other security providers and the soul of the police in terms of how it goes about its work may be in play today in more profound ways than are being recognized.

References

Australian Bureau of Statistics. "2006 Census of Population and Housing, Australia, Occupation by Sex (Based on Place of Employment)." Accessed February 11, 2010, at www .censusdata.abs.gov.au.

Bayley, David H. *Police for the Future.* New York: Oxford University Press, 1994.

Bayley, David H. *Changing the Guard: Developing Democratic Police Abroad.* New York: Oxford University Press, 2006.

Bayley, David H. and Clifford Shearing. *The New Structure of Policing: Description, Conceptualization, and Research Agenda.* Final report. Washington, D.C.: U.S. Department of Justice, National Institute of Justice, July 2001. NCJ 187083.

Bayley, David H. and David Weisburd. "Cops and Spooks: The Role of the Police in Counterterrorism." In *To Protect and Serve: Policing in an Age of Terrorism,* ed. David Weisburd, Thomas E. Feucht, Idit Hakimi, Lois Felson Mock and Simon Perry. New York: Springer, 2009:81–100.

Bieck, William and David A. Kessler. *Response Time Analysis.* Kansas City, Mo.: Board of Police Commissioners, 1977.

Bratton, William and Peter Knobler. *Turnaround: How America's Top Cop Reversed the Crime Epidemic.* New York: Random House, 1998.

Burrows, John. *Investigating Burglary: The Measurement of Police Performance.* Research Study 88. London: Home Office, 1986.

Cunningham, William C. and Todd H. Taylor. *The Hallcrest Report: Private Security and Police in America.* Portland, Ore.: Chancellor Press, 1985.

Eck, John E. *Solving Crimes: The Investigation of Burglary and Robbery.* Washington, D.C.: Police Executive Research Forum, 1982.

Eck, John E. and Edward Maguire. "Have Changes in Policing Reduced Violent Crime? An Assessment of the Evidence." In *The Crime Drop in America,* ed. Alfred Blumstein and Joel Wallman. New York: Cambridge University Press, 2000:207–265.

Emsley, Clive. *Policing and Its Context, 1750–1870.* London: Macmillan, 1983.

European Union. "Panoramic Overview of Private Security Industry in the 25 Member States of the European Union." Presentation at Fourth European Conference on Private Security Services, Brussels, Belgium. Confederation of European Security Services and UNI-Europa, 2004. Accessed February 11, 2010, at www .coess.org/pdf/ panormal.pdf.

Fridell, Lori, Robert Lunney, Drew Diamond and Bruce Kubu. *Racially Biased Policing: A Principled Response.* Washington, D.C.: Police Executive Research Forum, 2001.

Gascón, George and Todd Foglesong. "How to Make Policing More Affordable: A Case Study of the Rising Costs of Policing in the United States." Draft paper submitted to the Second Harvard

Executive Session on Policing and Public Safety, Cambridge, Mass., 2009.

Goldstein, Herman. *Problem Oriented Policing.* Philadelphia, Penn.: Temple University Press, 1990.

Greenwood, Peter W., Joan Petersilia and Jan Chaiken. *The Criminal Investigation Process.* Lexington, Mass.: D.C. Heath, 1977.

Gurr, Ted R. "On the History of Violent Crime in Europe and America." In *Violence in America: Historical and Comparative Perspectives,* ed. H.D. Graham and Ted R. Gurr. Beverly Hills, Calif.: Sage Publications, 1979:353–374.

International Association of Chiefs of Police. *Post 9-11 Policing: The Crime Control–Homeland Security Paradigm—Taking Command of New Realities.* Alexandria, Va.: IACP, 2005.

Joh, Elizabeth E. "The Paradox of Private Policing." *Journal of Criminal Law and Criminology* 95(1):(2004)49–131.

Johnston, Les. *The Rebirth of Private Policing.* London: Routledge, 1992.

Kelling, George L. "Order Maintenance, the Quality of Urban Life, and Police: A Different Line of Argument." *In Police Leadership in America,* ed. William A. Geller. New York: Praeger Publishers, 1985:309–321.

Kelling, George L. and Mark H. Moore. *The Evolving Strategy of Policing.* Harvard University, Kennedy School of Government, Perspectives on Policing Series, No. 4. Washington, D.C.: National Institute of Justice, November 1988. NCJ 114213.

Kelling, George L., Antony M. Pate, Duane Dieckman and Charles Brown. *The Kansas City Preventive Patrol Experiment: Summary Report.* Washington, D.C.: Police Foundation, 1974.

Koenig, Daniel J. *Do Police Cause Crime? Police Activity, Police Strength and Crime Rates.* Ottawa, Ontario: Canadian Police College, 1991.

Krahn, Harvey and Leslie Kennedy. "Producing Personal Safety: The Effects of Crime Rates, Police Force Size, and Fear of Crime." *Criminology* 23 (1985): 697–710.

Kroeker, Mark. Informal presentation to biannual meeting of the International Police Advisory Commission, Abuja, Nigeria, January 2007.

Lane, Roger. "Urban Police and Crime in Nineteenth-Century America." In *Crime and justice,* ed. N. Morris and Michael Tonry. Chicago: University of Chicago Press, 1980.

Laurie, Peter. *Scotland Yard.* New York: Holt, Rinehart & Winston, 1970.

Loftin, Colin and David McDowell. "The Police, Crime, and Economic Theory: An Assessment." *American Sociological Review* 47 (1982): 393–401.

Maguire, Kathleen and Ann L. Pastore, eds. *Sourcebook of Criminal Justice Statistics.* Years 2000–2007. Washington, D.C.: U.S. Department of Justice, Bureau of Justice Statistics. Accessed February 11, 2010, at www.albany.edu/sourcebook/about.html.

Morris, Pauline and Kevin Heal. *Crime Control and the Police: A Review of Research.* Research Study 67. London: Home Office, 1981.

Nadelman, Ethan A. "The Americanization of Global Law Enforcement: The Diffusion of American Tactics and Personnel." In *Crime and Law Enforcement in the Global Village,* ed. William F. McDonald. Cincinnati, Ohio: Anderson Publishing, 1997:123–138.

Nalla, Mahesh and Graeme Newman. "Public versus Private Control: A Reassessment." *Journal of Criminal Justice* 19 (1991): 537–549.

Police Foundation. *The Newark Foot Patrol Experiment.* Washington, D.C.: Police Foundation, 1981.

Prenzler, Tim and Rick Sarre. "Private and Public Security Agencies: Australia." In *Plural Policing: A Comparative Perspective,* ed. T. Jones and T. Newburn. London: Routledge, 2006:169–189.

President's Commission on Law Enforcement and the Administration of Justice. *The Challenge of Crime in a Free Society.* Washington, D.C.: U.S. Government Printing Office, 1967.

Reiner, Robert. *The Politics of the Police.* New York: St. Martin's Press, 1985.

Royal Commission on Criminal Procedure. Research Study 17. London: HMSO, 1981.

Shearing, Clifford D. "The Relation Between Public and Private Policing." In *Modern Policing,* ed. N. Morris and Michael Tonry. Chicago: University of Chicago Press, 1992.

Silberman, Charles. *Criminal Violence, Criminal Justice.* New York: Random House, 1978.

Singer, Peter W. *Corporate Warriors: The Rise of the Privatized Military Industry.* Cornell Studies in Security Affairs. Ithaca, N.Y.: Cornell University Press, 2003.

Skogan, Wesley and Kathleen Frydl. *Fairness and Effectiveness in Policing: The Evidence.* Washington, D.C.: National Academies Press, 2004.

Skolnick, Jerome H. and James Fyfe. *Beyond the Law.* New York: Free Press, 1993.

Snow, Thomas. "Competing National and Ethical Interests in the Fight Against Transnational Crime: A U.S. Practitioners Perspective." In *Crime and Law Enforcement in the Global Village,* ed. William F. McDonald. Cincinnati: Anderson Publishing, 1997:169–186.

Spelman, William and Dale K. Brown. *"Calling the Police": Citizen Reporting of Serious Crime.* Washington, D.C.: Police Executive Research Forum, 1981.

Stone, Christopher. "Strengthening Accountability in the New Global Police Culture." Presentation at conference on Crime and the Threat to Democratic Governance, Woodrow Wilson International Center for Scholars, Washington, D.C., 2003.

Tien, James M., James W. Simon and Richard C. Larson. *An Alternative Approach to Police Patrol: The Wilmington Split-Force Experiment.* Washington, D.C.: U.S. Government Printing Office, 1978.

Trojanowicz, Robert C. and Bonnie Bucqueroux. *Community Policing: A Contemporary Perspective.* Cincinnati: Anderson Publishing, 1990.

United Nations High Commissioner for Human Rights. *International Human Rights Standards for Law Enforcement: A Pocket Book on Human Rights for Police.* Geneva, Switzerland: UNHCHR, 1996.

U.S. Bureau of Labor Statistics, U.S. Department of Labor. "May 2005 Occupational Employment and Wage Estimates." Accessed February 11, 2010, at www.bls.gOv/oes/oes_dl/htm#2005_m.

U.S. Bureau of Labor Statistics, U.S. Department of Labor. "Security Guard Employment Before and After 2001." Summary 07–08 (August 2007). Accessed March 22, 2010, at www.bls.gov/opub/ils/pdf/opbils61.pdf.

Van Dijk, Jan. *The World of Crime.* Los Angeles: Sage Publications, 2008.

Walker, Samuel. "The New Paradigm of Police Accountability: The U.S. Justice Department 'Pattern or Practice' Suits in Context." *St. Louis University Public Law Review* 22(1) (2003):3–52.

Notes

1. The FBI, which provides the statistics on crimes known to the police, stopped calculating a rate for the entire Part I index after 2001. It did, however, continue to publish rates for both violent and property crime, from which a total rate for all Part I crime can be calculated.

2. Intelligence-led policing may be confused with evidence-based policing. Intelligence-led policing refers to the targeting of operations on the basis of specific information, whereas evidence-based policing refers to shaping of operational strategies on the basis of evaluations of their efficacy.

Critical Thinking

1. Why was community policing developed?
2. What factors are affecting the way policing is done today?
3. Does the increase of private policing present the possibility of problems?
4. What has been the public's reaction to the fact that crime has declined?

Create Central

www.mhhe.com/createcentral

Internet References

Law Enforcement Guide to the World Wide Web
   http://leolinks.com

National Institute of Justice/National Criminal Justice Reference Service
   www.ncjrs.gov/policing/man199.htm

DAVID H. BAYLEY is Distinguished Professor in the School of Criminal Justice at the State University of New York, Albany. **CHRISTINE NIXON** is APM Chair, Victorian Bushfire Reconstruction and Recovery Authority, and State Commissioner of Police, Victoria, Australia (Retired). The authors acknowledge valuable research assistance provided by Baillie Aaron, Research Assistant, in the Program in Criminal Justice and Police Management, John F. Kennedy School of Government, Harvard University.

From *New Perspectives in Policing*, http://goo.gl/dvnJ3 (September 2010). Copyright © by John F. Kennedy School of Government at Harvard University with funding by the National Institute of Justice. This article is available free of charge online at: http://cms.hks.harvard.edu/var/ezp_site/storage/fckeditor/file/pdfs/centers-programs/programs/criminal-justice/NPIP-The-Changing-Environment-for-Policing-1985–2008.pdf.

Article   Prepared by: Joanne Naughton

Judge Rejects New York's Stop-and-Frisk Policy

JOSEPH GOLDSTEIN

Learning Outcomes

After reading this article, you will be able to:

- Understand the objections to "stop-and-frisk"
- Describe the remedies ordered by the judge in *Floyd v. City of New York*.

In a repudiation of a major element in the Bloomberg administration's crime-fighting legacy, a federal judge has found that the stop-and-frisk tactics of the New York Police Department violated the constitutional rights of minorities in New York, and called for a federal monitor to oversee broad reforms.

In a decision issued on Monday, the judge, Shira A. Scheindlin, ruled that police officers have for years been systematically stopping innocent people in the street without any objective reason to suspect them of wrongdoing. Officers often frisked these people, usually young minority men, for weapons or searched their pockets for contraband, like drugs, before letting them go, according to the 195-page decision.

These stop-and-frisk episodes, which soared in number over the last decade as crime continued to decline, demonstrated a widespread disregard for the Fourth Amendment, which protects against unreasonable searches and seizures by the government, according to the ruling. It also found violations with the 14th Amendment's equal protection clause.

Judge Scheindlin found that the city "adopted a policy of indirect racial profiling by targeting racially defined groups for stops based on local crime suspect data." She rejected the city's arguments that more stops happened in minority neighborhoods solely because those happened to have high-crime rates.

"I also conclude that the city's highest officials have turned a blind eye to the evidence that officers are conducting stops in a racially discriminatory manner," she wrote.

Noting that the Supreme Court had long ago ruled that stop-and-frisks were constitutionally permissible under certain conditions, the judge stressed that she was "not ordering an end to the practice of stop-and-frisk. The purpose of the remedies addressed in this opinion is to ensure that the practice is carried out in a manner that protects the rights and liberties of all New Yorkers, while still providing much needed police protection."

City officials did not immediately comment on the ruling, or on whether they planned to appeal. Mayor Michael R. Bloomberg scheduled a news conference at 1 p.m. to discuss the decision.

To fix the constitutional violations, the judge designated an outside lawyer, Peter L. Zimroth, to monitor the Police Department's compliance with the Constitution.

Judge Scheindlin also ordered a number of other remedies, including a pilot program in which officers in at least five precincts across the city will wear body-worn cameras in an effort to record street encounters. She also ordered a "joint remedial process"—in essence, a series of community meetings—to solicit public input on how to reform stop-and-frisk.

The decision to install Mr. Zimroth, a partner in the New York office of Arnold & Porter, LLP, and a former corporation counsel and prosecutor in the Manhattan district attorney's office, will leave the department under a degree of judicial control that is certain to shape the policing strategies under the next mayor.

Relying on a complex statistical analysis presented at trial, Judge Scheindlin found that the racial composition of a census tract played a role in predicting how many stops would occur.

She emphasized what she called the "human toll of unconstitutional stops," noting that some of the plaintiffs testified that their encounters with the police left them feeling that they did not belong in certain areas of the cities. She characterized each stop as "a demeaning and humiliating experience."

"No one should live in fear of being stopped whenever he leaves his home to go about the activities of daily life," the judge wrote. During police stops, she found, blacks and Hispanics "were more likely to be subjected to the use of force than whites, despite the fact that whites are more likely to be found with weapons or contraband."

The ruling, in *Floyd v. City of New York*, follows a two-month nonjury trial in Federal District Court in Manhattan earlier this year over the department's stop-and-frisk practices.

Judge Scheindlin heard testimony from about a dozen black or biracial men and a woman who described being stopped, and she heard from statistical experts who offered their conclusions based on police paperwork describing some 4.43 million stops between 2004 and mid-2012. Numerous police officers and commanders testified as well, typically defending the legality of stops and saying they were made only when officers reasonably suspected criminality was afoot.

While the Supreme Court has long recognized the right of police officers to briefly stop and investigate people who are behaving suspiciously, Judge Scheindlin found that the New York police had overstepped that authority. She found that officers were too quick to deem as suspicious behavior that was perfectly innocent, in effect watering down the legal standard required for a stop.

"Blacks are likely targeted for stops based on a lesser degree of objectively founded suspicion than whites," she wrote.

She noted that about 88 percent of the stops result in the police letting the person go without an arrest or ticket, a percentage so high, she said, that it suggests there was not a credible suspicion to suspect the person of criminality in the first place.

Critical Thinking

1. Do you agree with the judge's ruling?
2. Despite the fact that the court's decision has been overturned on appeal, do you believe the incoming mayor should follow the judge's ruling, as he has said he will?

Create Central

www.mhhe.com/createcentral

Internet References

American Civil Liberties Union
www.aclu.org/racial-justice/racial-profiling

Jurist
http://jurist.org/paperchase/2013/11/federal-appeals-court-upholds-stop-and-frisk-ruling.php

Cameras on Cops: Stop-and-Frisk Ruling's NYPD Accountability Plan Worked in California by Patrick Wall, Jeff Mays, and James Fanelli

59

Article

Prepared by: Joanne Naughton

Cameras on Cops: Stop-and-Frisk Ruling's NYPD Accountability Plan Worked in California

PATRICK WALL, JEFF MAYS, AND JAMES FANELLI

Learning Outcomes

After reading this article, you will be able to:

- Discuss the use of small cameras worn by police officers in Rialto, California.

- Describe how the cameras would be used in New York.

The NYPD opposes court-ordered plans to equip its patrol cops with video cameras, but a study shows that it's a policy worth greenlighting.

The Manhattan federal judge who rebuked the NYPD's use of stop and frisks in a landmark ruling Monday has instructed the department to implement a pilot program in which officers wear cameras on their body.

While Mayor Bloomberg called Judge Shira Scheindlin's idea "a nightmare," she wrote in her decision that the cameras would benefit cops and civilians by providing an objective take during stops. As proof, she cited the success of a similar program in Rialto, Calif.

For the past year, as part of a study, the tiny town's police department equipped its officers with small cameras that recorded their interactions with civilians. Each day half of the department's 54 patrol officers wore the cameras while the other half didn't.

Rialto's police chief, William Farrar, partnered with Dr. Barak Ariel, a professor at the University of Cambridge's Institute of Criminology, to see if the cameras cut down on the use of force by police.

"We found interesting things," Ariel told DNAinfo.com New York. "The theory behind the camera is that they serve as a deterrent effect on both parties—on the officer and the member of the public. It's meant to cool down volatile situations."

The study found that the department received only three civilian complaints during the program's implementation, down from 24 during the same time a year earlier. The study also showed that cops who wore the cameras had eight incidents involving the use of force, while cops not wearing the devices had 17.

The cameras also saved the department cash, Ariel said.

Each camera costs about $1,200. Ariel said the high price is offset by the department spending less time and money on litigating complaints. He estimates that for every $1 spent on a camera, the department saved about $4.

Rialto has a population of 100,000 and spans about 28.5 square miles. Ariel said its police force is only the size of a single NYPD precinct. Still, he believes the pilot program will work in New York City.

"If it works, implement it," said Ariel, who is starting similar programs with the police department in the island country of Trinidad and Tobago and with Israel's transit police. "We shouldn't be so apprehensive about the cameras. I believe in testing things."

Under Scheindlin's program, the NYPD precinct in each borough with the highest number of stop and frisks must have its patrol cops wear the devices for a year. Then a court-appointed monitor, the NYPD and civil rights advocates would evaluate the benefits and the costs.

"The recordings may either confirm or refute the belief of some minorities that they have been stopped simply as a result of their race, or based on the clothes they wore, such as baggy pants or a hoodie," Scheindlin wrote.

The cameras would also vindicate cops who are wrongfully accused of bad behavior, she said.

The judge's take didn't sway Mayor Bloomberg.

"It would be a nightmare," he said at a press conference Monday, denouncing Scheindlin's ruling. "A camera on a [cop's] lapel—he turned the right way, he didn't turn the right way—it's not a solution to the problem."

An NYPD officer who works in the 40th Precinct in Mott Haven told DNAinfo New York on Monday that she welcomed the cameras, believing they would back up police accounts. But she didn't think the number of civilian complaints would drop in the precinct, which had the most stop and frisks in the Bronx in 2012.

"I think they're still going to argue. They argue because they can," the officer said.

Civilians supported the cameras, too.

J. Gomez, a lifelong resident of East Harlem, said she was in favor of police wearing cameras.

"I think the cameras would make a difference because people could see exactly what police are doing and why," said Gomez while standing near the 23rd Precinct, which stopped the highest number of people in Manhattan in 2012.

"I don't have good feelings about stop and frisk. Sometimes they stop people who aren't doing anything," she added.

Critical Thinking

1. Can the experience of Rialto be applied to the NYPD?
2. What results might be expected from the cameras?
3. What are the objections to the cameras from New York officials?

Create Central

www.mhhe.com/createcentral

Internet References

American Civil Liberties Union
www.aclu.org/technology-and-liberty/police-body-mounted-cameras-right-policies-place-win-all

National Public Radio
www.npr.org/2011/11/07/142016109/smile-youre-on-cop-camera

Article   Prepared by: Joanne Naughton

Understanding the Psychology of Police Misconduct

Brian D. Fitch

Learning Outcomes

After reading this article, you will be able to:

- Express your familiarity with the rationalizations that contribute to unethical behavior by police.

- Argue in favor of the importance of ethics training for law enforcement officers.

- Describe how police officers can reduce the psychological discomfort that might accompany their misconduct.

Law enforcement is a unique profession, with officers experiencing a host of freedoms not available to the general public, including the application of deadly force, high-speed driving, and seizing personal property. While these liberties may be necessary, they also can create opportunities for wrongdoing, especially if such behavior is likely to go undetected because of poor supervision. The embarrassment caused by misconduct can damage the public trust, undermine officer morale, and expose agencies to unnecessary—and, in many cases, costly—litigation.[1] Consequently, a clear understanding of the psychology underlying unethical behavior is critical to every law enforcement supervisor and manager at every level of an organization, regardless of one's agency or mission.

Law enforcement agencies go to great lengths to recruit hire, and train only the most qualified applicants—candidates who have already demonstrated a track record of good moral values and ethical conduct. Similarly, most officers support the agency, its values, and its mission, performing their duties ethically while avoiding any misconduct or abuse of authority. Yet despite the best efforts of organizations everywhere, it seems that one does not have to look very far these days to find examples of police misconduct particularly in the popular press.[2] Even more disturbing, however, is that many of the officers engaged in immoral or unethical behavior previously demonstrated good service records, absent any of the "evil" typically associated with corruption or abuse.

While it is probably true that at least some of the officers who engage in illicit activities managed somehow to slip through the cracks in the hiring process and simply continued their unethical ways, this account fails to explain how otherwise good officers become involved in misconduct. The purpose of this article is to familiarize law enforcement managers and supervisors with the cognitive rationalizations that can contribute to unethical behavior. The article also offers strategies and suggestions intended to mitigate misconduct, before it actually occurs, by developing a culture of ethics.

Moral Responsibility and Disengagement

Most law enforcement professionals are, at their core, good, ethical, and caring people. Despite the overuse of a popular cliché, many officers do in fact enter law enforcement because they want to make a positive difference in their communities. Officers frequently espouse strong, positive moral values while working diligently—in many cases, at great personal risk—to bring dangerous criminals to justice. Doing so provides officers with a strong sense of personal satisfaction and self-worth. As a result, most officers do not—and in many cases cannot—engage in unethical conduct unless they can somehow justify to themselves the morality of their actions.[3]

Decades of empirical research have supported the idea that whenever a person's behaviors are inconsistent with their attitudes or beliefs, the individual will experience a state of psychological tension—a phenomenon referred to as cognitive dissonance.[4] Because this tension is uncomfortable, people will modify any contradictory beliefs or behaviors in ways intended to reduce or eliminate discomfort. Officers can reduce psychological tension by changing one or more of their cognitions—that is, by modifying how they think about their actions and the consequences of those behaviors—or by adjusting their activities, attitudes, or beliefs in ways that are consistent with their values and self-image. Generally speaking, an officer will modify the cognition that is least resistant to change, which, in most cases, tends to be the officer's attitudes, not behaviors.

One of the simplest ways that officers can reduce the psychological discomfort that accompanies misconduct is to cognitively restructure unethical behaviors in ways that make them seem personally and socially acceptable, thereby allowing officers to behave immorally while preserving their self-image as ethically good people. The following is a partial list of common rationalizations that officers can use to neutralize or excuse unethical conduct.[5]

Denial of victim. Officers who rely on this tactic argue that because no victim exists, no real harm has been done. It is probably safe to suggest that officers do not generally regard drug dealers, thieves, and sexual predators as bona fide victims, regardless of the nature of an officer's conduct. An officer, for instance, who takes money from a suspected drug dealer during the service of a search warrant might argue that because the dealer acquired the currency illegally, the dealer was never actually entitled to the proceeds. Rather, the money belongs to whoever possesses it at the time.

Victim of circumstance. Officers who utilize this method convince themselves that they behaved improperly only because they had no other choice. Officers may claim that they were the victims of peer pressure, an unethical supervisor, or an environment where "everyone else is doing it," so what else could they possibly have done? Regardless of the context, these officers excuse their conduct by alleging that they had no alternative but to act unethically.

Denial of injury. Using this form of rationalization, officers persuade themselves that because nobody was actually hurt by their actions, their behavior was not really immoral. This explanation is especially common in cases involving drugs, stolen property, or large amounts of untraceable cash where it can be difficult, if not impossible, to identify an injured party. Officers who use this tactic may further neutralize their deviant conduct by comparing it to the harm being done by the drug dealer from whom the money was stolen.

Advantageous comparisons. Officers who depend on this explanation rely on selective social comparisons to defend their conduct. Officers who falsify a police report to convict a suspected drug dealer, for example, might defend their actions by minimizing their participation or the frequency of their unethical behavior, while at the same time vilifying a coworker as someone who "lies all the time on reports." In comparison to an officer who routinely falsifies reports, the first officer's conduct can seem less egregious.

Higher cause. Officers who practice this type of cognitive restructuring argue that sometimes, it may be necessary to break certain rules to serve a higher calling or to achieve a more important goal. An officer who conducts an unlawful search to uncover evidence against a suspected pedophile might reason that the nature of the crime justifies breaking the rules. "The ends justify the means," officers might assert—suggesting that they did what was necessary, regardless of the legality or morality of their conduct, to put a dangerous criminal behind bars. This form of rationalization can be especially disturbing because it goes beyond merely excusing or justifying deviant behavior to the point of actually glorifying certain forms of wrongdoing in the name of "justice" or "the greater good."

Table 1 Rationalizing Misconduct

Strategy	Description
Denial of Victim	Alleging that because there is no legitimate victim, there is no misconduct.
Victim of Circumstance	Behaving improperly because the officer had no other choice, either because of peer pressure or unethical supervision.
Denial of Injury	Because nobody was hurt by the officer's action, no misconduct actually occurred.
Advantageous Comparisons	Minimizing or excusing one's own wrongdoing by comparing it to the more egregious behavior of others.
Higher Cause	Breaking the rules because of some higher calling—that is, removing a known felon from the streets.
Blame the Victim	The victim invited any suffering or misconduct by breaking the law in the first place.
Dehumanization	Using euphemistic language to dehumanize people, thereby making them easier to victimize.
Diffusion of Responsibility	Relying on the diffusion of responsibility among the involved parties to excuse misconduct.

Blame the victim. An officer who uses this form of justification blames the victim for any misconduct or abuse. If, for instance, officers use unreasonable force on a suspected drug dealer, they can simply argue that the victim brought on this suffering by violating the law. "If the dealer doesn't want to get beat up, the dealer should obey the law," the officer might reason. "I'm not using force on law-abiding citizens, only on drug dealers; they give up their rights when they break the rules." By assigning blame to the victim, the officer not only finds a way to excuse any wrongdoing, but also a way to feel sanctimonious about doing so.

Dehumanization. The amount of guilt or shame officers feel for behaving unethically depends, at least in part, on how they regard the person being abused. To avoid the feelings of self-censorship or guilt that often accompany misconduct, officers can employ euphemistic language to strip victims of their humanity. Using terms like "dirtbag" to describe law violators has the effect of dehumanizing intended targets, generally making it easier for officers to justify, ignore, or minimize the harmful effects of their actions, while at the same time reducing their personal responsibility for behaving in ways that they know are wrong.

Diffusion of responsibility. An officer who uses this excuse relies on the shared participation—and, by extension, the shared guilt—of everyone involved in an incident of misconduct to excuse or reduce any personal culpability. With each additional accomplice, every individual officer is seen as that much less responsible for any wrongdoing that might have occurred. If, for instance, money is stolen from an arrestee, officers might assert that there were many officers at the crime scene who could have done this, so an individual cannot be blamed. Similarly, if ten officers were involved in the service of a search warrant, then each officer is only one-tenth responsible for any misconduct that occurs.

Misconduct's Slippery Slope

It is important to note that most officers do not jump headfirst into large-scale misconduct—instead, they weigh in gradually in a process referred to as incrementalism.[6] The strength and ease with which officers can rationalize unethical behavior also depends, at least in part, on how they view their conduct, the people harmed by their actions, and the consequences that flow from their actions. An officer's initial slide down the slippery slope of misconduct can begin with nothing more than simple policy violations that, if left unchecked, generate a mild feeling of psychological tension or discomfort. However, by learning to rationalize wrongdoing in ways that make it psychologically and morally acceptable, officers are able to relieve any feelings of distress or discomfort, effectively disengaging their moral compasses.

Officers can employ cognitive rationalizations prospectively (before the corrupt act) to forestall guilt and resistance, or retrospectively (after the misconduct) to erase any regrets. In either case, the more frequently an officer rationalizes deviant behavior, the easier each subsequent instance of misconduct becomes.[7] This is because the more frequently officers employ rationalizations, the easier it becomes to activate similar thought patterns in the future. With time and repeated experience, rationalizations can eventually become part of the habitual, automatic, effortless ways that officers think about themselves, their duties, and the consequences of their actions, eventually allowing officers to engage in increasingly egregious acts of misconduct with little, if any, of the guilt or shame commonly associated with wrongdoing.

As officers learn to pay less attention to the morality of their actions, the ways they think about misconduct—that is, their attitudes, beliefs, and values—may begin to change as well. Officers can begin defining behaviors that were once seen as unethical or immoral as necessary parts of completing their assigned duties. Even more troubling, however, is that once rationalizations become part of an agency's dominant culture, they can alter the ways officers define misconduct, particularly if wrongdoings are rewarded either informally by an officer's peer group or formally by the organization.

Ethics Education

Law enforcement agencies throughout the United States, as well as abroad, have begun to recognize the importance of ethics training. While such attention represents a significant step in the right direction, ethical instruction is often limited to little more than the discussion and development of proper moral values—an approach commonly referred to as character education.[8] Proponents of this method suggest that officers who possess the right values—and, by extension, the right character—will always do the right thing, regardless of

the circumstances. Although few people would argue with the importance of good moral values and character, ethical decisions are not always simple.

Before officers can act ethically, they must recognize the moral nature of a situation; decide on a specific and, hopefully, ethical course of action; possess the requisite moral motivation to take action; and demonstrate the character necessary to follow through with their decisions.[9] To further complicate matters, even the best of intentions can be thwarted by peer pressure or fear of retaliation. For example, the 2003 National Business Ethics Survey found that approximately 40 percent of those surveyed would not report misconduct if they observed it because of fear of reprisal from management.[10]

This cloud does, however, contain a silver lining. Research has demonstrated that ethics education can assist officers in better navigating moral challenges by increasing ethical awareness and moral reasoning—two critical aspects of ethical decision making.[11] However, conducting meaningful ethics education requires more than lengthy philosophical lectures on the importance of character. Rather, instructors should focus on facilitating a dialogue that challenges officers on key moral issues and assumptions; tests their reasoning and decision-making skills; and allows them to share their experiences in a safe, supportive environment.[12]

For ethics education to be truly effective, organizations must make moral discussions a regular part of the agency's training program. In the same way that officers routinely train in defensive tactics, firearms, and law to better prime them for field duties, officers should prepare equally well for any ethical issues they might encounter.[13] Supervisors can stimulate ethical discussions with a video documentary, news clip, or fictional story. Regardless of the stimulus, however, the more frequently officers discuss ethics, the better able they will be to recognize a moral dilemma, make the appropriate ethical decision, and demonstrate the moral courage necessary to behave honorably.

Next, law enforcement agencies must establish a clear code of ethical conduct, including a set of core values and a mission statement. Merely establishing a code of ethical conduct is not enough, however; the department's top management must lead by example. It is important to remember that a code of conduct applies equally to employees at all levels of an organization.[14] As most leaders can confirm from experience, officers can be surprisingly quick to point out any inconsistencies between the organization's stated values and the conduct of senior management. If leaders expect officers to behave ethically, leaders must model the way.

Departments must also work to create systems that reward ethical conduct and punish unethical behavior.[15] Core values and codes of conduct are of little value if they are not supported by wider agency objectives that reward ethical actions. Not only should law enforcement organizations reward officers for behaving ethically, they must also seriously address officers' ethical concerns by thoroughly investigating any allegations, while protecting the confidentiality of those reporting such incidents. And, finally, agencies should strive to create an open environment where ethical issues can be discussed without fear of punishment or reprisal.

In the end, mitigating and, hopefully, eliminating misconduct require regular ethics training, high ethical standards, appropriate reward systems, and a culture in which ethical issues are discussed freely. While the responsibility for creating a culture of ethics rests with leadership, individual officers must do their part to behave ethically, support the moral conduct of others, and challenge misconduct in all its forms. Only by remaining vigilant to the psychology of misconduct can law enforcement professionals focus attention back on the positive aspects of their profession, while enjoying the high levels of public trust necessary to do their jobs.

Notes

1. For a more complete discussion on the impact of police misconduct see Adam Dunn and Patrick J. Caceres, "Constructing a Better Estimate of Police Misconduct," *Policy Matters Journal* (Spring 2010): 10–16.

2. For a more complete description of police misconduct, media coverage, and public attitudes toward law enforcement see Joel Miller and Robert C. Davis, "Unpacking Public Attitudes to the Police: Contrasting Perceptions of Misconduct with Traditional Measures of Satisfaction," *International Journal of Police Science and Management* 10, no. 1 (2008): 9–22.

3. For a more complete report on the frequency of police misconduct see Mathew R. Durose, Erica L. Smith, and Patrick A. Lanan, *Contacts Between Police and the Public, 2005,* NCJ 215243, Bureau of Justice Statistics, Office of Justice Programs, Special Report (April 2007), http://bjs.ojp.usdoj.gov/content/pub/pdf/cppOS.pdf (accessed November 22, 2010).

4. For a discussion of research on cognitive dissonance, see Joel Cooper, Robert Mirabile, and Steven J. Scher, "Actions and Attitudes: The Theory of Cognitive Dissonance," in *Persuasion: Psychological Insights and Perspectives,* ed. Timothy C. Brock and Melaine C. Green (Thousand Oaks, California: Sage Publications Inc., 2005), 63–80.

5. For a more complete list of cognitive rationalizations, see Albert Bandura et al., "Mechanisms of Moral Disengagement in the Exercise of Moral Agency," *Journal of Personality and Social Psychology* 71, no. 2 (1996): 364–374; John F. Veiga, Timothy D. Golden, and Kathleen Dechant, "A Survey of the Executive's Advisory Panel: Why Managers Bend Company Rules," *Academy of Management Executive* 18, no. 2 (May 2004): 84–90; and Celia Moore, "Moral Disengagement in Processes of Organizational Corruption," *Journal of Business Ethics* 80 (June 2008): 129–139.

6. For a complete discussion of incrementalism, see Ehud Sprinzak, "The Psychopolitical Formation of the Extreme Left in Democracy: The Case of the Weathermen," in *Origins of Terrorism: Psychologies, Ideologies, Theologies, States of Mind,* ed. Walter Reich and Walter Laqueur (Cambridge, England: Cambridge University Press, 1990), 65–85.

7. For a discussion of implicit decision making, see Daniel Kahneman and Shane Frederick, "Representativeness Revisited: Attribute Substitution in Intuitive Judgment" in *Heuristics and Biases: The Psychology of Intuitive Judgment,* ed. Thomas Gilovich, Dale Griffin, and Daniel Kahneman (New York: Cambridge University Press), 20(G), 49–81.

8. See for example, Michael Josephson, *Becoming an Examplary Peace Officer. The Guide to Ethical Decision Making* (Los Angeles: Josephson Institute, 2009).

9. For further discussion on ethical decision making, see Russell Haines, Marc D. Street, and Douglas Haines, "The Influence of Perceived Importance of an Ethical Issue on Moral Judgment, Moral Obligation, and Moral Intent" *Journal of Business Ethics* 81 (2008): 387–399.

10. Ethics Resource Center, *2003 National Business Ethics Survey (NBES)* (May 21, 2003), www.ethics.org/resource/2003-national-business-ethics-survey-nbes (accessed November 24, 2010).

11. See, for example, Cubie L. L. Lau, "A Step Forward: Ethics Education Matters," *Journal of Business Ethics* 92 (2010): 565–584.

12. For a more complete discussion on facilitation, see Peter Renner, *The Art of Teaching Adults: How to Become an Exceptional Instructor and Facilitator* (Vancouver, Canada: Training Associates, 2005).

13. For a more complete discussion of ethics training, see Brian Fitch, "Principle-Based Decision Making," *Law and Order* 56 (September 2008): 64–70.

14. See, for example, Simon Webley and Andrea Werner, "Corporate Codes of Ethics: Necessary but Not Sufficient," *Business Ethics: A European Review* 17, no. 4 (October 2008): 405–415.

15. For further discussion on ethics and supervisory influence, see James C. Wimbush and Jon M. Shepard, "Toward an Understanding of Ethical Climate: Its Relationship to Ethical Behavior and Supervisory Influence," *Journal of Business Ethics* 3, no. 8 (1994): 637–647.

Critical Thinking

1. How can a police officer reduce the psychological discomfort that accompanies misconduct?

2. Explain the slippery slope theory regarding misconduct.

3. What can law enforcement agencies do to make ethics education truly effective?

Create Central

www.mhhe.com/createcentral

Internet References

Applying Social Learning Theory to Police Misconduct
http://ww2.odu.edu/~achappel/DB_article.pdf
Drury University
www.drury.edu/ess/irconf/dmangan.html

Dog Sniff Unconstitutional? Supreme Court Rules Drug Dog Sniffs Constitute Illegal Search

Dog sniff unconstitutional: Justice Antonin Scalia said a person has the Fourth Amendment right to be free from the government's gaze inside their home and in the area surrounding it, which is called the curtilage.

JESSE J. HOLLAND

Learning Outcomes

After reading this article, you will be able to:

- Show how dogs can do police work.
- Describe the factors that went into the Supreme Court's decision.

The Supreme Court ruled Tuesday that police cannot bring drug-sniffing police dogs onto a suspect's property to look for evidence without first getting a warrant for a search, a decision which may limit how investigators use dogs' sensitive noses to search out drugs, explosives and other items hidden from human sight, sound and smell.

The high court split 5–4 on the decision to uphold the Florida Supreme Court's ruling throwing out evidence seized in the search of Joelis Jardines' Miami-area house. That search was based on an alert by Franky the drug dog from outside the closed front door.

Justice Antonin Scalia said a person has the Fourth Amendment right to be free from the government's gaze inside their home and in the area surrounding it, which is called the curtilage.

"The police cannot, without a warrant based on probable cause, hang around on the lawn or in the side garden, trawling for evidence and perhaps peering into the windows of the home," Justice Antonin Scalia said for the majority. "And the officers here had all four of their feet and all four of their companion's, planted firmly on that curtilage—the front porch is the classic example of an area intimately associated with the life of the home."

He was joined in his opinion by Justices Clarence Thomas, Ruth Bader Ginsburg, Sonia Sotomayor and Elena Kagan.

On the morning of Dec. 5, 2006, Miami-Dade police detectives and U.S. Drug Enforcement Administration agents set up surveillance outside a house south of the city after getting an anonymous tip that it might contain a marijuana growing operation. Detective Douglas Bartelt arrived with Franky and the two went up to the house, where Franky quickly detected the odor of pot at the base of the front door and sat down as he was trained to do.

That sniff was used to get a search warrant from a judge. The house was searched and its lone occupant, Jardines, was arrested trying to escape out the back door. Officers pulled 179 live marijuana plants from the house, with an estimated street value of more than $700,000.

Jardines was charged with marijuana trafficking and grand theft for stealing electricity needed to run the highly sophisticated operation. He pleaded not guilty and his attorney challenged the search, claiming Franky's sniff outside the front door was an unconstitutional law enforcement intrusion into the home.

The trial judge agreed and threw out the evidence seized in the search, but that was reversed by an intermediate appeals court. In April a divided Florida Supreme Court sided with the original judge.

The Supreme Court's decision upholds that ruling.

"A drug detection dog is a specialized device for discovering objects not in plain view (or plain smell)," Kagan wrote in a concurring opinion. "That device here was aimed at a home—the most private and inviolate (or so we expect) of all the places and things the Fourth Amendment protects. Was this activity a trespass? Yes, as the court holds today. Was it also an invasion of privacy? Yes, that as well."

The four justices who dissented were Chief Justice John Roberts, Justice Stephen Breyer, Justice Anthony Kennedy and Justice Samuel Alito.

It's not trespassing when a mail carrier comes on a porch for a brief period, Alito said. And that includes "police officers who wish to gather evidence against an occupant," Alito said. "According to the court, however, the police officer in this case, Detective Bartelt, committed a trespass because he was accompanied during his otherwise lawful visit to the front door of the respondent's house by his dog, Franky. Where is the authority evidencing such a rule?"

Alito also said that the court's ruling stretches expectations of privacy too far. "A reasonable person understands that odors emanating from a house may be detected from locations that are open to the public, and a reasonable person will not count on the strength of those odors remaining within the range that, while detectable by a dog, cannot be smelled by a human."

Critical Thinking

1. What was the reasoning behind the Supreme Court's ruling?
2. Do you agree with Justice Alito's comparison of a mail carrier with a police officer wishing to gather evidence?

Create Central

www.mhhe.com/createcentral

Internet References

Flex Your Rights
www.flexyourrights.org/faqs/when-can-police-use-drug-dogs
Norml
http://norml.org/news/2013/04/04/us-supreme-court-limits-warrantless-use-of-drug-sniffing-dogs

Unit 4

UNIT

Prepared by: Joanne Naughton

The Judicial System

The courts are an equal partner in the American justice system. Just as the police have the responsibility of guarding our liberties by enforcing the law, the courts play an important role in defending these liberties by applying and interpreting the law. The courts are the battlegrounds where civilized "wars" are fought without bloodshed, to protect individual rights and to settle disputes.

Today, there are several issues and complexities concerning the judicial process that range from issues of false confessions of crimes, to Miranda rights, to the credibility of neurological evidence, to the misconduct of officials and prosecutors, and to the controversial issues of the use of torture. Our judicial process is an adversary system of justice, and the protagonists—the state and the defendant—are usually represented by counsel.

Article   Prepared by: Joanne Naughton

"I Did It"

Why Do People Confess to Crimes They Didn't Commit?

ROBERT KOLKER

Learning Outcomes

After reading this article, you will be able to:

- Explain what could motivate an innocent person to plead guilty.

- Argue that a criminal suspect should not agree to be interviewed by police.

The woman was naked from the waist down, her pants and underwear tossed into the weeds. Her down jacket was pulled to her chest, exposing her left breast to the autumn chill. Her head and face had been pummeled, and embedded in the blows were pellets from a BB gun; smashed shards of the gun were found nearby in the brush. Her hair was so gummed with blood that the hunter who stumbled on her body couldn't tell that it had once been all white.

By nightfall on November 29, 1988, the whole upstate village of Hilton was talking about Viola Manville—74 years old and a grandmother, a free spirit, outspoken, and now a homicide victim. Hilton is a small, blue-collar farm town on the edge of Lake Ontario west of Rochester where a good number of people once worked on the assembly lines at Kodak. The town can be rough—one neighbor from a wealthier suburb calls it "a little Appalachia here in New York"—but Hilton had never seen a murder like this. The Monroe County Sheriff's Office interviewed dozens of people: neighbors, family members, an ex-boyfriend, troubled teenagers. They learned that Manville often had been seen walking along the same set of abandoned railroad tracks where her body was found, even after having been the victim of an attempted rape there three years earlier. The man arrested in that attack, Glen Sterling, was still in prison.

Glen Sterling had a brother named Frank. He was tall but hunched and painfully shy. Frank Sterling grew up just 100 yards from the abandoned railroad tracks, a mile from the spot where the victim's body was found. Both his parents were janitors, and Frank was the middle child, a chain-smoker so lonely that as a teenager he'd do almost anything to make a friend. His classmates at Hilton Central High called him Bug Chower, after a story got around that he ate insects to get

attention. The name stuck. "He was the kid in school that everybody berated," says a former classmate, Rob Cusenz. "An easy mark."

At the time of the murder, Frank was 25 and still living at home, working as a school-bus monitor. He had a clean criminal record, but to the police, he had the makings of a motive. What if Frank had been angry that his brother Glen was in jail? What if he'd been nursing a grudge against Manville ever since she accused his brother of trying to rape her? What if this wasn't a sex-related murder but revenge? It was all just speculation, and indeed when the police questioned Sterling, they found his alibi was solid—he'd been seen working on the school bus all morning, and he recited the plots of the *Smurfs* and *Chipmunks* episodes he'd watched that afternoon. There was no physical evidence linking him to the crime, and Sterling was not arrested. Within a few months, other leads also dried up, and the Manville murder went unsolved.

Almost three years later, on July 10, 1991, an unmarked police car with two plainclothes detectives pulled up to the Sterling family's house. This was the third time in four years that the police had come to see him. He was now almost 28. He had become a truck driver and moved to Alabama for a year, then came back when work dried up. That afternoon, he was tired; he'd just finished a job that took him through a half-dozen states over two days. The detectives said they'd been assigned to reinterview people of interest in the case, and they realized Sterling had never been polygraphed. They asked him to come with them to a Rochester police station. He agreed.

At 7 P.M., Sterling followed a polygraph technician, Mark Sennett, into a small room on the fourth floor, where he sat at a table and waited. Before hooking up Sterling to the lie detector, Sennett spent more than two hours asking him questions: Did he know why he was there? Why would the police think he might have killed Vi Manville? Early on, Sennett told him that Glen had told his fellow inmates that one of his brothers had killed Manville—a lie he'd made up on the spot to see how the suspect might react. Sterling was startled; he said (maybe a little too defensively, Sennett thought) that there was no way his brother would have said that. Sennett told Sterling he was in for a long night. When the polygraph man left the room at 10:45 P.M., Sterling began to panic. If he stayed, he feared, the police wouldn't stop—but asking to leave or for a lawyer, he thought, would be as good as admitting he was a murderer.

At 11:20 P.M., another interrogator came to see Sterling. Patrick Crough, a young, confident detective, had worked just two homicide cases before the Manville murder, but he had already shown a natural talent for bonding with suspects. Crough spoke softly and leaned in close to Sterling, taking his time explaining his theory of the case. He talked about the love Sterling must have had for his brother and the anger he must have felt about his not being home for Thanksgiving. He told Sterling he thought he might have bottled up his anger about Glen being in jail. Maybe, Crough said, it was the reason for his upset stomach, his bad teeth.

Sterling admitted to Crough that he was angry enough to have "killed the bitch"—and threw his lighter across the room, saying, "I didn't kill her, but I sure as hell could have." Still, as midnight approached, Sterling maintained his innocence—and even asked to be hypnotized to prove he wasn't hiding anything. At about 12:45 A.M., Sennett returned and suggested what he called a "relaxation technique." He had Sterling lie down on the floor and keep his feet elevated on his chair. He told him to take four deep breaths, then slid his own chair up to Sterling and held his hand. He asked Sterling if he could picture himself on those railroad tracks, running into a lady with white hair, arguing with her, seeing her lying naked in the bushes. He asked him how he felt about seeing her this way. "Happy," Sterling said.

Seconds later, Sterling jumped to his feet and snapped, "This is a bunch of bullshit! I didn't do nothing!"

"You're right, this is bullshit," Sennett said before walking out of the room. "I think you killed this lady, and I'm going to prove it."

Sterling was trembling now, verging on hysteria. He had been in the small room for close to eight hours. Crough came in again at 2:40 A.M. and started rubbing Sterling's back. "I was whispering," Crough said later, "simply that we would not dislike him, that we were here for him, we understood—we felt he should tell the truth to get it off his chest." Crough's partner, Thomas Vasile, held Sterling's other hand, and the two detectives huddled around him for a long time, gently reassuring him. Finally, according to the police report, Sterling blurted out, "I did it . . . I need help."

Just before dawn, at 5:22, Sterling made a videotaped statement. Onscreen for just over twenty minutes, Sterling can be seen speaking in a slow, defeated monotone, the ash of his cigarette burning to the nub. With Sennett working the camera, Sterling nods and agrees to every detail Crough and Vasile ask about—the BB gun, the naked body—breaking into sobs now and then as the two officers console him. He mentions the purple color of Manville's jacket—a crime-scene detail police said no one else could have known. Sterling's motive, he explains on the videotape, is exactly what Crough had said: "I was already upset about not having my brother home for Thanksgiving. Turned out later she was that one my brother was in prison for. She said the wrong thing at the wrong time. Things transpired . . . After she said, 'Your brother got what he deserved,' I hit her."

Without witnesses or physical evidence linking him to the crime scene, prosecutors made the videotaped confession the centerpiece of their case. On September 29, 1992, Frank Sterling was convicted of murder and later sentenced to 25 years to life in prison, and sent to the state prison in Elmira. And several days after the trial, when a number of people in Hilton came forward saying that a 19-year-old man named Mark Christie was telling everyone he knew that he'd just gotten away with murder, the police didn't pay them much attention. The killer, after all, had confessed.

In the criminal-justice system, nothing is more powerful than a confession. Decades of research on jury verdicts have demonstrated that no other form of evidence—not eyewitnesses, not a video record of the crime, not even DNA—is as convincing to a jury as a defendant who says "I did it." The police, of course, understand the power of confessions and rely on interrogation techniques to produce them quickly so they can clear their cases. This is the stuff of countless TV procedurals—the small interrogation room with a bare table and two-way mirror; the good-cop-bad-cop routine; the deployment of outright lies like "You failed the polygraph" or "Your prints are on the knife." As a society, we have come to view these as acceptable, if blunt, tools of justice. We count on the integrity of police and safeguards like Miranda rights to prevent abuses, and we take it on faith that innocent people would never confess to crimes they haven't committed.

But, of course, they do. In recent years, the use of DNA evidence has allowed experts to identify false confessions in unprecedented and disturbing numbers. In the past two decades, researchers have documented some 250 instances of false confessions, many resulting in life sentences and at least four in wrongful executions. Of the 259 DNA exonerations tracked by a major advocacy group, 63 of them—or one out of every four—was found to have involved a false confession. Counting just the homicide cases, the proportion shoots up to 58 percent of all exonerations. Even this number could be an underestimate. "Most of the documented false confessions have been in highly publicized murder cases," says Steven Drizin, of Northwestern Law School's Center on Wrongful Convictions. "There is no reason not to think the same tactics would be as effective if not more effective in lesser cases, where the punishment that could flow from a confession would be less." False confessions appear to be particularly common in New York State, in which twelve of the 27 DNA-based exonerations have turned out to be based on bogus admissions of guilt.

Researchers who study false confessions say the roots of the problem lie in the interrogation tactics themselves. The most influential such method is the Reid technique, a decades-old, nine-step procedure designed to isolate and persuade a suspect to reveal his deceptions. Virtually every police department in the country has been influenced, directly or indirectly, by the Reid technique. Its defenders see it as the cornerstone of good police work, but its detractors say it places too much power in the hands of interrogating officers. In light of the new research documenting the scope of the problem, reformers in New York and elsewhere are calling for a wholesale reevaluation of the way the police question suspects. Frank Sterling's story should help their cause; it demonstrates just what can go wrong with the science of interrogation.

In 1940, a burly, clean-cut, Irish Catholic cop named John E. Reid was thinking of quitting the Chicago police force. Reid was tough, a former guard on the DePaul University football team, but was never comfortable carrying a gun. At the last minute, he applied for a transfer to a desk job at the Chicago crime lab. He arrived in the midst of a technological revolution in police work. In 1931, a presidential panel known as the Wickersham Commission had exposed abuses brought by the "third degree," the use of force by police to extract confessions. Police across the country had held suspects' heads underwater, hung them out of windows, and beaten them. In 1936, the Supreme Court decision *Brown v. Mississippi*—the brutal case of three black men who were beaten and whipped until they confessed—effectively outlawed confessions brought by brute force. Crime labs like Chicago's began developing new, more scientific means to solve cases: ballistics, document examination, and lie detection.

As much as anyone, John Reid can be credited with leading American law enforcement into the modern age. Reid's advances began with the lie detector. In 1945, he designed a chair that used inflated rubber bladders to detect a subject's jitters. In 1947, he essentially created the modern polygraph procedure with the "control-question technique," a way of measuring a suspect's reaction to provocative questions. That same year, Reid left the crime lab and founded John E. Reid & Associates, which went on to train scores of polygraph analysts, including members of the CIA and the Mossad.

Reid's most influential work focused on the art of the interrogation. Soft-spoken and sincere, he had a knack for gently persuading suspects to confess. "It was almost a priestlike approach," says George Lindberg, who worked for Reid for thirteen years. "He'd hold your hand and say, 'You should really get this off your chest.'" Reid played an important role in a number of high-profile Chicago murder trials, and other cities shuttled him in as a closer for their most sensitive cases. He was credited with personally helping to solve some 300 murders and coaxing 5,000 thieves to confess. Some in law-enforcement circles called him the most famous name next to J. Edgar Hoover. Reid's aim wasn't always true—in 1955, he got a Nebraska man named Darrel Parker to admit to killing his wife, and the real killer confessed 33 years later—but his faith in his own ability, and in the professionalization of his craft, led him to believe interrogations could be systematized to the point of being foolproof. "It's almost as if every crook reads the same book on what to do and say to give themselves away," he liked to say.

In 1962, Reid and his mentor, a Northwestern Law professor named Fred Inbau, co-wrote the first edition of *Criminal Interrogation and Confessions*. Criminologists and law historians credit their method with defining the culture of police-interrogation training for the past half-century. The procedure basically involves three stages meant to break down a suspect's defenses and rebuild him as a confessor. First, the suspect is brought into custody and isolated from his familiar surroundings. This was the birth of the modern interrogation room. Next the interrogator lets the suspect know he's guilty—that he knows it, the cops know it, and the interrogator doesn't want to hear any lies. The interrogator then floats a theory of the case, which the manual calls a "theme." The theme can be supported by evidence or testimony the investigator doesn't really have. In the final stage, the interrogator cozies up to the subject and provides a way out. This is when the interrogator uses the technique known as "minimization": telling the suspect he understands why he must have done it; that anyone else would understand, too; and that he will feel better if only he would confess. The interrogator is instructed to cut off all denials and instead float a menu of themes that explain why the suspect committed the crime—one bad, and one not so bad, but both incriminating, as in "Did you mean to do it, or was it an accident?"

Reid was hailed in his time as the man who made the third degree obsolete. But if his method wasn't physically coercive, it was certainly psychologically so. The Supreme Court's 1966 Miranda decision singled out the Reid method for creating a potentially coercive environment, citing it as one reason suspects needed to be informed of their right to remain silent. Reid and Inbau made minor modifications to the program, adding some language about Miranda to the 1967 edition of their manual, but they remained true believers. *Criminal Interrogation and Confessions* asserts that Reid investigators could judge truth and deception with 85 percent accuracy, a higher rate than anyone else has ever claimed to have achieved—or, as Reid once put it, "better results than a priest."

In Elmira, Frank Sterling kept to himself, spending most of his time in what was called the college block, where inmates can study toward degrees. His family visited for a time, but his father died in 1995, and his mother stopped coming to see him after she developed heart problems and moved to Texas to live with her son Gary. Sterling had his own health issues. The dust at Elmira made it difficult for him to breathe, and some of the prisoners referred to him as Shaky because he trembled. "Each time I'd see Frank upon coming back from being at another prison, I'd see he had aged more—his face, his eyes," says fellow inmate Jeff Deskovic.

Sterling had tried to recant his confession almost immediately after he gave it. He told his lawyer he was so worn down by the police that he didn't even remember what had happened that night. But the authorities weren't moved by that claim. Right after Sterling's trial, Sterling's lawyer filed to vacate the conviction on other grounds: He argued that the rumors surrounding Mark Christie, the man who had been heard bragging about killing Vi Manville after Sterling was convicted, provided sufficient justification to investigate whether he was the real killer. Christie, whose alibi fell apart under new scrutiny, was asked to take a polygraph and agreed. He fidgeted too much for the first test to be considered conclusive but took it again the next day and passed. On December 23, 1992, a judge refused to overturn Sterling's conviction. Christie, the judge said, was simply a young man who liked to brag.

In 1996, four years into Sterling's sentence, Mark Christie reentered the picture. If Sterling had been the weird kid in Hilton, Christie had a creepier reputation: He wore combat fatigues every day and took an eighteen-inch Bowie knife with him wherever he went. Now Christie had confessed to another murder, the brutal killing of a 4-year-old Rochester-area girl named Kali Ann Poulton. His confession prompted Sterling's appeals lawyer, Don Thompson, to file a new motion to overturn Sterling's conviction. If Christie were capable of killing Poulton, couldn't he have killed Vi Manville? A State Supreme

Court judge rejected the motion. "Only Sterling confessed to authorities," read the decision. "Only Sterling had a motive to kill Manville. Only Sterling knew facts that had not been publicized."

Sterling and Thompson filed a total of four motions to vacate Sterling's conviction over the next eight years, but all of them failed. Then, in 2004, Thompson sought the help of the Innocence Project—the Benjamin Cardozo School of Law–based group led by Barry Scheck and Peter Neufeld that has won wide acclaim for its work in freeing the wrongly convicted. The first time Neufeld watched Sterling's confession, even he thought he was guilty. But he soon came to see how everything pointed toward Christie. In 2005, Monroe County District Attorney Michael Green agreed to let the Innocence Project conduct DNA tests on some of Manville's clothing from the crime scene. In the fall of 2008, after three years of testing and legal maneuvering, word came back with what seemed like a match. The samples contained so-called touch DNA—a few skin cells—instead of the more definitive evidence found in blood and semen samples. Still, Neufeld says, "the profile had a very rare type. And Christie has that type."

In spite of the apparent match, a year passed, and the Monroe County D.A. still didn't take action. Last fall, an Innocence Project staff attorney named Vanessa Potkin personally visited Christie in prison to try to persuade him to own up to the murder. She spent part of two days talking to Christie, and while he almost seemed to acknowledge his role, and perhaps even to taunt her a bit, he admitted nothing. "His attitude was he's not responsible for Frank being there in prison," Potkin says. "Frank's the one who talked."

Sterling's team decided on a new tactic. On January 22, Potkin visited Christie again, this time with a polygraph and interrogation expert named Richard Byington who worked for the leading company in the field: John E. Reid & Associates. Neufeld had been waiting for the right case to ask the Reid people for pro bono help—a sort of Nixon-in-China move—and the company's president, Joseph Buckley, had agreed. The hope was that Byington, an experienced and highly regarded interrogator, could persuade Christie to confess.

At first, Christie appeared to relish the visit. He boasted to Byington that he had stolen a copy of the Reid-Inbau manual from the Hilton library to try and beat the polygraph he'd been asked to take after the Manville verdict. Of course, he'd aced it. Byington spent several hours trying to get Christie to warm up to him. Eventually, Christie seemed to grow impatient. "What do you want?" Byington remembers Christie saying.

Byington turned more aggressive. "I said, 'Listen, here's the deal. There's no doubt that you committed the Manville murder. The physical evidence says it, and the DNA basically says it. Now you need to do the right thing so Frank, who hasn't done anything, can go home.'" But Christie, who still harbored thoughts of getting out one day, still wasn't inclined to talk. "Why should I say anything?" he told Byington.

Then Byington played another card. In a strange coincidence, the detective who had procured Christie's confession in the Kali Ann Poulton case was Patrick Crough, the same man who had gotten Frank Sterling to confess. Byington pulled out a copy of a newly published memoir Crough had written about child-abduction cases called *The Serpents Among Us* and pointed to the page where Crough calls Christie not just a child-killer but, he believed, a child molester. Christie became furious. After thirteen years in prison, he had no real sense of how well he was remembered in the outside world, and he had hoped Kali Ann's murder, and his role in it, might have been forgotten. Now he saw that Crough was working to keep the case alive—and accusing him of raping the young victim as well. He knew he'd never lead a normal life outside of prison now.

"You know more about this than you're telling me," Byington said to Christie. And shortly after, Christie's confession began.

Earlier this year, on April 28, Frank Sterling was set free. He wept at the courthouse, hugged Don Thompson, and expressed disbelief. Peter Neufeld took a shot at the cops who interrogated Sterling eighteen years earlier. "There's no question that in this case," Neufeld said, "the police officers had tunnel vision."

In the early days of DNA exoneration, even the lawyers working the cases didn't know what to make of the surprising number of false confessions they came across. "It wasn't until the late nineties that we began to see patterns emerge," says Neufeld. "But still, it was running against 25 years of my own experience. Why would an innocent person confess?"

That question was eventually taken up by a handful of researchers, including the University of San Francisco School of Law's Richard Leo, Berkeley sociologist Richard Ofshe, John Jay College's Saul Kassin, and Northwestern Law School's Steven Drizin. False confessions now are generally understood to break down into three categories. There are voluntary false confessions, in which innocent people come forward on their own. Some, like John Mark Karr in the JonBenet Ramsey case, do it for the attention—others to self-punish or because they've lost touch with reality. Then there are what Leo calls "persuaded false confessions," in which people are convinced by the interrogator that they actually committed the crime. In New York, 17-year-old Marty Tankleff famously falsely confessed to killing his parents in 1988 after being convinced he must have blocked it out. Finally, there are compliant false confessions, in which the suspect is psychologically coerced to confess even while believing he's innocent. They do it, Kassin writes, "to escape a stressful situation, avoid punishment, or gain a promised or implied reward . . . often coming to believe that the short-term benefits of confession relative to denial outweigh the long-term costs." This appears to be what happened in the infamous Central Park jogger case. It also seems to explain Frank Sterling's confession.

Critics say the Reid technique is a major source of the problem. What was once seen as the vanguard of criminal science, they argue, is nothing more than a psychological version of the third degree. Even beyond the Reid method, the courts have given police "carte blanche in the interrogation room for any tactics shy of physical abuse," says Drizin. Others believe police shouldn't be able to mislead suspects with lies or manipulate them by suggesting that what they did isn't so bad. Great Britain's police aren't allowed to employ those tactics, and Kassin says the best available data suggest the efficacy with which they arrest and convict criminals isn't diminished by that.

Reid detractors also say that police often feed evidence to suspects, which accounts for why false confessors sometimes know details about a crime that they wouldn't otherwise know. In a recently published study, University of Virginia law professor Brandon Garrett found that in 97 percent of the false-confession cases he studied from the DNA era, the wrongly accused suspects were said to have supplied such telling details—facts either picked up elsewhere or provided by police. Interrogators also tend to be overconfident of their abilities to spot guilty suspects. No study so far (aside from Reid's own research) has shown the police to be any better than average at picking out liars. In fact, they're sometimes worse. In one 1987 study, police officers watched videotaped statements of witnesses, and their record at identifying deceptive testimony was no better than the average person's. Over confidence can blind investigators to evidence suggesting that the suspect is innocent. The pressure to resolve cases quickly and tidily can have a similar effect, especially in high-profile cases. Simply wearing suspects down is another issue: At some point, a given suspect will say anything just to make the immediate discomfort stop. "Why don't they beat people anymore?" asks Don Thompson. "It's not because they're particularly enlightened now. It's because the psychological coercion is so much more effective."

Frank Sterling's confession, Thompson believes, was marked by a number of these problems. After Sterling says he hit Vi Manville, Patrick Crough asks Sterling what he hit her with. Sterling says, "My hand." A moment later, Crough says, "Frank, as best as you can remember, and I know this is difficult for you, did something happen with that BB gun?" Only after being prompted that way does Sterling say, "Yeah, I started hitting her with it." Mark Sennett, the polygraph examiner, lied to Sterling about his brother Glen. Crough teased out the motive and alternately pressured and consoled Sterling. Sterling knew about the supposedly telling crime-scene detail of Manville's purple jacket, but Thompson says many people in Hilton would have seen her on her daily walks in that jacket. Finally, there was Sterling's state of mind. Having been held alone, without counsel, in a small interrogation room and questioned for twelve hours, he became isolated, exhausted, and vulnerable to manipulation. Over the years, Thompson and Crough had crossed paths in Rochester, running into each other around town or at the supermarket. "I'm never really comfortable when I'm talking to him," Thompson says. "He's an accomplished interrogator, which translates to being an accomplished manipulator."

Shortly after Sterling's release, I had dinner with Crough in Rochester. Calm and self-assured, he did what he could to sound gracious about Sterling's ordeal. But he couldn't help but also be defensive. He insisted he did good work that night in 1991. "His responses kept the interview going," he told me. "As a homicide detective, you don't walk out on an interview when the person's giving you a little something." Crough pointed out that he was the one who visited Christie in prison—he volunteered to do it and talked him into giving his DNA sample when Christie didn't have to do that—and it was his book that helped persuade Christie to confess. After a while, though, some contrition bled through. "Like that hasn't haunted me?" he told me. "I've been doing interrogations in major crimes for twenty

years. This is the first time I've ever had one go bad on me. That's not a bad statistic, you know."

The law-enforcement community insists current interrogation techniques are sound. The courts have upheld tactics like deceit and minimization, Reid president Joseph Buckley notes, and without such methods police would have a far more difficult time eliciting confessions from suspects who are, in fact, guilty. When false confessions do happen, Byington says it's not the Reid technique that's to blame but the misapplication of it. The police's main mistake with Frank Sterling, he says, was starting in on their suspect before they were reasonably sure he was guilty. Then, when Sterling gave Crough and the others questionable information, they blindly barreled ahead. "When they ask Frank what he was wearing, he says he thinks he was wearing a T-shirt and jeans," Byington says. "Well, if Frank was wearing a T-shirt and jeans, he'd have frozen to death." In Byington's opinion, Sterling had essentially been fed information over twelve long hours, then encouraged to spout it back over twenty minutes of video. In a good confession, Byington says, the suspect should do about 80 percent of the talking, narrating their experience for the benefit of the police, not saying yes and no to a series of prompts.

To prevent false confessions, interrogation critics say there's a solution so simple that it's remarkable it hasn't happened already: videotaping every minute of every police interrogation. Where the idea was once impractical, they note, the digital era changed that. Some law-enforcement officials fear that if juries see how the sausage is made, they might blanch at convicting even guilty suspects. In fact, Kassin's recent research indicates that when people see two versions of a false confession—one with just the confession and another that includes the entire interrogation—they become more effective jurors, correctly acquitting the innocent and convicting the guilty. Still, eighteen states and more than 800 jurisdictions have already started taping interrogations. New York has moved slowly—when they videotape at all, police tend to tape only confessions, not whole interrogations—but the New York State Bar Association has called for taping the full questioning session.

Earlier this year, the NYPD announced with some fanfare that it would test recording interrogations in two precincts. Last week, spokesman Paul Browne told me the bids have been selected, and that the 67th Precinct in Brooklyn and 48th Precinct in the Bronx will soon be outfitted with interrogation rooms ready for digital recording. Tests should start after the first of the year. Commissioner Ray Kelly "is open to seeing what we learn," Browne says, though in the spring, Kelly told me deploying such a system throughout the NYPD was a complicated endeavor, and that it wasn't clear to him yet that the effort would be worth the results.

One group solidly against tape-recording in New York is the Detectives' Endowment Association, whose president, Michael Palladino, holds on to the belief that what happens in an interrogation room is too messy for some jurors to tolerate. He also worries that juries won't be the only ones influenced. "Every taped interrogation can be used as a training film for criminals on what to expect from the police during an interrogation," he says. "Certainly, the element of surprise is gone."

Curiously enough, however, research shows that police and prosecutors forced to tape their interrogations often wind up supporting the practice. One Minnesota prosecutor famously called it "the best thing we've ever had rammed down our throats." A taped record can mean fewer motions to suppress and fewer claims that suspects were unduly deceived or abused. Joseph Buckley says the Reid method and taping can go hand in hand. "When somebody claims there was coercion, the record speaks for itself," he says. Even Patrick Crough says he believes in it, calling it "a tool to let the jury see what we see."

Don Thompson has thought a great deal about what would have happened in 1992 if the jury had been able to see the whole Sterling interrogation and not just the final twenty minutes. "You can't describe to a jury the effects of isolation over a twelve-hour period," he says. "I'd make them sit through the whole twelve hours. Because at that point, even for the jurors sitting in the jury box, it begins to feel like a hostage crisis."

Frank Sterling is standing on the railroad tracks in Hilton behind his old house—a small ranch-style building on a two-lane road, about a quarter-mile from the high school. "When we first moved here, the trains were still running through," he says, pointing at the tracks. "Then they disbanded it."

As we walk down the gravel path, Sterling points in the direction of the Big M supermarket he walked to on the afternoon Vi Manville was killed. To get to the store, he had to cross a train trestle over a creek and then leave the tracks, walking along the opposite creek bed. To get to where Manville was killed, Sterling would have had to continue on the tracks away from the market— "another mile and a half down the road," he says, laughing.

Sterling is heavier now than he was when he was sent to prison. His teeth were neglected for so long that a week before his release, he had nine of them pulled. At the time, he joked to his lawyers that he put them under his pillow for the Exoneration Fairy. He can't drive a truck because of medical issues, but he hopes to find computer work. For now, he is living with friends one town over from Hilton. He drives to Rochester when he needs to see his lawyers about finding health benefits, job training, and donated clothes. Sterling says he's angry, but he tries not to dwell on it. "I don't want it to tear me up." He hasn't decided whether to file a civil suit for wrongful conviction. The first night he was out, he says, he woke up in the middle of the night to the sound of rain on a windowpane. "It was something I couldn't hear for eighteen years," he says. "It's amazing. Something so simple that happens every day. Something everyone complains about."

Is it difficult being back here? "No," Sterling says. "I enjoyed growing up here." The creek is where he liked to fish for salmon. The train trestle is where kids liked to drink and where Frank walked his dogs Outlaw and Shebia. For a time, he says, he considered Vi Manville a friendly presence on the tracks. "She'd reach into her pocket and give the dogs a cookie."

When Crough and his partner first came to Sterling's house in 1991, he says, "they claimed they were looking at others. But I have a feeling they were focused on, 'Okay, we'll make it look like we're looking into others but he's the one who probably did it for revenge.'" He agreed to the polygraph he says "because I didn't do it. I thought, *Okay, well, I've got nothing to hide, so I should pass with flying colors.*"

So why did he confess? "They just wore me down," he says, shaking his head. "I was just so tired. Remember, I hadn't had any sleep since about 2:30 Tuesday night."

He tries to explain what it was like to spar with the police for twelve hours.

"It's like, 'Come on, guys, I'm tired—what do you want me to do, just confess to it?'

'No, we want the truth.'

'Well you're not fucking listening to the truth, I'm telling you. What more do you want me to say?'

'We want to know what happened.'"

Sterling says the police never asked him to say in his own words what happened. "'Yes' and grunts—that's basically what the whole confession is about." Regarding the color of Manville's coat, he says, "I knew in the fall she always wore her purple jacket."

I ask him what he thinks when he watches the twenty-minute confession video now. "When you look, you'll notice I shake a little bit," he says. "But to hold on to the whole cigarette and let the whole cigarette go to ash and never take a drag off of it? I'm a smoker. Normally, I would be sitting there dragging on it, not letting the whole cigarette just sit there burning down. Yeah, I was not in the right mind, looking back at it now."

He knows some people will never understand why he admitted to a crime he didn't commit. "They say, 'Why confess if you didn't do it?' But they don't have the whole understanding of what I was going through at the time. It's like, yeah—I wanted to get it over with, get home, and get some sleep."

He laughs softly. "Eighteen years and nine months later, I finally get to go home."

Critical Thinking

1. What is the Reid technique of interviewing?
2. What did the Supreme Court say about the Reid technique in *Miranda v. Arizona*?
3. What could be done to prevent false confessions?
4. Do you believe it is advisable for a criminal suspect to agree to speak to police?

Create Central

www.mhhe.com/createcentral

Internet References

Futurity
www.futurity.org/innocent-confess

PsychCentral
http://psychcentral.com/news/2013/09/12/why-people-confess-even-if-they-didnt-do-it/59450.html

Article   Prepared by: Joanne Naughton

In Miranda Case, Supreme Court Rules on the Limits of Silence

Justices uphold the murder conviction of a Texas man who refused to answer a question. The 5–4 ruling says suspects must invoke their legal rights.

DAVID G. SAVAGE

Learning Outcomes

After reading this article, you will be able to:

- Illustrate how the 5th Amendment didn't help Salinas.
- Discuss the Court's approach to the Miranda decision.

Crime suspects need to speak up if they want to invoke their legal right to remain silent, the Supreme Court said Monday in a ruling that highlights the limited reach of the famous Miranda decision.

The 5–4 ruling upheld the murder conviction of a Texas man who bit his lip and sat silently when a police officer asked him about the shotgun shells that were found at the scene of a double slaying. They had been traced to the suspect's shotgun.

At his trial, prosecutors pointed to the defendant's silence as evidence of his guilt. In affirming the conviction of Genovevo Salinas, the court's majority admitted that some suspects might think they had a right to say nothing.

"Popular misconceptions notwithstanding," the Constitution "does not establish an unqualified 'right to remain silent,'" said Justice Samuel A. Alito Jr.

Rather, he said, the 5th Amendment says no one may be "compelled in any criminal case to be witness against himself." Since the Miranda decision in 1966, the court has said police must warn suspects of their rights when they are taken into custody.

But the Miranda decision covers only suspects who are held in custody and are not free to leave.

In the Texas case, Salinas was asked to come to the police station, and he agreed to do so. "All agree that the interview was noncustodial," Alito said, so the police were not required to read him his rights under the Miranda decision.

And although Salinas had a qualified right to remain silent under the 5th Amendment, a suspect must invoke his rights and say he wants to remain silent, the court ruled Monday.

Salinas "alone knew why he did not answer the officer's question, and it was therefore his burden to make a timely assertion of the privilege," Alito said.

The decision is consistent with the high court's grudging approach to the Miranda decision and related 5th Amendment questions over recent decades. The court's conservative-leaning justices have not been willing to overturn the Miranda precedent, but they have repeatedly narrowed its scope.

Chief Justice John G. Roberts Jr. and Justices Antonin Scalia, Anthony M. Kennedy and Clarence Thomas voted with Alito to uphold the conviction in *Salinas vs. Texas.*

Alito noted that during a trial, defendants may refuse to testify, and prosecutors may not use their silence in court as evidence against them, citing the court's 1965 ruling in *Griffin vs. California.* In a concurring opinion, Thomas and Scalia said the Griffin case was mistaken and should be overruled.

Meanwhile, in another case, Thomas spoke for himself and four liberal justices to require a jury to find a defendant guilty of every facet of a crime that could lead to a mandatory prison term.

In *Alleyne vs. United States,* the court ruled that before a judge imposes an extra mandatory prison term on a defendant for conduct such as brandishing a firearm, a jury must find the defendant guilty of that offense. To do otherwise violates the defendant's basic right to a jury trial with his guilt proven beyond a reasonable doubt, Thomas said.

Thomas has long maintained that juries, not judges, must decide whether a defendant is guilty of all the elements of a crime that warrant extra punishment. And in a rare show of unity with the court's more liberal members, he overruled earlier decisions that left this power in the hands of a judge.

In the case before the court, Allen Alleyne was given four years in prison for helping his girlfriend rob the manager of a convenience store. Following the prosecution's recommendation, the judge gave him an extra seven years for having brandished a firearm. But Alleyne said he had not brandished a gun, and the jury had not convicted him of that extra offense.

The 5–4 ruling overturns the extra seven-year term. The dissenters faulted the majority for overruling a precedent from 2002 that allowed judges to make such decisions.

Critical Thinking

1. How does the 5th Amendment protect us?
2. Who does the 5th Amendment protect?
3. Why didn't the 5th Amendment protect Salinas?

Create Central

www.mhhe.com/createcentral

Internet References

Miranda Rights
www.mirandarights.org/righttoremainsilent.html

NWSidebar
http://nwsidebar.wsba.org/2013/06/26/salinas-v-texas-miranda-rights

Article   Prepared by: Joanne Naughton

Neuroscience in the Courtroom

Brain scans and other types of neurological evidence are rarely a factor in trials today. Someday, however, they could transform judicial views of personal credibility and responsibility.

MICHAEL S. GAZZANIGA

Learning Outcomes

After reading this article, you will be able to:

- Be skeptical about reports of eye witness identification of a suspect.

- State why brain scans might be valuable in a criminal case.

B y a strange coincidence, I was called to jury duty for my very first time shortly after I started as director of a new MacArthur Foundation project exploring the issues that neuroscience raises for the criminal justice system. Eighty of us showed up for selection in a case that involved a young woman charged with driving under the influence, but most of my fellow citizens were excused for various reasons, primarily their own DUI experiences. Finally, I was called to the judge. "Tell me what you do," he said.

"I am a neuroscientist," I answered, "and I have actually done work relevant to what goes on in a courtroom. For example, I have studied how false memories form, the nature of addiction, and how the brain regulates behavior."

The judge looked at me carefully and asked, "Do you think you could suspend all that you know about such matters for the course of this trial?" I said I could try. And with that, he said I was excused.

I was dismayed but should not have been. In the interest of fairness, judges and attorneys are supposed to seek jurors who will be guided solely by what they hear in the courtroom and to steer clear of those whose real or imagined outside expertise might unduly influence fellow jurors. Yet, in a way, the judge's dismissal of me also paralleled the legal system's wariness today of the tools and insights of neuroscience. Aided by sophisticated imaging techniques, neuroscientists can now peer into the living brain and are beginning to tease out patterns of brain activity that underlie behaviors or ways of thinking. Already attorneys are attempting to use brain scans as evidence in trials, and the courts are grappling with how to decide when such scans should be admissible. Down the road, an ability to

link patterns of brain activity with mental states could upend old rules for deciding whether a defendant had control over his or her actions and gauging to what extent that defendant should be punished. No one yet has a clear idea of how to guide the changes, but the legal system, the public and neuroscientists need to understand the issues to ensure that our society remains a just one, even as new insights rock old ideas of human nature.

Unacceptable Evidence (For Now)

With the growing availability of images that can describe the state of someone's brain, attorneys are increasingly asking judges to admit these scans into evidence, to demonstrate, say, that a defendant is not guilty by reason of insanity or that a witness is telling the truth. Judges might approve the request if they think the jury will consider the scans as one piece of data supporting an attorney's or a witness's assertion or if they think that seeing the images will give jurors a better understanding of some relevant issue. But judges will reject the request if they conclude that the scans will be too persuasive for the wrong reasons or will be given too much weight simply because they look so impressively scientific. In legal terms, judges need to decide whether the use of the scans will be "probative" (tending to support a proposition) or, alternatively, "prejudicial" (tending to favor preconceived ideas) and likely to confuse or mislead the jury. So far judges—in agreement with the conventional wisdom of most neuroscientists and legal scholars—have usually decided that brain scans will unfairly prejudice juries and provide little or no probative value.

Judges also routinely exclude brain scans on the grounds that the science does not support their use as evidence of any condition other than physical brain injury. Criminal defense attorneys may wish to introduce the scans to establish that defendants have a particular cognitive or emotional disorder (such as flawed judgment, morality or impulse control), but— for now at least—most judges and researchers agree that science is not yet advanced enough to allow those uses.

Functional magnetic resonance imaging (fMRI) offers an example of a process that can provide good scientific information, of which fairly little is legally admissible. This technology is a favorite of researchers who explore which parts of the brain are active during different processes, such as reading, speaking or day-dreaming. It does not, however, measure the firing of brain cells directly; it measures blood flow, which is thought to correlate to some extent with neuronal activity. Further, to define the imaging signal associated with a particular pattern of brain activity, researchers must usually average many scans from a group of test subjects, whose individual brain patterns may diverge widely. A defendants fMRI scan may appear to differ greatly from an average value presented in court but could still be within the statistical boundaries of the data set that defined that average.

Moreover, scientists simply do not always know the prevalence of normal variations in brain anatomy and activity in the population (or groups within it). Showing a defendant's brain scan without data from an appropriate comparison group might profoundly mislead a jury. Judges have already had a hard time evaluating whether to admit physical brain-scan evidence of neurological or psychiatric problems that might bear on a defendant's culpability; they may face more difficulty in the years ahead when deciding whether to allow brain images to serve as indicators for more complex mental states, such as a witness's credibility or truthfulness.

Since the early 20th century, when psychologist and inventor William Moulton Marston first claimed that a polygraph measuring blood pressure, pulse, skin conductivity and other physiological signs could determine whether someone is lying, lie detection has been a hot topic in legal circles. U.S. courts have largely dismissed polygraph results as inadmissible, but other technologies are being developed, and courts will surely be forced eventually to evaluate their admissibility as well. These tools include brain-imaging methods that aim to detect mental states reflective of truthful behavior.

Detecting Lies and Determining Credibility

Recent work by Anthony D. Wagner and his colleagues at Stanford University, for instance, has revealed that under controlled experimental conditions fMRI, combined with complex analytical algorithms called pattern classifiers, can accurately determine that a person is remembering something but not whether the content of the detected memory is real or imagined. In other words, we might be able to use fMRI to detect whether individuals believe that they are recalling something, but we cannot tell whether their beliefs are accurate. Wagner concludes that fMRI methods may eventually be effective in detecting lies but that additional studies are needed.

Other experiments help to expose the nature of honesty: Does honesty result from the absence of temptation or from the exercise of extra willpower to resist it? In 2009 Joshua D. Greene and Joseph M. Paxton of Harvard University gave test subjects placed in a scanner a financial incentive to

overstate their accuracy in a coin toss; the researchers were able to obtain fMRI images of individuals deciding whether or not to lie. Dishonest behavior correlated with extra activity in certain brain regions involved in impulse control and decision making. Yet Greene and Paxton noted that some subjects who told the truth also exhibited that same brain activity, so the fMRI images may capture only their extra struggle to resist temptation, not their ultimate truthfulness. The researchers therefore urge judges to be cautious about allowing these kinds of data in today's courtroom.

Their view is not universal, however. Frederick Schauer, professor of law at the University of Virginia and an expert on legal evidence, points out that courts now routinely admit many types of evidence that are far more dubious than the lie-detection science that is being excluded. The current approach to assessing whether witnesses or others are telling the truth is inaccurate and based on misconceptions about dishonest behavior: demeanor, for example, does not always provide reliable clues to honesty. The law has its own standards for determining admissibility into a court, and those standards are more lenient than scientific standards. Schauer argues that jurors should be allowed to consider the result of a lie-detection test that has a 60 percent accuracy rate because it could provide reasonable doubt as to guilt or innocence.

One of the first cases to tackle the use of brain-scanning technology for lie detection recently ended in a federal district court in Tennessee. In *United States v. Semrau*, a magistrate judge found that the evidence offered by a commercial fMRI lie-detection company should be excluded in part because of Federal Rule of Evidence 403, which holds that evidence must be probative and not prejudicial.

Furthermore, the judge explained why he found that the unfair prejudicial influence of the technology in the case substantially outweighed its probative value. The magistrate's main objection was that the defense expert conducting the lie-detection test could not tell the court whether the answer to any particular question was true or false. In fact, the expert testified that he could tell only whether the defendant was answering the set of questions about the case truthfully overall.

The use of neuroscience to assess the character and overall honesty of defendants may eventually trump its use for probing their truthfulness on any one matter.

One must wonder: In future cases, might the results be admissible with the more limited goal of simply determining whether or not the defendant was being deceptive in general? The use of neuroscience to assess the character and overall honesty of defendants may eventually trump its use for probing their truthfulness on any one matter in the courtroom. Federal Rule 608(b) provides that once the character of a witness has been attacked, counsel can introduce as evidence opinions about the witness's "character for truthfulness or untruthfulness." Today this type of evidence consists simply of testimony by others about the character of the witness. But what about tomorrow? Will juries want to know how a witness scores on a test of probable dishonesty? Will the evidence that someone tends toward dishonesty be more prejudicial if it comes out of a fancy machine? My guess is that such evidence will eventually be used and that it will initially tend to be prejudicial but that as society acquires more experience with the technology, the prejudicial effect will diminish.

Scanning for Psychopaths

Judges and attorneys are already being forced to work out the role of brain scans in the courtroom. In the long run, however, the greatest impact of neuroscience on the legal system will surely come from deeper insights into how our brain shapes our behavior. Even in infancy humans manifest innate senses of fairness and reciprocity, as well as desires to comfort the mistreated and punish transgressors. We are judge and jury from birth. On top of these instincts we have built our enlightened view of how culture should regard and punish antisocial behavior. Someday neuroscience could well force the legal system to revise its rules for determining culpability and for meting out sentences. It could also shake up society's understanding of what it means to have "free will" and how best to decide when to hold someone accountable for antisocial actions.

Consider the psychiatric and legal standing of psychopaths, who constitute less than 1 percent of the general population but roughly 25 percent of those in prison. That label, though used popularly as a catchall for many violent and nonviolent criminals, is properly reserved for those with a well-defined psychiatric condition diagnosed through a test called the Hare Psychopathy Checklist—Revised (PCL-R).

Psychopaths often display superficial charm, egocentricity, grandiosity, deceitfulness, manipulativeness, and an absence of guilt or empathy, all of which the PCL-R can assess. Yet psychometric tests such as the PCL-R are only proxies for measuring the neurological dysfunctions underlying these people's disturbed mental lives. Neuroimaging measurements of brain processes should therefore, at least in theory, provide a much better way to identify psychopaths.

To date, numerous studies have associated psychopathy with unusual brain activity. Psychopaths seem to exhibit, for example, abnormal neurological responses to stimuli that demand close attention and to words with emotional, concrete or abstract meanings. But such responses may also be found in people who have suffered damage to an area known as the medial temporal lobe—meaning they cannot be used as definitive signs of psychopathy. Other studies suggest psychopaths may have damage to the deep-brain structures of the limbic system, which helps to give rise to emotions, but the finding is preliminary.

Scientists are also beginning to look for abnormal connections in psychopaths' brains. Marcus E. Raichle, Benjamin Shannon and their colleagues at Washington University in St. Louis, along with Kent Kiehl of the University of New Mexico, analyzed fMRI data from scans of adult inmates and of juvenile offenders, all of whom were also assessed for psychopathy with the PCL-R. The adults, they found, had a variety of unusual connections between regions in their brains, although no one alteration predominated. Striking differences appeared more consistently and exclusively in the young offenders—and the degree of those changes increased along with their individual levels of impulsivity. One interpretation is that the impulsive juveniles lack some of the normal neural constraints on their choices of actions. Perhaps among juveniles who go untreated a brain abnormality that promotes impulsiveness eventually becomes more widespread, resulting in the diverse neural abnormalities seen in adults. Such a difference may also help explain why psychiatric treatments for psychopathy in juveniles are more successful than in adults, who are largely unresponsive.

Controversially, psychopathy is not now a recognized basis for an insanity defense. Instead psychopaths are seen as more dangerous than offenders without the pathology, and they receive longer or harsher sentences. A neuroimaging tool or method that could reliably identify psychopaths would be useful at the sentencing phase of a trial because it could help determine whether the defendant might deserve medical confinement and treatment rather than punitive incarceration. Getting the public to accept that people identified in this way should be committed to a mental hospital instead of a prison may be a tough sell, but with enough evidence the practice could eventually become legal doctrine. By then, one hopes, neuroscience will also have come up with better ways to help rehabilitate or cure them.

Neuroscience and Criminal Defenses

Criminal law currently accepts only a short list of possible defenses—will modern neuroscience begin to add to it? For example, the courts have consistently refused to accept a formal "battered woman defense" from defendants who retaliated with lethal force against spouses who regularly and violently beat them. Nevertheless, in some states the courts do allow experts to testify that battered-woman syndrome is a type of post-traumatic stress disorder, which judges and juries can take into consideration when assessing the credibility of a woman's claim that she acted to protect herself. Such precedents open a door to wider judicial uses of neuroscience.

How one defines a defendant's *mens rea,* or mental state, in a given context has a major effect on how much responsibility to ascribe to him or her. In ongoing fMRI-based research, Read Montague of Baylor College of Medicine and Gideon Yaffe, a law professor at the University of Southern California, study whether certain addicted individuals suffer from a subtle form of "risk blindness." Reasonable people learn not to rob stores by realizing that committing the crime would jeopardize their ability to enjoy a life with friends and family, pursue rewarding careers, and so on. Montague and Yaffe see indications, however, that at least some addicts cannot think through the benefits of those alternative courses of action. Potentially their findings could justify modifying the "reasonable person" standard in criminal law so addicts could be judged against what a reasonable addict, rather than a reasonable nonaddict, would have done in a given situation; such a finding might then lead to acquittal or reduction in punishment for an addicted defendant.

When the foregoing examples are taken together, profound questions emerge about how our culture and the courts will manage antisocial behavior. As neuroscientist William T. Newsome of Stanford University has asked, Will each of us have a personalized "responsibility" ranking that may be called on should we break the law? If we soon all carry our personal medical histories on a memory stick for reference, as some experts predict, will we also perhaps include a profile derived from knowledge of our brain and behavior that captures our reasonableness and irresponsibility? Would this development be good for society and advance justice, or would it be counterproductive? Would it erode notions of free will and personal responsibility more broadly if all antisocial decisions could seemingly be attributed to some kind of neurological deviation?

Would it erode notions of free will and personal responsibility if all antisocial decisions could seemingly be attributed to some kind of neurological deviation?

I feel it is important to keep scientific advances on how the brain enables mind separate from discussions of personal responsibility. People, not brains, commit crimes. As I have spelled out elsewhere, the concept of personal responsibility is something that arises out of social interactions. It is a part of the rules of social exchange, not a part of the brain.

Proceed with Caution

In spite of the many insights pouring forth from neuroscience, recent findings from research into the juvenile mind highlight the need to be cautious when incorporating such science into the law. In 2005 in the case *Roper v. Simmons,* the U.S. Supreme Court held that the execution of a defendant who committed a murder at age 17 or younger was cruel and unusual punishment. It based its opinion on three differences between juveniles and adults: juveniles suffer from an impetuous lack of maturity and responsibility; juveniles are more susceptible to negative influences and lack the independence to remove themselves from bad situations; and a juvenile's character is less formed than an adult's. Although the court realized it was drawing an arbitrary line, it ruled that no person who was younger than 18 at the time of a crime could receive the death penalty.

In May 2010 the court expanded that limitation. In *Graham v. Florida,* it held that for crimes other than homicide, a sentence of life without the possibility of parole for a person under the age of 18 violated the Constitution's prohibition of cruel and unusual punishment. Citing information provided by the American Medical Association, the court stated that "psychology and brain science continue to show fundamental differences between juvenile and adult minds."

But how consistently do neuroscience and psychology support that opinion? A study by Gregory S. Berns, Sara Moore and C. Monica Capra of Emory University explored whether the irrefutable tendency of juveniles to engage in risky behavior resulted from immaturity in the cognitive systems that regulate emotional responses. This team tested the theory using a technology called diffusion tensor imaging (DTI) to examine the tracts of white matter that connect different control regions of the cortex in 91 teenage subjects. Surprisingly, the juveniles who engaged in risky behavior had tracts that looked *more adult* than did those of their more risk-averse peers.

Advanced neuroimaging has thus presented a finding directly contrary to the conventional scientific and legal perspectives on the capacity of juveniles. If further research supports those conclusions, then the law, by its own logic, might need to hold juvenile delinquents to adult criminal standards. Alternatively, justice might require that convicted juveniles undergo DTI or a successor technology to determine whether their white matter structure is adultlike. The results of such a test could then provide guidance to the court on sentencing. The scope of these consequences highlights why the courts should not incorporate insights from neuroscience into the law until a substantial body of studies have confirmed them.

Exciting as the advances that neuroscience is making every day are, all of us should look with caution at how they may gradually come to be incorporated into our culture. The legal relevance of neuroscientific discoveries is only part of the picture. Might we someday want brain scans of our fiancées, business partners or politicians, even if the results could not stand up in court? As the scientific understanding of human nature continues to evolve, our moral stance on how we wish to manage a just society will shift as well. No one I know wants to rush into a new framework without extreme care being given to each new finding. Yet no one can ignore the changes on the horizon.

More to Explore

Patterns of Neural Activity Associated with Honest and Dishonest Moral Decisions. Joshua D. Greene and Joseph M. Paxton in *Proceedings of the National Academy of Sciences USA,* vol. 106, no. 30, pages 12,506–12,511; July 28, 2009.

Adolescent Engagement in Dangerous Behaviors Is Associated with Increased White Matter Maturity of Frontal Cortex. Gregory S. Berns, Sara Moore and C. Monica Capra in *PLoS ONE,* vol. 4, no. 8, e6773; August 26, 2009.

Altered Functional Connectivity in Adult and Juvenile Psychopathy: A Rest-State fMRI Analysis. Benjamin Shannon et al. Abstract from the 16th Annual Meeting of the Organization for Human Brain Mapping. Barcelona, 2010.

Detecting Individual Memories through the Neural Decoding of Memory States and Past Experience. Jesse Rissman, Henry T. Greely and Anthony D. Wagner in *Proceedings of the National Academy of Sciences USA* vol. 107, no. 21, pages 9,849–9,854; May 25, 2010.

Who's in Charge? Free Will and the Science of the Brain. Michael S. Gazzaniga. Ecco HarperColins, 2011.

The Law and Neuroscience Project: www.lawandneuroscience project.org.

Critical Thinking

1. How could brain scans assist criminal defendants?
2. Should courts allow brain scans into evidence?

Create Central

www.mhhe.com/createcentral

Internet References

Clinical Neurological Sciences
www.cnsuwo.ca/ebn

Frontiers
www.frontiersin.org/journal/10.3389/fpsyg.2012.00385/abstract

Article   Prepared by: Joanne Naughton

Torturer's Apprentice

The new science of interrogation is not, in fact, so new at all: "Extraordinary rendition" and "enhanced interrogation" and "waterboarding" all spring directly from the practices of the medieval Roman Catholic church. The distance, in both technique and ideology, between the Inquisition's interrogation regime and 21st-century America's is uncomfortably short—and provides a chilling harbinger of what can happen when moral certainty gets yoked to the machinery of torture.

CULLEN MURPHY

Learning Outcomes

After reading this article, you will be able to:

- Show how some modern interrogation methods spring from the medieval Roman Catholic church practices of the Inquistion.

- Discuss how the use of torture as a tool came to be justified in the search for truth.

- Show that some defenses of torture by the CIA were invented by the Inquisition.

Umberto Eco, in his best-selling 1980 novel, *The Name of the Rose,* summons to life a dark and compelling character: Bernard Gui, a bishop and papal inquisitor. In the movie, he is played with serpentine menace by F. Murray Abraham. The year is 1327, and Gui has come to an abbey where a series of murders has been committed. It falls to him to convene a tribunal and examine the suspects. Eco describes the inquisitor's bearing as the tribunal gets under way:

He did not speak: while all were now expecting him to begin the interrogation, he kept his hands on the papers he had before him, pretending to arrange them, but absently. His gaze was really fixed on the accused, and it was a gaze in which hypocritical indulgence (as if to say: Never fear, you are in the hands of a fraternal assembly that can only want your good) mixed with icy irony (as if to say: You do not yet know what your good is, and I will shortly tell you) and merciless severity (as if to say: But in any case I am your judge here, and you are in my power).

Bernard Gui is a historical figure. He was a Dominican priest, and in 1307 he was indeed made an inquisitor by Pope Clement V, with responsibility for a broad swath of southern France. Over a period of 15 years, Gui pronounced some 633 men and women guilty of heresy. We know the disposition of these cases because Gui wrote everything down—the record survives in his *Liber sententiarum,* his "Book of Sentences." It is a folio-size volume, bound in red leather. File a request at the British Library, in London, and before long the document will be delivered to the Manuscripts Reading Room, where you can prop it up on a wedge of black velvet. The writing, in Latin, is tiny and heavily abbreviated.

Inquisition records can be highly detailed and shockingly mundane. An itemized accounting of expenses for the burning of four heretics in 1323 survives from Carcassonne:

For large wood 55 sols, 6 deniers.

For vine-branches . . . . . 21 sols, 3 deniers.

For straw 2 sols, 6 deniers.

For four stakes 10 sols, 9 deniers.

For ropes to tie the convicts . . . . . 4 sols, 7 deniers.

For the executioner, each 20 sols . . . . . 80 sols.

In all 8 livres, 14 sols, 7 deniers.

An event like this would typically have occurred on a Sunday, in the course of a ceremony known as a *sermo generalis.* A throng would gather, and the various sentences would be read aloud by the inquisitor. The recitation of capital crimes came last, and the prisoners were then turned over—*relaxed* was the euphemistic term—by the spiritual authorities to the secular ones: churchmen did not wish to sully themselves with killing. To emphasize that his hands were clean, the inquisitor would read a pro forma prayer, expressing hope that the condemned might somehow be spared the pyre—though there was no hope of that. Bernard Gui's most productive day was April 5, 1310, when he condemned 17 people to death.

Late in 2010, Google Labs introduced something called the NGram Viewer, which allows users to search a database of millions of published works and discover how often particular words have been used from year to year. If you search for the word *inquisition,* you'll get a graph showing a sharp upward climb beginning about a decade ago. The word comes up more and more because people have been invoking it as a casual metaphor when writing about our own times—for instance, when referring to modern methods of interrogation, surveillance, torture, and censorship. The original Inquisition was initiated by the Church in the 13th century to deal with heretics and other undesirables, and continued off and on for 600 years. But it's a mistake to think of the Inquisition as just a metaphor, or as relegated to the past. For one thing, within the Church, it has never quite ended; the office charged today with safeguarding doctrine and meting out discipline occupies the Inquisition's old palazzo at the Vatican. More to the point, the Inquisition had all the hallmarks of a modern institution—with a bureaucracy, a memory, a procedure, a set of tools, a staff of technocrats, and an all-encompassing ideology that brooked no dissent. It was not a relic but a harbinger.

You can see this in the work of someone like Bernard Gui. Few personal details are known about the man himself, but Eco's fictional characterization gets at something authentic. He was methodical, learned, clever, patient, and relentless—all of this can be inferred from the paper trail. Gui was a prodigious writer. Among other things, he compiled a lengthy manual for inquisitors called *Practica officii inquisitionis heretice pravitatis,* or "Conduct of the Inquisition Into Heretical Depravity." The manual covers the nature and types of heresy an inquisitor might encounter and also provides advice on everything from conducting an interrogation to pronouncing a death sentence.

Gui would never have put it this way, but his aim in the *Practica* was to create something like a science of interrogation. He was well aware that interrogation is a transaction between two people—a high-stakes game—and that the person being interrogated, like the person asking the questions, brings an attitude and a method to the process. The accused may be wily and disputatious. Or he may seem humble and accommodating. He may feign insanity. He may resort to "sophistries, deceit, and verbal trickery." The inquisitor, Gui advised, needed a variety of "distinct and appropriate techniques."

Gui's was not the Inquisition's first interrogation manual, but it was one of the most influential. A generation after Gui, another Dominican, Nicholas Eymerich, produced the *Directorium inquisitorum,* which built on the work of his predecessor and achieved even greater renown. In our own times, the techniques of interrogation have been refined by psychologists and criminologists, by soldiers and spies. Place the medieval techniques alongside those laid out in modern handbooks, such as *Human Intelligence Collector Operations,* the U.S. Army interrogation manual, and the inquisitors' practices seem very up-to-date.

The inquisitors were shrewd students of human nature. Like Gui, Eymerich was well aware that those being questioned would employ a range of stratagems to deflect the interrogator. In his manual, he lays out 10 ways in which heretics seek to "hide their errors." They include "equivocation," "redirecting the question," "feigning astonishment," "twisting the meaning of words," "changing the subject," "feigning illness," and "feigning stupidity." For its part, the Army interrogation manual provides a "Source and Information Reliability Matrix" to assess the same kinds of behavior. It warns interrogators to be wary of subjects who show signs of "reporting information that is self-serving," who give "repeated answers with exact wording and details," and who demonstrate a "failure to answer the question asked."

But the well-prepared inquisitor, Eymerich writes, has ruses of his own. To confront an unforthcoming prisoner, he might sit with a large stack of documents in front of him, which he would appear to consult as he asked questions or listened to answers, periodically looking up from the pages as if they contradicted the testimony and saying, "It is clear to me that you are hiding the truth." The Army manual suggests a technique called the "file and dossier approach," a variant on what it terms the "we know all" approach:

> The HUMINT [human intelligence] collector prepares a dossier containing all available information concerning the source or his organization. The information is carefully arranged within a file to give the illusion that it contains more data than is actually there . . . It is also effective if the HUMINT collector is reviewing the dossier when the source enters the room.

Another technique suggested by Eymerich is to suddenly shift gears, approaching the person being interrogated in a seeming spirit of mercy and compassion, speaking "sweetly" and solicitously, perhaps making arrangements to provide something to eat and drink. The Army manual puts it this way:

> At the point when the interrogator senses the source is vulnerable, the second HUMINT collector appears. [He] scolds the first HUMINT collector for his uncaring behavior and orders him from the room. The second HUMINT collector then apologizes to soothe the source, perhaps offering him a beverage and a cigarette.

Eymerich and the Army describe many other techniques. You can try to convince the prisoner that resistance is pointless because others have already spilled the beans. You can take the line that you know the prisoner is but a small fish, and if only you had the names of bigger fish, the small one might swim free. You can play on the prisoner's feelings of utter despair, reminding him that only cooperation with the interrogator offers a path to something better. The Army manual refers to this as the "emotional futility" approach:

> In the emotional-futility approach, the HUMINT collector convinces the source that resistance to questioning is futile. This engenders a feeling of hopelessness and helplessness on the part of the source. Again as with the other emotional approaches, the HUMINT collector gives the source a "way out" of the helpless situation.

And then there is the matter of torture. Pope Innocent IV authorized its use by the Inquisition in 1252 in the papal bull *Ad extirpanda.* Few words summon the Dark Ages as quickly as *torture,* but the uncomfortable reality is that the emergence of torture as an instrument of justice marks the advent of a modern way of thinking: the truth can be ascertained without God's help.

Torture as a tool of jurisprudence was little known in the darkest part of the Dark Ages. The ability of human beings to discover the truth was thought to be limited. Thus the reliance not on judges or juries but on *iudicium Dei*—the judgment of an all-knowing God—to determine guilt or innocence. This often took the form of trial by ordeal. The accused would be submerged in water, or made to walk on red-hot coals, or forced to plunge an arm into boiling water. If he or she suffered no harm, or if the wounds healed sufficiently within a certain period of time, then it was the judgment of God that the accused was innocent. This regime was common in Europe for many centuries. It was unquestionably primitive and certainly barbaric. In its favor, it was devoid of hubris about what mere mortals can ever really know.

The late-medieval revolution in legal thinking—manifest everywhere, from Church courts to secular ones—took the pursuit of justice out of God's hands and put it into the hands of human beings. In his book *Torture,* the historian Edward Peters explains that the medieval legal revolution was based on one big idea: when it came to discovering guilt or innocence—or, more broadly, discovering the truth about something—there was no need to send the decision all the way up the chain of command, to God. These matters were well within human capacity.

But that didn't quite settle the issue, Peters goes on. When God is the judge, no other standard of proof is needed. When human beings are the judges, the question of proof comes to the fore. What constitutes acceptable evidence? How do you decide between conflicting accounts? In the absence of a confession—the most unassailable form of evidence, the "queen of proofs"—what form of questioning can properly be applied to induce one? Are there ways in which the interrogation might be . . . enhanced? And in the end, how do you know that the full truth has been exposed—that a bit more isn't waiting to be discovered some little way beyond, perhaps with some additional effort? So it's not hard to understand, Peters concludes, how torture comes into the picture.

From time to time, exhibits of torture instruments go on tour. The effect is oddly Disneyfied—a theme-park view of interrogation. The very names of the instruments reinforce a sense of distant fantasy: Brazen Bull, Iron Maiden, Judas Cradle, Saint Elmo's Belt, Cat's Paw, Brodequins, Thummekings, Pilliwinks, Heretic's Fork, Spanish Tickler, Spanish Donkey, Scold's Bridle, Drunkard's Cloak. They could just as easily be the names of pubs, or brands of condoms, or points of ascent on a climbing map.

The Inquisition rarely resorted to these specific instruments. It relied on three different techniques, all of them used today. Before a session began, the person to be interrogated would be brought into the torture chamber and told what was about to be done. The experience of being *in conspectus tormentorum* was often enough to compel testimony. If not, the session commenced. A physician was generally in attendance. Meticulous records were kept; the usual practice was for a notary to be present, preparing a minutely detailed account. These documents survive in large numbers; they are dry, bureaucratic expositions whose default tone of clinical neutrality is punctuated matter-of-factly—"Oh! Oh!"—by quoted screams.

The first technique used by the Inquisition was known in Spanish as the *garrucha* ("pulley") and in Italian as the *strappado* ("pull" or "tug"). It was a form of torture by suspension, and worked through simple gravity. Typically, the hands of the person to be interrogated were tied behind his back. Then, by means of a rope threaded through a pulley or thrown over a rafter, his body would be hoisted off the ground by the hands, and then be allowed to drop with a jerk. The strain on the shoulders was immense. The weight of the body hanging from the arms contorted the pleural cavity, making breathing difficult (asphyxiation was the typical cause of death in crucifixion, for the same reason).

Under various names, the *garrucha* appears frequently in more-recent history. Senator John McCain was subjected to a version of it, called "the ropes," by the North Vietnamese, after his airplane was shot down during the Vietnam War. It has been employed in the interrogation of prisoners in U.S. custody. One well-known case is that of Manadel al-Jamadi, who died during interrogation at Abu Ghraib in 2003. His hands had been tied behind his back, and he had then been suspended by the wrists from the bars of a window five feet off the ground. Michael Baden, the chief forensic pathologist for the New York State Police at the time, explained the consequences to Jane Mayer of *The New Yorker:*

> "If his hands were pulled up five feet—that's to his neck. That's pretty tough. That would put a lot of tension on his rib muscles, which are needed for breathing. It's not only painful—it can hinder the diaphragm from going up and down, and the rib cage from expanding. The muscles tire, and the breathing function is impaired."

The second technique employed by the Inquisition was the rack. In Spanish the word is *potro,* meaning "colt," the reference being to a small platform with four legs. Typically the victim was placed on his back, with legs and arms fastened tautly to winches at each end. Every turn of the winches would stretch him by some additional increment. Ligaments might snap. Bones could be pulled from their sockets. The sounds alone were sometimes enough to encourage cooperation in those brought within hearing distance. Here is an account of a suspected heretic who had been placed on the *potro* and was being questioned by inquisitors in the Canary Islands in 1597. The winches had just been given three turns. The suspect would confess after six more. The recording secretary preserved the moment:

> On being given these he said first, "Oh God!" and then, "There's no mercy": after the turns he was admonished, and he said, "I don't know what to say, oh dear God!" Then three more turns of the cord were ordered to be given, and after two of them he said, "Oh God, oh God, there's no mercy, oh God help me, help me!"

The third technique involved water. *Toca,* meaning "cloth," was the Spanish name, referring to the fabric that plugged a victim's upturned mouth, and upon which water was poured. The effect was to induce the sensation of asphyxiation by drowning. *Waterboarding* is the English term commonly used today. The modern term in Spanish is *submarino.* One historian writes:

> Even a small amount of water in the glottis causes violent coughing, initiating a fight-or-flight response, raising the heart

rate and respiratory rate and triggering desperate efforts to break free. The supply of oxygen available for basic metabolic functions is exhausted within seconds. While this is sometimes called "an illusion of drowning," the reality is that death will follow if the procedure is not stopped in time.

The CIA has acknowledged that one of its detainees, Khalid Sheikh Mohammed, the mastermind of the 9/11 attacks, was waterboarded 183 times in a single month. Defenders of the practice contend that this figure is misleading—that 183 refers to the number of individual "pours," and that they occurred in the context of no more than five "sessions."

As it happens, the Inquisition invented that defense. In theory, torture by the Church was strictly controlled. It was not supposed to put life in jeopardy or cause irreparable harm. And torture could be applied only once. But inquisitors pushed the boundaries. For instance, what did *once* mean? Maybe it could be interpreted to mean once for each charge. Or, better, maybe additional sessions could be considered not as separate acts but as "continuances" of the first session. Torture would prove difficult to contain. The potential fruits always seemed so tantalizing, the rules so easy to bend.

The public profile of torture is higher than it has been for many decades. Arguments have been mounted in its defense with more energy than at any other time since the Middle Ages. The documentary record pried from intelligence agencies could easily be mistaken for Inquisition transcripts. The lawyer Philippe Sands, investigating the interrogation (which used a variety of techniques) by the United States of a detainee named Mohammed al-Qahtani, pulled together key moments from the official classified account:

> Detainee spat. Detainee proclaimed his innocence. Whining. Dizzy. Forgetting things. Angry. Upset. Yelled for Allah. Urinated on himself. Began to cry. Asked God for forgiveness. Cried. Cried. Became violent. Began to cry. Broke down and cried. Began to pray and openly cried. Cried out to Allah several times.

The Inquisition, with its stipulation that torture and interrogation not jeopardize life or cause irreparable harm, actually set a more rigorous standard than some proponents of torture insist on now. The 21st century's *Ad extirpanda* is the so-called Bybee memo, issued by the Justice Department in 2002 (and later revised). In it, the Bush administration put forth a very narrow definition, arguing that for an action to be deemed torture, it must produce suffering "equivalent in intensity to the pain accompanying serious physical injury, such as organ failure, impairment of bodily function, or even death." To place this in perspective: the administration's threshold for when an act of torture *begins* was the point at which the Inquisition stipulated that it must *stop*.

The regulation of torture never really works—it just points the practitioners in new directions. Darius Rejali, one of the most prominent scholars of torture, puts the matter simply: "When we watch interrogators, interrogators get sneaky." The phenomenon is sometimes called "torture creep." Inquisitors were well aware of the dynamic. We see it today when interrogators, queasy about extracting information by means

of torture, send prisoners to be interrogated in countries without such scruples. The process is known as "extraordinary rendition"—a way of keeping your own hands clean, the equivalent of the Church's "relaxing" the condemned to the secular authority. (During the past decade, the United States has handled an estimated 150 suspected terrorists this way.) In medieval times, torture was at first limited to *crimina excepta*—crimes of the utmost gravity—but that category was eventually broadened, and the threshold of permissibility lowered. In the aftermath of the killing of Osama bin Laden, in May 2011, a number of commentators claimed that the al-Qaeda leader's hideout had been discovered owing to information gleaned from torture—demonstrating how worthwhile torture can be. The claim was false, but the fact that it was made illustrates a falling threshold: where once torture had been justified only by some urgent "ticking time bomb" scenario, now it is seen as an acceptable way to obtain intelligence of a more ordinary kind.

Amoral brutes certainly commit torture, but in their hands it doesn't become part of a legally sanctioned system. Torture becomes legitimized in the hands of a different sort of person—one who is determined to use the powers of reason, and believes in the rightness of his cause. This is what the writer Michael Ignatieff means when he calls torture chambers "intensely moral places." Those who wish to justify torture don't do so by *avoiding* moral thinking; rather, they override the obvious immorality of a specific act by the presumptive morality of the larger endeavor. The Bybee memo maintained that interrogators could not be prosecuted if they were acting in good faith: "The absence of specific intent negates the charge of torture." It is the same logic advanced by the inquisitors. Citing Thomas Aquinas, they argued that purity of motive forgave the crossing of any line.

Which, in the end, is the most dangerous inquisitorial impulse of all—that sense of moral certainty. In America today, religion asserts itself repeatedly and increasingly. Oklahoma and a dozen other states have introduced legislation to ban the use of Islamic sharia law in any way within their jurisdictions, despite the fact that it has become a problem exactly nowhere. Schoolbooks in Texas have been revised by government fiat to downplay the idea of separation of church and state. During the past decade, public libraries have faced challenges on moral grounds to more than 4,000 books in their collections. The notion of America as a "Christian nation" has emerged as a theme—explicitly or by innuendo—in the current presidential campaign. When President Obama, in 2009, maintained in a speech that what united Americans was not a specific religious tradition but "ideals and a set of values," he was attacked by a wide range of public figures.

But religion is not the only culprit. The Enlightenment, which was supposed to be the antidote to this sort of thinking, gave rise to uncompromising outlooks of its own. For some, the higher power is not God but the forces of history, or democracy, or reason, or technology, or genetics. Fundamentally, the inquisitorial impulse arises from some vision of the ultimate good, some conviction about ultimate truth, some confidence in the quest for perfectibility, and some certainty about the path to the desired place—and about whom to blame for obstacles in the way. These are powerful inducements. Isaiah Berlin foresaw where they would lead:

> To make mankind just and happy and creative and harmonious forever—what could be too high a price to pay for that? To make such an omelette, there is surely no limit to the number of eggs that should be broken—that was the faith of Lenin, of Trotsky, of Mao, for all I know, of Pol Pot . . . You declare that a given policy will make you happier, or freer, or give you room to breathe; but I know that you are mistaken, I know what you need, what all men need; and if there is resistance based on ignorance or malevolence, then it must be broken and hundreds of thousands may have to perish to make millions happy for all time.

Pasted into the front of Gui's *Liber sententiarum* is a sheaf of 17th-century correspondence that describes how the book came to the British Library in the first place. It was discovered by the philosopher John Locke in the late 1670s, in the archives of Montpellier. Locke understood the importance of what he had found, and arranged for the manuscript to be sent to the historian Philipp van Limborch, in the Netherlands, who was compiling a history of the Inquisition. "When you see what it contains," Locke wrote his friend, "I think you will agree with us that it ought to see the light." Limborch published Gui's document as an appendix. Years later, a buyer was found for the manuscript on behalf of the British Library. Locke wrote

his famous *Letter Concerning Toleration in 1685*. He made the case for freedom of thought and expression—and a certain humility regarding one's own cherished beliefs—on the grounds that, no matter how much certainty is in our hearts, human beings cannot know for sure which truths are true, and that believing we can leads us down a terrible path.

The correspondence tucked into Gui's manuscript offers a reminder of what Locke understood. The Inquisition is not a closed chapter. It is an open book.

Critical Thinking

1. Can torture be justified when interrogating criminal suspects?

2. What techniques from the Inquisition are still used today?

3. What, if anything, is wrong with a nation having a sense of moral certainty?

Create Central

www.mhhe.com/createcentral

Internet References

Balanced Politics
   www.balancedpolitics.org/prisoner_torture.htm
Center for Justice and International Law
   http://cejil.org

Article   Prepared by: Joanne Naughton

Lasting Damage: A Rogue Prosecutor's Final Case

JOAQUIN SAPIEN

Learning Outcomes

After reading this article, you will be able to:

- Show how some prosecutors place a greater value on winning a case than doing justice.
- Know how prosecutors are penalized when they violate their oath to do justice.

Among the thousands of prosecutors who have tried cases in the name of the people of New York City, Claude Stuart came to hold a handful of unfortunate distinctions:

- He was a serial abuser of his authority. State appellate courts reversed three convictions based on his wrongdoing.
- His misconduct actually led to disciplinary action by his superiors. He lost his job, and eventually his law license, after an appellate court determined he had lied to a judge about the whereabouts of a key witness.
- The particulars of his disciplinary proceedings became public, opening a window into the typically secretive panels that are supposed to police the state's lawyers.

Stuart declined repeated requests for comment for this story.

It's worth it, then, to appreciate the impact of Stuart's career in greater detail, how the misconduct took place, how it has complicated the continuing pursuit of justice, and how the consequences of Stuart's misconduct still linger, years after the man himself was exposed and disgraced.

The People v. Tyronne Johnson, Stuart's last trial as a prosecutor in Queens, is a perfect case to trace those issues.

The Crime

On Feb. 24, 2000, Queens prosecutors charged 23-year-old Tyronne Johnson with the murder of Leroy Vann. Three weeks earlier, Vann, an owner of a nightclub that Johnson frequented in Jamaica, Queens, had been shot in the stomach at 3:20 A.M. while standing in front of his home.

Vann stumbled inside, tumbled behind a couch and called for his elderly mother, Mary Puryear. His mother later testified that Vann had told her that a man named "Tyronne" from a nearby housing project had shot him in a botched robbery attempt with at least one other man, according to court records.

Police officer John Blandino said he interviewed Vann as an ambulance sped them to a local hospital.

"Leroy, listen here, you have a big hole in your chest," Blandino said, according to court testimony. "There is a chance you might not make it, but let us catch this person that did this to you. Tell me about Tyronne."

Vann, coughing and sputtering blood, repeated what he told his mother and added that Tyronne drove a white Lincoln Navigator, according to the officer.

When Johnson was questioned that morning, he volunteered to go to the precinct for questioning and told police he "wouldn't shoot Leroy, he's a friend," according to court records. He was released after police interrogated him for several hours.

Two weeks later, Daniel Small, a man in police custody for a separate offense identified Johnson in a photo array, saying he had confessed the crime to him. Johnson was arrested days later. Thirteen years after that arrest, Johnson maintains what he asserted at the time: He had played no role in the killing.

The Trial

By the time pre-trial proceedings began in spring 2002, Small had died.

Stuart, lacking any physical evidence, told the court and Johnson's defense lawyer that he would rely chiefly on the testimony of Blandino and Puryear to make his case.

But the day before the trial, Stuart dropped what amounted to a bomb, telling the defense he intended to present a third witness: a 22-year-old man named Henry Hanley, who lived across the street from Vann and had fled when police first tried to interview him days after the murder.

Hanley was arrested in March 2000 on a probation violation and questioned about the murder. He said he was paid to be a lookout while Johnson and another man murdered Vann in an attempt to rob him. He agreed to testify against Johnson in exchange for a light sentence for his involvement.

Hanley wasn't Stuart's only late surprise. He also waited until just before trial to share with Johnson's lawyer a potentially critical piece of evidence: the police statement of Shanise Knight, a relative of Hanley's.

Knight had told investigators that she had seen a man confront Vann minutes before the shooting. She described the man as about 35 years old, six feet tall and 230 pounds. Johnson was 23, stood 5 feet, 6 inches, and had a much slighter build, weighing about 140 pounds. Knight had not identified Johnson when she was shown a photo array of possible suspects that included his picture.

Johnson's lawyer, understandably, wanted to call Knight as a witness, but he could not locate her. He asked Stuart repeatedly during the trial if he knew where she was. Stuart said he didn't.

Court records show that on June 4, 2002, Judge Jaime Rios, who was overseeing the trial, also asked Stuart if he knew where Knight was. Stuart again said he didn't, adding that he, too, was trying to find her.

Johnson was convicted the next day of second-degree murder. He was sentenced to 20 years to life.

In an interview at Sing Sing Correctional Facility, Johnson's face was grim when he recalled hearing the verdict read.

"I felt broken inside," he said.

The Reversal

The verdict was only hours old when Johnson's family and lawyer set about mounting an appeal.

And it didn't take long for that effort to provide a shocking revelation. Michael Race, a private investigator hired by the family, tracked down Knight. Knight, for the first time, told her story to Johnson's side. And there was much more to it than she had initially told police.

Knight said she could discredit Hanley's critical testimony. She told Johnson's investigator that Hanley had been neither an accomplice to the crime nor a witness to it. She said he had been staying with her and was downstairs, asleep, when the shooting occurred. Knight said she woke him when she heard the gunshots. She ultimately signed an affidavit to that effect.

But she had one more explosive bit of information. She said in her sworn statement that Stuart not only had known where she was during the trial, but that he and two police detectives had visited her at her job just days before Stuart had insisted to Judge Rios that he did not know where she was.

More of Stuart's case soon seemed to crumble, as well. When Race went to see Hanley in prison, Hanley signed an affidavit in which he recanted his trial testimony and alleged that he was pressured by Stuart to accuse Johnson.

"I did not witness this incident into the death of Leroy Vann," Hanley's affidavit said. "I want the court to know and understand what I have previously done was a great error."

A television station aired an interview with Knight in which she described her meeting with Stuart. The segment also featured Hanley's girlfriend, Sharmaine Ramdass, who confirmed that she and Hanley were asleep at the time of the murder.

Later that year, Stuart's supervisors agreed to have Johnson's conviction vacated. Queens District Attorney Richard Brown wrote a letter to Judge Rios saying as much, adding that Stuart's conduct could not "be condoned."

The Disciplinary Process

It is impossible to know how many prosecutors get reported to the state's disciplinary panels for alleged misconduct. What is clear is that the appellate judges who overturn convictions because of misconduct don't routinely refer the offending prosecutors to the disciplinary committees. Defense lawyers, for their part, are often reluctant to complain formally, fearful that they will incur the wrath of prosecutors they will have to deal with again and again.

But Stuart's conduct in the Johnson case did provoke a referral. The trial judge, after vacating the conviction, sent District Attorney Brown's letter to the disciplinary panel, known formally as the Second Department Grievance Committee.

Brown had been blunt in his letter: He said Stuart's handling of the Johnson case "was totally inconsistent with the high ethical standards that I expect from my assistants" and that his office would pursue an investigation. "If disciplinary action against the assistant is appropriate, it will be taken."

Brown did act against Stuart, forcing his resignation.

When investigators with the disciplinary panel began to dig into Stuart's record, they found he had actually been reprimanded years before for another flawed prosecution.

In 1995, Stuart insinuated that a gun in the possession of the defendant at the time of his arrest was the same gun used in an attempted murder and robbery. But Stuart had a ballistics report showing that wasn't true: Bullet casings found at the scene of the crime didn't match the gun.

The defendant, Jay Walters, was convicted and sentenced to up to 25 years in prison. He served nearly four years before his conviction was overturned by an appellate court, which found that Stuart advocated "a position which he knew to be false"— an "abrogation of his responsibility as a prosecutor."

The investigation of the 1995 case ended with the disciplinary panel issuing Stuart a so-called letter of caution warning him not to breach ethical boundaries again. It was never made public. Stuart's bosses in the Queens District Attorney's office say they did not know about it.

Years later, when the panel looking into the Johnson case asked about the Walters matter, Stuart blamed his misconduct on inexperience. He then asserted that in the Johnson case, while he should have acknowledged seeing the key missing witness, he did not intend to mislead the court.

"I certainly made an error or mistake in judgment," he said. He claimed that he had telephoned Knight the day before he was asked about her whereabouts by Judge Rios, but that he had not reached her. He said he based his reply to the judge solely on that.

"I answered the question very narrowly," he said.

Melissa Broder, counsel for the disciplinary committee, dismissed Stuart's explanation.

Stuart had told the court a "flat-out lie," she said, because he was afraid the witness' testimony would undermine his case or that Rios would decide Stuart had withheld potentially exculpatory evidence.

In September 2005—more than 18 months after it had opened its investigation of Stuart—the committee suspended Stuart's license to practice law.

After his resignation, he landed a job in private practice doing civil litigation, a job he then lost along with his license.

"I was disappointed that I had to let him go," said David Brand, a partner at the Long Island firm Stuart had joined. "He was actually a good, effective trial lawyer."

In March 2010, New York's appellate division denied Stuart's application to renew his law license, saying he "does not demonstrate the requisite fitness and character to practice law."

Stuart—who still has an active license to practice law in New Jersey—today works as a math teacher at Queens Vocational and Technical High School.

Johnson, who remains to this day in a prison cell in part because of Stuart, said he feels sorry for the former prosecutor.

"I wish he just learned a lesson, but he didn't have to pay for it with his whole career," Johnson said of the severity of Stuart's discipline. "You're held to a high standard. Don't set people up . . . if there is evidence of someone's innocence, explore it . . . They know when something's not right."

The Retrial

Eugene Reibstein, a high-level Queens assistant district attorney who had tried dozens of homicides and felonies, was tasked with mounting the second prosecution of Johnson in July 2003.

Reibstein visited Hanley in prison and got him to recant his recantation. Despite his sworn affidavit claiming he had lied at the first trial, Hanley told the same story again during the second trial.

This time, however, Johnson's lawyer got to put Knight on the stand. She testified that Johnson couldn't have been responsible for the crime because he was far smaller than the man she saw that night. She also stuck to her earlier sworn statements that Hanley, the alleged eyewitness, had been asleep in her apartment at the time of the shooting. Ramdass, Hanley's girlfriend at the time, testified that she was in fact asleep with Hanley during the shooting.

It was not enough. Reibstein said that Knight and Ramdass were lying in his summation.

But ultimately it was Vann's mother, Mary Puryear, who shifted the balance of the trial.

A *New York Daily News* story described the jury as "transfixed" when Puryear, Vann's mother, testified from a wheelchair and tearfully described how Vann told her "Mama, I've been shot. Tyronne did it."

Johnson was convicted again and sentenced to 20 years to life.

The controversy around the case did not end there.

After the trial, Judge Rios' law clerk wrote a letter to the New York State Commission on Judicial Conduct, accusing him of coaching the prosecution in private discussions during the second trial.

Johnson's lawyers petitioned for yet another trial. At a hearing, Rios admitted to speaking to Reibstein in his chambers, but said he could not remember the details of the conversation.

Brooklyn Supreme Court Judge Matthew D'Emic ruled that while the conversation "strayed into improper territory," it did not prejudice the verdict against Johnson.

Now 36, Johnson has spent the last 13 years behind bars. His lawyers maintain he never received a fair trial. And they have now applied to a federal court to grant him yet one more trial.

"It doesn't get easier," Johnson said in the interview at Sing Sing last year. "You see your Mom get old. You see your children getting older. Relationships fall apart. People die. It gets harder as you go along. My son was five years old when I got locked up. My son is 17 on Friday."

If he's eligible for parole, Johnson's soonest possible release date would be in 2020. But to qualify, inmates usually have to express remorse for their crimes. He says he'll never do that.

"I'll never admit to something I didn't have anything to do with."

Critical Thinking

1. Was Stuart's punishment too severe?
2. If you were on the jury of Johnson's retrial, would you have had a reasonable doubt after hearing Knight, Ramdass, and Puryear testify?

Create Central

www.mhhe.com/createcentral

Internet References

Center for Prosecutor Integrity
www.prosecutorintegrity.org/wp-content/uploads/EpidemicofProsecutorMisconduct.pdf

Fair Trials International
www.fairtrials.org

Article

Prepared by: Joanne Naughton

U.S. Reviewing 27 Death Penalty Convictions for FBI Forensic Testimony Errors

SPENCER S. HSU

Learning Outcomes

After reading this article, you will be able to:

- Understand that any human endeavor is subject to the possibility of error, including forensic science.
- Comprehend the value of media scrutiny of government entities.
- Know that hair analysis cannot be used as positive identification, despite the fact that a prosecution witness may say it can.
- Discuss the death penalty as it relates to wrongful convictions.

An unprecedented federal review of old criminal cases has uncovered as many as 27 death penalty convictions in which FBI forensic experts may have mistakenly linked defendants to crimes with exaggerated scientific testimony, U.S. officials said.

The review led to an 11th-hour stay of execution in Mississippi in May.

It is not known how many of the cases involve errors, how many led to wrongful convictions or how many mistakes may now jeopardize valid convictions. Those questions will be explored as the review continues.

The discovery of the more than two dozen capital cases promises that the examination could become a factor in the debate over the death penalty. Some opponents have long held that the execution of a person confirmed to be innocent would crystallize doubts about capital punishment. But if DNA or other testing confirms all convictions, it would strengthen proponents' arguments that the system works.

FBI officials discussed the review's scope as they prepare to disclose its first results later this summer. The death row cases are among the first 120 convictions identified as potentially problematic among more than 21,700 FBI Laboratory files being examined. The review was announced last July by the FBI and the Justice Department, in consultation with the Innocence Project and the National Association of Criminal Defense Lawyers (NACDL).

The unusual collaboration came after *The Washington Post* reported last year that authorities had known for years that flawed forensic work by FBI hair examiners may have led to convictions of potentially innocent people, but officials had not aggressively investigated problems or notified defendants.

At issue is a once-widespread practice by which some FBI experts exaggerated the significance of "matches" drawn from microscopic analysis of hair found at crime scenes.

Since at least the 1970s, written FBI Laboratory reports typically stated that a hair association could not be used as positive identification. However, on the witness stand, several agents for years went beyond the science and testified that their hair analysis was a near-certain match.

The new review listed examples of scientifically invalid testimony, including claiming to associate a hair with a single person "to the exclusion of all others," or to state or suggest a probability for such a match from past casework.

Whatever the findings of the review, the initiative is pushing state and local labs to take similar measures.

For instance, the Texas Forensic Science Commission on Friday directed all labs under its jurisdiction to take the first step to scrutinize hair cases, in a state that has executed more defendants than any other since 1982.

Separately, FBI officials said their intention is to review and disclose problems in capital cases even after a defendant has been executed.

"We didn't do this to be a model for anyone—other than when there's a problem, you have to face it, and you have to figure how to fix it, move forward and make sure it doesn't happen again," FBI general counsel Andrew Weissmann said. "That tone and approach is set from the very top of this building," he said, referring to FBI Director Robert S. Mueller III.

David Christian "Chris" Hassell, director of the FBI Laboratory, said the review will be used to improve lab training, testimony, audit systems and research, as it has done when previous breakdowns were uncovered. The lab overhauled scientific practices when whistleblowers revealed problems in 1996 and again after an FBI fingerprint misidentification in a high-profile 2003 terrorism case, he said.

"One of the things good scientists do is question their assumptions. No matter what the field, what the discipline, those questions should be up for debate," Hassell said. "That's as true in forensics as anything else."

Advocates for defendants and the wrongly convicted called the undertaking a watershed moment in police and prosecutorial agencies' willingness to re-open old cases because of scientific errors uncovered by DNA testing.

Peter J. Neufeld, co-founder of the Innocence Project, which supports inmates who seek exoneration through DNA testing, applauded the FBI, calling the review historic and a "major step forward to improve the criminal justice system and the rigor of forensic science in the United States."

Norman L. Reimer, executive director of the NACDL, also praised the effort, predicting that it would have "an enormous impact on the states" and calling on the defense bar to represent indigent convicts.

"That's going to be a very big job as this unfolds," said Reimer, whose group has spent 1,500 hours identifying cases for the second round of review.

Under terms finalized with the groups last month, the Justice Department will notify prosecutors and convicted defendants or defense attorneys if an internal review panel or the two external groups find that FBI examiners "exceeded the limits of science" when they claimed to link crime scene hair to defendants in reports or testimony.

If so, the department will assist the class of prisoners in unprecedented ways, including waiving statutes of limitations and other federal rules that since 1996 have restricted post-conviction appeals. The FBI also will test DNA evidence if sought by a judge or prosecutor.

The review will prioritize capital cases, then cases in which defendants are imprisoned.

Unlike DNA analysis, there is no accepted research on how often hair from different people may appear the same.

The federal inquiry came after the Public Defender Service helped exonerate three D.C. men through DNA testing that showed that three FBI hair examiners contributed to their wrongful convictions for rape or murder in the early 1980s.

The response has been notable for the department and the FBI, which in the past has been accused of overprotecting its agents. Twice since 1996, authorities conducted case reviews largely in secret after the scientific integrity of the FBI Lab was faulted.

Weissmann said that although earlier reviews lawfully gave prosecutors discretion to decide when to turn over potentially exculpatory material to the defense, greater transparency will "lessen skepticism" about the government's motives. It also will be cheaper, faster and more effective because private parties can help track down decades-old cases.

Scientific errors "are not owned by one side," he said. "This gives the same information to both sides, and they can litigate it."

The review terms could have wide repercussions. The FBI is examining more than 21,000 federal and state cases referred to the FBI Lab's hair unit from 1982 through 1999—by which time DNA testing of hair was routine—and the bureau has asked for help in finding cases before lab files were computerized in 1985.

Of 15,000 files reviewed to date, the FBI said a hair association was declared in about 2,100 cases. Investigators have contacted police and prosecutors in more than 1,200 of those cases to find out whether hair evidence was used in a conviction, in which case trial transcripts will be sought. However, 400 of those cases have been closed because prosecutors did not respond.

On May 7, Mississippi's Supreme Court stayed the execution of Willie Jerome Manning for a 1992 double homicide hours before he was set to die by lethal injection.

FBI cases may represent only the tip of the problem.

While the FBI employed 27 hair examiners during the period under review, FBI officials confirmed for the first time this week that records indicate that about 500 people attended one-week hair comparison classes given by FBI examiners between 1979 and 2009. Nearly all of them came from state and local labs.

State and local prosecutors handle more than 95 percent of violent crimes.

In April, the accreditation arm of the American Society of Crime Laboratory Directors declined to order state and local labs to conduct reviews, but issued a public notice recommending that each laboratory evaluate the impact of improper statements on past convictions, reminding them of their ethical obligation to act in case of a potential miscarriage of justice.

FBI Lab officials say they have not been contacted by other labs about their review or who completed the FBI classes.

Critical Thinking

1. In light of what we now know about how these cases were prosecuted, do you think the death penalty remains an appropriate penalty in any case?

2. Why do you think these errors occurred?

3. Do you think we have ever executed innocent people?

Create Central

www.mhhe.com/createcentral

Internet References

Prison-Justice for America
   http://prison-justice.org

Think Progress
   http://thinkprogress.org/justice/2013/07/19/2330071/federal-forensics-investigation-calls-into-question-hundreds-of-convictions

Article   Prepared by: Joanne Naughton

Freed Amid Scandal, They Soon Found Trouble Again

Thousands of drug case convictions were abruptly open to challenge after state chemist Annie Dookhan was accused of misconduct. Many released have committed new crimes, but not the tidal wave feared.

WILLIAM FROTHINGHAM AND SCOTT ALLEN

Learning Outcomes

After reading this article, you will be able to:

- Demonstrate some of the ramifications of denying criminal defendants fair trials.
- Understand why criminal justice professionals on the front lines of the drug war are not surprised about the re-arrest of many Dookhan defendants.

Annie Dookhan seemed like the answer to Carlton Haynes's prayers.

The convicted cocaine dealer, 43, had been filing motion after handwritten motion in a vain attempt to get out of the maximum security prison in Walpole. But his luck changed late last August when news broke that Dookhan, a former state chemist, had allegedly mishandled evidence in thousands of drug cases, including his.

Haynes demanded a new trial—"The integrity of our constitution the courts and the liberties of all mankind are at stake," he wrote—and a judge agreed to release him from his cell 2½ years early as long as he wore a GPS bracelet to monitor his movements.

But it wasn't long before Haynes started getting into trouble again. And again. And again, including two arrests for selling drugs on Boston Common and an alleged assault on his girlfriend's young son.

Haynes, now back behind bars, is part of the crime wave that law enforcement officials predicted a year ago when judges began releasing inmates—some with long records of drug-dealing and violence—over concerns about Dookhan's role in their cases. The only question, said Boston Police Commissioner Edward F. Davis last October, is "how much damage Ms. Dookhan has done to our crime-reduction efforts."

Now, a *Globe* analysis shows that the scandal has led to measurably increased crime in cities such as Boston and Brockton.

While the Dookhan defendants' release has not unleashed the tidal wave some feared, offenders returned to the street have already figured in three killings, either as suspects or victims.

One year after the public first learned about the alleged misdeeds of Annie Dookhan, the *Globe* review of court records shows that more than 600 so-called Dookhan defendants have had convictions against them erased or temporarily set aside, or they've been released on bail pending a new trial. Of those, at least 83 have been re-arrested—about 13 percent of the total—and 16 have been arrested more than once for crimes ranging from possessing a pound of cocaine to vandalizing cars outside a Hyannis pub.

Donta Hood of Brockton, who allegedly shot a man to death in a drug dispute, may be the most notorious of the re-arrested, but at least 15 others are accused of new violent crimes, including one who allegedly shot at two state troopers and a passenger in their vehicle. Twenty-three more are facing new drug charges in Suffolk County, home to 61 of the re-arrested Dookhan defendants. Two other released defendants were themselves murdered.

And there may be many more to come. A special counsel to Governor Deval Patrick concluded this week that Dookhan's negligent or dishonest work as a drug analyst at the Hinton state lab in Jamaica Plain affected more than 40,000 drug defendants in nine years. Though most either never went to jail or have already been released, hundreds remain locked up. Many of those are now clamoring for freedom because of Dookhan's role in their cases.

To defense lawyers and the American Civil Liberties Union of Massachusetts, the scandal represents the greatest miscarriage of justice in the state in many years, tainting every case Dookhan touched regardless of the defendant's record.

"Regardless of any other issues Mr. Haynes has, Annie Dookhan's misconduct and widespread problems at the Hinton drug lab have made it such that Mr. Haynes received an unfair trial and the Commonwealth obtained unfair convictions on these drug charges," said Haynes's lawyer, Kathryn Hayne Barnwell.

But the spike in crime since the Dookhan scandal also offers a grim snapshot of the drug war's revolving door as people who have been handed the ultimate get-out-of-jail card get right back into legal trouble again, sometimes with astonishing speed:

- Rakeem Austin of Dorchester, 27, allegedly broke into three vehicles or residences in a single 24-hour span last November just five weeks after a judge stayed his three-year sentence for cocaine distribution and turned him loose. The GPS he was required to wear as a condition of his release led directly to his arrest, allegedly putting him at the scene of the crime in all three break-ins.

- Dekara Anderson of Dorchester, 38, won his freedom last October when a judge stayed his seven-year sentence for cocaine distribution due to Dookhan's work with case evidence. Six months later, when Framingham police finally chased Anderson down and tasered him, they say they found a plastic bag full of crack cocaine clenched tightly between his buttocks.

- Enrique Camilo of Roslindale, 39, was already out on bail from a Dookhan-related cocaine trafficking case last October when police recovered almost a pound of cocaine at his home. Camilo was arrested at Logan International Airport as he returned from the Dominican Republic, but he promptly made bail and fled, forfeiting $75,000 in bail. He remains a fugitive.

- Michael Gladunov of Boston, 33, was—by contrast—fairly easy to catch in the months after he was released in a Dookhan-related case. He was arrested twice for skipping court dates, and also picked up new charges of theft as well as resisting arrest. He seemed aware, however, that he was blowing his chance, reportedly telling police, "That's all right, I got a case with Dookhan . . . Put me in a cage. I belong in a cage."

To the police, prosecutors, probation officers, and others on the front lines of the drug war, the high rate of re-arrest among Dookhan defendants comes as no surprise. The average age of the 61 people who have been re-arrested in Suffolk County is 35, much too old to be a youthful offender, suggesting that many of them have a considerable history of dealing drugs. Getting into trouble is what they know.

Vincent DeMore, one of three assistant district attorneys in Suffolk County handling Dookhan-tainted cases, said that by the time drug defendants get to the point of being sentenced to jail, most have already accumulated a long record of drug possession and dealing.

"They almost all have 100 percent recidivism rates," said DeMore, who works at the weekly drug court sessions in Suffolk Superior Court where defendants in Dookhan cases make their pleas to be released or have convictions reversed. "They wouldn't be in Superior Court if that wasn't the case. By their very definition they are subsequent offenders."

Defense lawyers agree that, while some guilty drug defendants will undoubtedly walk free, the lack of a fair trial is the greater miscarriage of justice. Albert Cullen III, who represents several Dookhan defendants, said it is vital for prosecutors to play by the rules no matter the defendant.

"We rely on the Commonwealth to follow the law, and they didn't," Cullen said. " But these are not cases of mistaken identities or DNA. This is not adjudication of innocence, so far from that."

Despite the gloomy, if predictable, statistics on re-arrested Dookhan defendants, DeMore and others in the justice system know the crime wave is so far not as big as many feared in the early days after the scandal broke.

At the time, Dookhan admitted that she had committed a cardinal offense in her profession—testing drugs by visual inspection rather than doing chemical analysis—to make the work go faster. She also said she sometimes forged colleagues' signatures. In at least one case, prosecutors said, a defendant faced cocaine trafficking charges based on Dookhan's testing when he was actually peddling fake cocaine.

"I messed up bad. It's my fault, " Dookhan said in Aug. 28, 2012, remarks to State Police that she now wants suppressed from her upcoming trial on 27 felony counts because she had not been told of her right to remain silent.

Two days after Dookhan's confession, State Police closed the entire lab; it remains closed, all 90,000 drug tests done by chemists there in the last nine years now under a cloud. The Legislature set aside $30 million for the added costs of relitigating potentially thousands of drug cases, an amount many suspect won't be enough.

A mass prison exodus was feared, but what followed was, while disturbing, considerably more modest. About 2,000 of the affected defendants were still incarcerated at that time, but many were ineligible for release on the basis of Dookhan's alleged misconduct because they had been convicted of other charges.

"In Massachusetts, you really have to work at it to get incarcerated," prosecutor DeMore explained, meaning that most of the Dookhan defendants were "already on the streets anyway, so the amount of people who were returning to the street I think was a relatively small number. There just weren't that many of them."

Moreover, state prison and probation officials stepped up efforts to work with the Dookhan defendants to find housing, jobs, and substance abuse counseling—three key factors in whether criminals re-offend when they are released. In addition, Boston police have made a priority of monitoring Dookhan defendants who get out of jail, meeting with them individually to let them know they would be watched.

"People had feared that we were just going to open the doors to the prisons. The system really got organized so that wouldn't happen," said Probation Commissioner Edward J. Dolan. "It wasn't like prisoners went to the lobby of Souza-Baranowski [a state prison] and called a cab. I think that has contributed to the fact it wasn't a bigger public safety issue."

Beyond that, district attorneys have fought hard to keep some of the highest-risk Dookhan defendants from getting out in the first place, looking for legal arguments to preserve the convictions.

For instance, in some cases where Dookhan performed the drug testing, the lab preserved the drugs, opening the possibility of retesting the samples. In Suffolk County this year, prosecutors convicted two Dookhan defendants for heroin distribution, Julio Medina and Travis Curry, after the drugs were re-tested by another lab.

Today, many of the Dookhan defendants who were behind bars when the scandal broke are still there. For instance, 87 of the 292 Dookhan defendants who have begun the appeals process in Suffolk Superior Court were still locked up as of early summer.

Those 87 include 19 cases in which prosecutors persuaded a judge to deny the defendants' request for a new trial or at least a stay of their prison sentence.

Prosecutors also drove a hard bargain with many defendants they agreed to release, offering them a choice between accepting a plea bargain in which they go free, but carry a criminal conviction, or contesting their conviction and getting out of prison with a GPS device on their ankle. That precaution alone led to arrest warrants for several, including one who cut off the bracelet so he could take a dip in a hot tub.

Jake Wark, spokesman for Suffolk District Attorney Dan Conley said that there were, in the end, only 15 cases that prosecutors felt were so compromised by Dookhan's alleged misconduct that they dropped the charges entirely.

"The thought seemed to be that it's just a matter of the paperwork to get these convictions vacated, that I can just file this boiler plate motion and away we go, and it's not really working out that way. We're litigating them," DeMore said.

Essex District Attorney Jonathan Blodgett took a similarly aggressive approach, successfully challenging five of the seven Dookhan defendants who asked for a new trial and appealing to the Supreme Judicial Court in an effort to limit the authority of special judicial magistrates to release Dookhan defendants.

In all, the *Globe* review found that, as of early summer, 613 Dookhan defendants had either had their criminal sentences put on hold, been released on bail pending a new trial, or prosecutors had dropped the charges entirely. Suffolk County alone accounted for nearly half of the released defendants, 320, followed by Plymouth County with 113, and Norfolk County with 53.

That is more than enough drug offenders to cause a perceptible wave of crime, especially in places such as Suffolk County—home to three-quarters of Dookhan defendants who have been re-arrested—and in Brockton, where two recently released Dookhan defendants are accused of some of the most violent crimes.

That includes back-to-back assaults in May when Malcolm Desir allegedly shot at undercover police and then Donta Hood, 23, allegedly killed Charles Evans.

Plymouth District Attorney Timothy Cruz said this week the Dookhan defendants have contributed to a rise in violent crime in Brockton, including the late December shooting death of Dookhan defendant Tashawn Leslie and last week's stabbing death of Dookhan defendant Jeffery Cicerano.

"There have been significant issues with the drug lab," said Cruz at a press conference on the rising number of murders in the city. "Many times, we hear about the nonviolent drug offenders, I guess they're not here in the city of Brockton because, unfortunately, a lot of them are protecting their turf with weapons and they have no remorse about shooting other people or shooting at police officers, which makes them much more dangerous."

Overshadowed by the violent outbursts, some Dookhan defendants are approaching their unexpected freedom as a second chance, but they are learning how difficult it can be to go straight after a life of selling and using illegal drugs.

Not only do they carry the stigma of drug convictions and often lack qualifications for good work, they also face practical hurdles such as learning to live with a GPS ankle bracelet.

Ferdinand Rivera, 35, lost his job at a flooring company after customers saw the GPS device on his ankle and did not feel comfortable with him in their home. Although his boss knew about the bracelet beforehand, Rivera was fired after the episode.

Rivera has a lengthy criminal record dating back to his juvenile years, but he said his family values have changed and he is determined to make his most recent release from prison his last. He currently lives with his fiance and 8-year-old daughter in Dorchester and was recently accepted into Local 7, an iron workers union where he will work five days a week and take classes two nights a week as part of a three-year apprenticeship program.

"A lot of guys want to do the right thing, but there's nothing for them, so they go back to doing the same thing," Rivera said, mentioning how fortunate he is to have the strong support system others lack. "Some guys are worse off than if they just stayed in jail."

In fact, some Dookhan defendants have decided to remain in prison for now, hoping that a much-anticipated investigation of the Hinton lab by the state inspector general will be so damning that they can get their convictions erased and leave prison without an ankle bracelet.

Defendants and prosecutors alike are looking forward to Oct. 10 when the Supreme Judicial Court is scheduled to hear arguments in five Dookhan cases that could establish the guidelines for which convictions should stand and which should be tossed out because of her involvement. After the court's decision, expected in December, both sides expect the pace of Dookhan cases coming through the drug court to quicken.

Thousands of cases affected

The criminal cases of 40,323 people may have been tainted by the actions of Annie Dookhan, the alleged rogue state drug lab chemist who was arrested in September 2012. Of those:

613

Freed from jail or prison since the drug lab scandal unfolded in 2012.

83

Arrested again after release. Sixteen have been arrested more than once.

Boston Police Commissioner Davis looks back over the past year with some relief because the fall-out from the drug lab scandal could have been worse, but he is not letting his guard down.

"We're still vigilant, we're still concerned about this, the crisis has not passed," said Davis in an interview. But the crime wave this summer was not as severe as he had feared, "and I think that's a hopeful sign."

Critical Thinking

1. How do you explain why about 13% of the people whose convictions were erased or set aside, or who have been released on bail, have gotten into trouble again?

2. Do you think incarcerating drug law violators is an effective way to deal with drug abuse problems?

Create Central

www.mhhe.com/createcentral

Internet References

The Boston Globe

www.bostonglobe.com/metro/2013/11/22/annie-dookhan-former-state-chemist-who-mishandled-drug-evidence-agrees-plead-guilty/7UU3hfZUof4DFJGoNUfXGO/story.html

The Raw Story

www.rawstory.com/rs/2013/11/23/massachusetts-state-chemist-jailed-for-forging-drug-evidence

Unit 5

UNIT

Prepared by: Joanne Naughton

Juvenile Justice

Although there were variations within specific offense categories, the overall arrest rate for juvenile violent crime remained relatively constant for several decades. Then, in the late 1980s, something changed; more and more juveniles charged with a violent offense were brought into the justice system. The juvenile justice system is a twentieth-century response to the problems of dealing with children in trouble with the law, or children who need society's protection.

Juvenile court procedure differs from the procedure in adult courts because juvenile courts are based on the philosophy that their function is to treat and to help, not to punish and abandon the offender. Recently, operations of the juvenile court have received criticism, and a number of significant Supreme Court decisions have changed the way that the courts must approach the rights of children. Despite these changes, however, the major thrust of the juvenile justice system remains one of diversion and treatment, rather than adjudication and incarceration, although there is a trend toward dealing more punitively with serious juvenile offenders.

Article

Prepared by: Joanne Naughton

Violence in Adolescent Dating Relationships

"The early- to mid-teenage years mark a time in which romantic relationships begin to emerge. From a developmental perspective, these relationships can serve a number of positive functions. However, for many adolescents, there is a darker side: dating violence."

ERNEST N. JOURILES, CORA PLATT, AND RENEE MCDONALD

Learning Outcomes

After reading this article, you will be able to:

- State risk factors for adolescent dating.
- Discuss what the various studies show about teenage dating violence.

For many, the early- to mid-teenage years mark a time in which romantic relationships begin to emerge. From a developmental perspective, these relationships can serve a number of positive functions. However, for many adolescents, there is a darker side: dating violence. In this article, we discuss the definition and measurement of adolescent dating violence, review epidemiological findings regarding victimization, and describe correlates of victimization experiences. We end with a discussion of prevention and intervention programs designed to address adolescent dating violence and highlight important gaps in our knowledge.

Defining and Measuring Adolescent Dating and Dating Violence

"Dating" among adolescents is complicated to define and measure, in part because the nature of dating changes dramatically over the course of adolescence (Connolly et al., 1999; Feiring, 1996). In early adolescence, dating involves getting together with small groups of friends of both sexes to do things together as a group. From these group experiences, adolescents progress to going out with or dating a single individual. Initial single-dating relationships are typically casual and short-term; more

serious, exclusive, and longer-lasting relationships emerge in mid- to late-adolescence.

"Dating" among adolescents is complicated to define and measure.

In research on adolescent dating violence, adolescents are often asked to respond to questions about a "boyfriend" or "girlfriend" or someone with whom they have "been on a date with or gone out with." However, what constitutes a boyfriend or girlfriend or a dating partner is not clear, and these judgments are likely to vary tremendously across adolescents. These judgments are probably also influenced by a number of factors including the amount of time spent with each other, the degree of emotional attachment, and the activities engaged in together (Allen, 2004). They are also likely to change over the course of adolescence, as youth mature and become more experienced with dating.

Most everyone has a general idea about what constitutes "violence" in adolescent dating relationships, but not everyone conceptualizes and defines it the same way. In the empirical literature, multiple types of dating violence have been studied, including physical, sexual, and psychological violence. Definitions for these different types of violence vary from study to study, but each is typically based on adolescents' reports of the occurrence of specific acts. For example, physical violence often refers to adolescents' reports of hits, slaps, or beatings; sexual violence refers to forced kissing, touching, or intercourse; and psychological violence to reports of insults, threats, or the use of control tactics. These different types of violence are sometimes further subdivided. For example, indirect aggression (also referred to as relational or social aggression), which includes spreading hurtful rumors or telling cruel stories about a dating partner, has recently begun to be conceptualized as a form of dating violence that may be distinct from more overt forms of psychological or emotional abuse (Wolfe, Scott, Reitzel-Jaffe et al., 2001). As another example, in a recent prevalence study, sexual assault was distinguished from drug- or alcohol-facilitated rape, with the latter defined as sexual assault that occurred while the victim was "high, drunk, or passed out from drinking or taking drugs" (Wolitzky-Taylor et al., 2008).

In the bulk of studies on adolescent dating violence, the youth are surveyed about the occurrence of specific acts of violence within a particular time period, for example, during the previous 12 months. These surveys are typically administered on a single occasion, in either a questionnaire or interview format. Some include only one or two questions about violence; others include comprehensive scales of relationship violence with excellent psychometric properties (e.g., Wolfe et al., 2001). A handful of investigators have attempted to study adolescent dating violence using other methods, such as laboratory observations (e.g., Capaldi, Kimm, & Shortt, 2007), and repeated interviews over a short, circumscribed period of time (e.g., Jouriles et al., 2005). However, studies using alternatives to one-time, self-report survey assessments are few and far between.

This first section highlights some of the complexities involved in conceptualizing adolescent dating violence and describes how different types of dating violence are often defined and measured, providing a backdrop for understanding and interpreting empirical findings in the literature. As illustrated in the section below, different conceptualizations and definitions of dating violence lead to different research findings and conclusions. Similarly, various data collection methods (such as using more questions and/or repeated questioning) also yield different results. At the present time, there is no gold standard with respect to defining or measuring adolescent dating violence; the field is still developing in this regard.

Prevalence of Adolescent Dating Violence

Over the past decade, data from several different national surveys have been used to estimate the prevalence of the various forms of adolescent dating violence. Surveys conducted by the Centers for Disease Control suggest that 9–10% of students in grades 9–12 indicate that a boyfriend or girlfriend has hit, slapped, or physically hurt them on purpose during the previous 12 months, and approximately 8% report having been physically forced to have sexual intercourse against their wishes (Howard, Wang, & Yan, 2007a, 2007b). The 2005 National Survey of Adolescents (NSA) indicates that 1.6% of adolescents between 12 and 17 years of age have experienced "serious dating violence" (Wolitzky-Taylor et al., 2008). Serious dating violence was defined as experiencing one or more of the following forms of violence from a dating partner: physical violence (badly injured, beaten up, or threatened with a knife or gun), sexual violence (forced anal, vaginal, or oral sex; forced penetration with a digit or an object; forced touching of genitalia), or drug/alcohol-facilitated rape.

Table 1 Prevalence of Dating Violence in Same-Sex and Opposite-Sex Romantic Relationships

Data from National Longitudinal Study of Adolescent Health		
In the previous 18 months partner had been:	Opposite-sex relationship	Same-sex relationship
Physically violent	12%	11%
Psychologically violent	29%	21%

Halpern, Oslak, Young, Martin, & Kupper, 2001; Halpern, Young, Waller, Martin, & Kupper, 2004.

Most studies in this area ask about male-to-female and female-to-male violence or include gender-neutral questions without assessing whether a respondent is in an opposite-sex or same-sex relationship. The National Longitudinal Study of Adolescent Health is unique in that it reports data on violence in opposite-sex as well as same-sex romantic relationships. As can be seen in Table 1, prevalence rates for both physical and psychological violence are similar in opposite-sex and same-sex romantic relationships among adolescents in grades 7–12.

Prevalence rates for both physical and psychological violence are similar in opposite-sex and same-sex romantic relationships among adolescents in grades 7–12.

The prevalence of physical dating violence appears to be fairly similar across studies of national samples. Variation across estimates most likely reflects differences in how violence is defined, and perhaps differences in the samples from which the estimates were derived (e.g., different age ranges sampled). It should be noted that prevalence estimates based on smaller, less representative, localized samples tend to be higher than those based on national samples. In fact, a number of researchers have reported prevalence estimates for physical dating violence among adolescents (over a one-year period or less) to be over 40% (Hickman, Jaycox, & Aronoff, 2004). These elevated estimates might stem directly from sampling differences, but also perhaps from differences in the conceptualization and measurement of dating violence. For example, in many of the smaller samples, investigators assessed dating violence more extensively (such as using more questions and/or through repeated questioning), which might contribute to higher prevalence estimates.

Taken together, the results across studies yield some general conclusions about the nature and scope of adolescent dating violence. Regardless of how it is defined, it appears that a substantial number of United States youth are affected by dating violence. Even with very conservative definitions, such as the one used in the NSA, it was projected that approximately 400,000 adolescents have been victims, at some point in their lives, of serious dating violence (Wolitzky-Taylor et al., 2008). Psychological violence appears to be much more common than either physical or sexual violence. Data are mixed on the relative prevalence of physical and sexual violence, but some of the national surveys suggest that they are approximately equal in prevalence.

Onset and Course

Dating violence appears to emerge well before high school. For example, cross-sex teasing and harassment, which involve behaviors often construed as either psychological or sexual violence, is evident among 6th graders and increases in prevalence over time (McMaster et al., 2002). One-third of a sample of 7th graders who indicated that they had started dating also reported that they had committed acts of aggression (physical, sexual, or psychological) toward a dating partner; in over half of these cases, physical or sexual aggression was involved (Sears et al., 2007). In the NSA, serious dating violence victimization was not reported by 12-year-olds, but it was by 13-year-olds (Wolitzky-Taylor et al., 2008).

Longitudinal data on the course of adolescent dating violence are scarce, but there is evidence that psychological aggression predicts subsequent physical aggression (O'Leary & Slep, 2003). In fact, different types of dating violence commonly co-occur within adolescent relationships, with the occurrence of one type of violence (physical, psychological, or sexual) associated with an increased likelihood of other types of violence (Sears, Byers, & Price, 2007). In research on interpersonal victimization in general, victims of violence are known to be at increased risk for subsequent victimization. This appears to be true for victims of adolescent dating violence as well (Smith, White, & Holland, 2003).

Demographics of Adolescent Dating Violence

Certain demographic variables including age, race and ethnicity, geographic location, and sex are associated with increased risk for victimization. Specifically, the risk for dating violence victimization increases with age, at least through the middle and high school years. This trend appears to be true for physical, psychological, and sexual violence (e.g., Halpern et al., 2001; Howard et al., 2007a, 2007b; Wolitzky-Taylor et al., 2008). This might be attributable to a number of things, including the changing nature of dating over the course of adolescence. Some evidence has emerged pointing to racial and ethnic differences in adolescents' experiences of dating violence, but other recent, large-scale studies call these findings into question. For example, a number of investigators have found Black adolescents to be more likely than their White counterparts to experience physical and sexual dating violence (e.g., Howard et al., 2007a, 2007b). However, these differences have sometimes

disappeared when other variables, such as prior exposures to violence, are considered (Malik, Sorenson, & Aneshensel, 1997). Moreover, recent, well-designed studies of very large samples have found no evidence of racial or ethnic differences in adolescent victimization (e.g., O'Leary et al., 2008; Wolitzky-Taylor et al., 2008). There do appear to be regional differences in dating violence, with adolescents in southern states at substantially greater risk for experiencing dating violence than adolescents in other regions of the U.S. (Marquart, et al., 2007). Although the reasons for regional differences are not known, it is interesting to note that the South has a higher prevalence rate of overall violence than other regions in the U.S. In short, there may be factors in the Southern U.S. that facilitate the promotion, acceptance, or tolerance of violent behavior.

When violence is defined broadly, prevalence rates for male and female victimization tend to be similar (e.g., Halpern et al., 2001). However, narrower definitions of violence point to some sex differences in the experience of violence. For example, female adolescents are more likely than males to experience severe physical violence (violent acts that are likely to result, or actually have resulted, in physical injuries) and sexual violence (e.g., Molidor & Tolman, 1998; Wolitzky-Taylor et al., 2008). Females are also more likely than males to experience fear, hurt, and the desire to leave the situation for self-protection (Molidor & Tolman, 1998; Jackson, Cram, & Seymour, 2000). In addition, females are more likely to report physical injuries and more harmful and persistent psychological distress after being victimized (O'Keefe, 1997).

Correlates of Adolescent Dating Violence

Most of the findings on the correlates of adolescent dating violence come from studies in which data were collected at a single point in time. Thus, it is difficult to discern if observed correlates are precursors or consequences of the violence, or if they are simply related to experiencing violence, but not in a cause-and-effect manner. Although it is tempting to interpret some of these associations in a causal, unidirectional manner, more often than not, alternative explanations can also be offered. For example, the documented association between dating violence and psychological distress is typically interpreted to mean that experiencing dating violence causes psychological distress (e.g., Howard et al., 2007a, 2007b; Molidor & Tolman, 1998). However, it is not too difficult to imagine how feelings of psychological distress might influence an adolescent's decision about whom to go out with (i.e., adolescents who are psychologically distressed, compared with those who are not, may make different choices about whom to date) and, perhaps, lead an adolescent to an abusive relationship.

Many adolescents engage in antisocial or illegal activities, but those who do so consistently and frequently are at increased risk of dating violence victimization (e.g., Howard et al., 2007a, 2007b). In addition, simply having antisocial friends increases risk for victimization. For example, females who associate with violent or victimized peers appear to be at increased risk for dating violence victimization (Gagne, Lavoie, & Hebert, 2005). Similarly, male and female adolescents exposed to peer-drinking activities within the past 30 days (e.g., "Hanging out with friends who drank") were victimized more often than their counterparts who were not exposed to such activities (Howard, Qiu, & Boekeloo, 2003).

Many other adolescent experiences have also been associated with dating violence victimization. For example, earlier exposures to violence, both within and outside of the family, are associated with victimization (e.g., Gagne et al., 2005; Malik et al., 1997). Negative parent-child interactions and parent-child boundary violations at age 13 predict victimization at age 21 (Linder & Collins, 2005). Trauma symptoms, which may result from violence exposure and untoward parent-child interactions, are posited to interfere with emotional and cognitive processes important in interpreting abusive behavior, and possibly to heighten tolerance for abuse (Capaldi & Gorman-Smith, 2003). Having had prior sexual relationships with peers increases adolescent females' risk for experiencing relationship violence (e.g., Howard et al., 2007a, 2007b). Also, the likelihood of victimization increases as the number of dating partners increases (Halpern et al., 2001).

Several different dimensions of adolescent relationships have been examined in relation to dating violence. For example, physical violence is often reciprocated within relationships, meaning that when dating violence is reported, both partners are typically violent toward one another (e.g., O'Leary, Slep, Avery-Leaf, Cascardi, 2008). Relationship violence is more likely to happen in serious or special romantic relationships, rather than more casual ones (O'Leary et al., 2008; Roberts, Auinger, & Klein, 2006). It is also more likely to occur in relationships with problems, conflict, and power struggles (Bentley et al., 2007; O'Keefe, 1997).

Relationship violence is more likely to happen in serious or special romantic relationships, rather than more casual ones.

Although there are many risk factors for adolescent dating violence, some protective factors have emerged as well. For instance, having high-quality friendships at age 16 is associated with reduced likelihood of experiencing dating violence in romantic relationships at age 21 (Linder & Collins, 2005). High-quality friendships are characterized by security, disclosure, closeness, low levels of conflict, and the effective resolution of conflict that does occur. Also, adolescents who do well in school and those who attend religious services are at decreased risk for experiencing dating violence (Halpern et al., 2001; Howard et al., 2003).

Prevention and Intervention

Much of the prevention research in this area is directed at an entire population (e.g., 9th grade at a school) with the goal of preventing violence from occurring. However, the prevalence data indicate that a sizable number of adolescents in high school, and even middle school, have already perpetrated and/or experienced dating violence. Thus, in most cases the research is not technically universal prevention, from the standpoint of preventing violence before it ever occurs. Rather, it is an attempt to reduce dating violence, by preventing its initial occurrence as well as preventing its re-occurrence among those who have already experienced it.

A sizable number of adolescents in high school, and even middle school, have already perpetrated and/or experienced dating violence.

Many of the school-based prevention programs share a number of commonalities, in addition to the joint focus on prevention and intervention (Whitaker et al., 2006). Most are designed to address perpetration and victimization simultaneously. Many are incorporated into mandatory health classes in middle or high school. Most are based on a combination of feminist and social learning principles, and involve didactic methods to increase knowledge and change attitudes regarding dating violence. Despite these similarities, there are potentially important differences in the structure (e.g., duration) and content of these various programs. Unfortunately, most of these school-based programs have not undergone rigorous empirical evaluation to determine whether they actually reduce occurrences of violence.

A notable exception is Safe Dates, a program developed for 8th and 9th grade students (Foshee, Bauman, Arriaga et al., 1998) that has undergone a fairly rigorous evaluation. Safe Dates includes: (a) ten interactive classroom sessions covering topics such as dating violence norms, gender stereotyping, and conflict management skills, (b) group activities such as peer-performed theater productions and a poster contest, and (c) information about community resources for adolescents in abusive relationships. Evaluation results indicate that Safe Dates reduces psychological and physical violence perpetration, but not victimization, among the students who participated in the program. At first glance, this result might be puzzling: How can the perpetration of violence go down, without a commensurate reduction in victimization? This might be explained, in part, by the fact that not all individuals who participated in Safe Dates dated other Safe Date participants. Although the Safe Dates participants were less likely to commit acts of dating violence after completing the program, they were not necessarily less likely to date individuals who commit violent acts.

Evaluations of other school-based programs using techniques similar to those employed in Safe Dates have not had demonstrable effects on violence perpetration or victimization. Some of these evaluations simply did not include measures of perpetration or victimization as outcomes. Others, however, have attempted to measure intervention effects on violent behavior and victimization, but have found no effects (e.g., Avery-Leaf et al., 1997; Hilton et al., 1998). Many of these school-based programs, however, *have* achieved changes in knowledge or attitudes regarding dating violence (e.g., Avery-Leaf et al., 1997; Hilton et al., 1998; Krajewski et al., 1996; Weisz & Black, 2001).

Another program with demonstrated results is The Youth Relationships Project (YRP) (Wolfe et al., 2003). YRP is a community-based intervention designed for 14–16 year olds who were maltreated as children and were thus at increased risk of being in abusive relationships in the future. YRP is an 18-session, group-based program with three primary components: (a) education about abusive relationships and power dynamics within these relationships, (b) skills development, and (c) social action. The skills targeted in this program include communication skills and conflict resolution. The social action portion of the program includes, among other things, allowing program participants the opportunity to become familiar with and to practice utilizing resources for individuals in violent relationships, as well as the chance to develop a project to raise awareness of dating violence within the community. Sessions include skills practice, guest speakers, videos, and visits to relevant community agencies. Evaluation results indicate that YRP reduces physical dating violence perpetration and physical, emotional, and threatening abuse victimization.

It is encouraging that Safe Dates and the YRP have yielded promising results in reducing dating violence among adolescents. However, given the current state of the prevention literature in this area, it would be erroneous to suggest that we know how to prevent adolescent dating violence. Systematic reviews of this literature indicate that the vast majority of studies attempting to evaluate a dating violence prevention program have *not* found intervention effects on behavioral measures, and even though changes in knowledge and attitudes are often documented, it is not really clear if such changes lead to changes in either perpetration or victimization (Hickman et al., 2004; Whitaker et al., 2006). The promising findings of the Safe Dates and YRP programs require replication, and more information is needed on how these programs accomplished their positive effects. Researchers and practitioners can use these programs as a starting point in their own efforts at preventing relationship violence, but it is still important to continue exploring new ideas about prevention in this area.

Concluding Remarks

It is clear that violence in adolescent dating relationships is a prevalent problem with potentially devastating consequences. We also know a great deal about correlates of such violence. On the other hand, there are still important gaps in our knowledge. For example, longitudinal research on this topic is extremely scarce; thus, we know little about the emergence and unfolding of dating violence and victimization over time. This is particularly true for high-risk groups, such as children from violent homes and other groups potentially at risk. In addition, we know very little about how to address the problem of adolescent dating violence effectively. This might be due, in part, to the dearth of well-designed longitudinal studies on this topic, which are necessary to develop a solid knowledge base on the

causes of relationship violence and targets for intervention. Although there are promising and notable efforts in the area of understanding and preventing violence in adolescent dating relationships, we still have much to learn.

> **Longitudinal research on this topic is extremely scarce; thus, we know little about the emergence and unfolding of dating violence and victimization over time.**

References

Allen, L. (2004). "Getting off" and "going out": Young people's conceptions of (hetero) sexual relationships. *Health & Sexuality, 6,* 463–481.

Avery-Leaf, S., Cascardi, M., O'Leary, K.D., & Cano, A. (1997). Efficacy of a dating violence prevention program on attitudes justifying aggression. *Journal of Adolescent Health, 21,* 11–17.

Bentley, C.G., Galliher, R.V., & Ferguson, T.J. (2007). Associations among aspects of interpersonal power and relationship functioning in adolescent romantic couples. *Sex Roles, 57,* 483–495.

Capaldi, D.M., & Gorman-Smith, D. (2003). The development of aggression in young male/female couples. In P. Florsheim (Ed.), *Adolescent Romantic Relations and Sexual Behavior: Theory, Research, and Practical implications* (pp. 243–278). Lawrence Erlbaum Associates, Publishers.

Capaldi, D.M., Kim, H.K., & Shortt, J.W. (2007). Observed initiation and reciprocity of physical aggression in young, at risk couples. *Journal of Family Violence, 22,* 101–111.

Connolly, J., Craig, W., Goldberg, A., & Pepler, D. (1999). Conceptions of cross-sex friendships and romantic relationships in early adolescence. *Journal of Youth and Adolescence, 28,* 481–494.

Feiring, C. (1996). Concept of romance in 15-year-old adolescents. *Journal of Research on Adolescence, 6,* 181–200.

Foshee, V., Bauman, K.E., Arriaga, X.B., Helms, R.W., Koch, G.G., & Linder, G.F. (1998). An evaluation of safe dates, an adolescent dating violence prevention program. *American Journal of Public Health, 88,* 45–50.

Gagne, M., Lavoie, F., & Hebert, M. (2005). Victimization during childhood and revictimization in dating relationships in adolescent girls. *Child Abuse & Neglect, 29,* 1,155–1,172.

Halpern, C.T., Oslak, S.G., Young, M.L., Martin, S.L., & Kupper, L.L. (2001). Partner violence among adolescents in opposite-sex romantic relationships: Findings from the national longitudinal study of adolescent health. *American Journal of Public Health, 91,* 1,679–1,685.

Halpern, C.T., Young, M.L., Wallet, M.W., Martin S.L., & Kupper, L.L. (2004). Prevalence of partner violence in same-sex romantic and sexual relationships in a national sample of adolescents. *Journal of Adolescent Health, 35,* 131.

Hickman, L.J., Jaycox, L.H., & Aranoff, J. (2004). Dating violence among adolescents: Prevalence, gender distribution, and prevention program effectiveness. *Trauma, Violence, and Abuse, 5,* 123–142.

Hilton, N.Z., Harris, G.T., Rice, M.E., Krans, T.S., & Lavigne, S.E. (1998). Antiviolence education in high schools: Implementation and evaluation. *Journal of Interpersonal Violence, 13,* 726–742.

Howard, D.E., Qiu, Y., & Boekeloo, B. (2003). Personal and social contextual correlates of adolescent dating violence. *Journal of Adolescent Health, 33,* 9–17.

Howard, D.E., Wang, M.Q., & Yan, F. (2007a). Psychosocial factors associated with reports of physical dating violence among U.S. adolescent females. *Adolescence, 42,* 311–324.

Howard, D.E., Wang, M.Q., & Yan, F. (2007b). Prevalence and psychosocial correlates of forced sexual intercourse among U.S. high school adolescents. *Adolescence, 42,* 629–643.

Jackson, S.M., Cram, F., & Seymour, F.W. (2000). Violence and sexual coercion in high school students' dating relationships. *Journal of Family Violence, 15,* 23–36.

Jouriles, E.N., McDonald, R., Garrido, E., Rosenfield, D., & Brown, A.S. (2005). Assessing aggression in adolescent romantic relationships: Can we do it better? *Psychological Assessment, 17,* 469–475.

Krajewsky, S.S., Rybarik, M.F., Dosch, M.F., & Gilmore, G.D. (1996). Results of a curriculum intervention with seventh graders regarding violence in relationships. *Journal of Family Violence, 11,* 93–112.

Linder, J.R., & Collins, W.A. (2005). Parent and peer predictors of physical aggression and conflict management in romantic relationships in early adulthood. *Journal of Family Psychology, 19,* 252–262.

Malik, S., Sorenson, S.B., & Aneshensel, C.S. (1997). Community and dating violence among adolescents: Perpetration and victimization. *Journal of Adolescent Health, 21,* 291–302.

Marquart, B.S., Nannini, D.K., Edwards, R.W., Stanley, L.R., & Wayman, J.C. (2007). Prevalence of dating violence and victimization: Regional and gender differences. *Adolescence, 42,* 645–657.

McMaster, L.E., Connolly, J., Pepler, D., & Craig, W.M. (2002). Peer to peer sexual harassment in early adolescence: A developmental perspective. *Development and Psychopathology, 14,* 91–105.

Molidor, C., & Tolman, R.M. (1998). Gender and contextual factors in adolescent dating violence. *Violence Against Women, 4,* 180–194.

O'Keefe, M. (1997). Predictors of dating violence among high school students. *Journal of Interpersonal Violence, 12,* 546–568.

O'Leary, K.D., & Slep, A.M.S. (2003). A dyadic longitudinal model of adolescent dating aggression. *Journal of Clinical Child and Adolescent Psychology, 32,* 314–327.

O'Leary, K.D., Slep, A.M., Avery-Leaf, S., & Cascardi, M. (2008). Gender differences in dating aggression among multiethnic high school students. *Journal of Adolescent Health, 42,* 473–479.

Roberts, T.A., Auinger, M.S., & Klein, J.D. (2006). Predictors of partner abuse in a nationally representative sample of adolescents involved in heterosexual dating relationships. *Violence and Victims, 21,* 81–89.

Sears, H.A., Byers, E.S., & Price, E.L. (2007). The co-occurrence of adolescent boys' and girls' use of psychologically, physically, and sexually abusive behaviours in their dating relationships. *Journal of Adolescence, 30,* 487–504.

Smith, P.H., White, J.W., & Holland, L.J. (2003). A longitudinal perspective on dating violence among adolescent and college-age women. *American Journal of Public Health, 93,* 1,104–1,109.

Weisz, A.N., & Black, B.M. (2001). Evaluating a sexual assault and dating violence prevention program for urban youths. *Social Work Research, 25,* 89–102.

Whitaker, D.J., Morrison, S., Lindquist, C., Hawkins, S.R., O'Neil, J.A., Nesius, A.M., Mathew, A., & Reese, L. (2006). A critical review of interventions for the primary prevention of perpetration of partner violence. *Aggression and Violent Behavior, 11,* 151–166.

Wolfe, D.A., Scott, K., Reitzel-Jaffe, D., Wekerle, C., Grasley, C., & Straatman, A.-L. (2001). Development and validation of the conflict in adolescent dating relationships inventory. *Psychological Assessment, 13,* 277–293.

Wolfe, D.A., Wekerle, C., Scott, K., Straatman, A.L., Grasley, C., & Reitzel-Jaffe, D. (2003). Dating violence prevention with at-risk youth: A controlled outcome evaluation. *Journal of Consulting and Clinical Psychology, 71,* 279–291.

Wolitzky-Taylor, M.A., Ruggiero, K.J., Danielson, C.K., Resnick, H.S., Hanson, R.F., Smith, D.W., Saunders, B.E., & Kilpatrick, D.G. (2008). Prevalence and correlates of dating violence in a national sample of adolescents. *Journal of the American Academy of Child and Adolescent Psychiatry, 47,* 755–762.

Critical Thinking

1. How would you define violence in dating?
2. Why do you think it is difficult to reduce the number of violent dating incidents?
3. What would you do if a friend of yours was victimized by a violent dating partner?

Create Central

www.mhhe.com/createcentral

Internet References

National Criminal Justice Reference Service
www.ncjrs.gov/teendatingviolence/publications.html

Reclaiming Futures
www.reclaimingfutures.org/blog/teen-dating-violence

ERNEST N. JOURILES, PhD is Professor in the Department of Psychology and Co-Director of the Family Research Center at Southern Methodist University. CORA PLATT is a doctoral student in the Department of Psychology at Southern Methodist University. RENEE MCDONALD, PhD is Associate Professor in the Department of Psychology and Co-Director of the Family Research Center at Southern Methodist University.

From *The Prevention Researcher,* February 2009. Copyright © 2009 by Integrated Research Services, Inc. Reprinted by permission.

Article   Prepared by: Joanne Naughton

Juvenile Recidivism—Measuring Success or Failure: Is There a Difference?

COLETTE S. PETERS AND SHANNON MYRICK

Learning Outcomes

After reading this article, you will be able to:

- Distinguish between a juvenile offender whose life is now crime-free and one who is leading a successful life.
- Discuss the consequences of mental health problems for some children.

Consider the situations of two young offenders, both of whom are real individuals who were released several years ago from a youth correctional facility. They were sentenced to a juvenile correctional facility for felonies involving person-to-person assaults. They both had some strengths on which to build—they had completed treatment while in custody and received high school diplomas. They also both faced some challenges—neither had family or a home to return to after being released.

"Aaron"[1] has made positive connections with community members who are helping him negotiate the paths to independence and reentry. Since the date of his parole, the community has wrapped its arms around this young man. Community members have helped him find housing, helped him enroll in college, and aided him in finding part-time work. He has remained crime-free and continues working toward his undergraduate degree at a local university.

"Brad" has not fared as well. His community did not have the resources available to help him continue to build on his successes while in custody. Despite ongoing attempts to find a job, he remains unemployed. He has ended up homeless, couch-surfing through a series of friends' apartments while receiving federal food assistance. Like Aaron, Brad also has remained crime-free, but he continues to struggle with finances and depression.

By any measure besides recidivism, there is just one success story here. But if the only way a juvenile corrections agency measures performance is through recidivism rates, both young men are equally successful. Both are crime-free. The agency has "done its job."

Pros and Cons of Measuring Recidivism

Measuring and reporting recidivism rates are important responsibilities of juvenile correctional agencies and historically have been the primary measures used to track performance. Recidivism is an easy, cost-effective measure to track, and it resonates with members of the public and legislators who are concerned about crime rates. However, focusing exclusively on recidivism data reflects a deficit-based approach to delinquency intervention and juvenile corrections, rather than a strengths-based approach. When used as the primary indicator of an agency's performance, recidivism does not reflect the full range of the work that juvenile correctional agencies, youths, families, schools and communities perform on a daily basis.

Recidivism reveals whether juvenile offenders who leave custody go on to lead crime-free lives, but not whether they lead productive crime-free lives. Recidivism does not measure whether these young adults demonstrate successful pro-social behavior and contribute in a positive way to their communities. To really understand which programs and treatments are effective in reforming young offenders and placing them on a firm footing in life, juvenile correctional agencies are beginning to track not only what goes wrong, but also what goes right by tracking positive youth outcomes.

Pros and Cons of Measuring Success

Research and experience have suggested that successful transitions from childhood to adolescence and then adolescence to adulthood require positive development in several areas. These areas include education, pro-social family and peer relationships, health and well-being, and work and life skills.[2]

Much of the day-to-day work in correctional agencies and other areas of the juvenile justice system acknowledges and embraces an approach to reducing delinquency through youth development. Although some agencies more explicitly express their youth development goals, every agency conducts assessments to identify risk and protective factors in several domains such as substance abuse history, familial relationships, living arrangements, school or employment history and mental health. Case plans strategize ways to reduce dynamic risk factors and increase protective factors. Youths, families and staff work to build on youths' strengths while reducing risk factors.

Agencies are seeking positive youth outcomes that go beyond just remaining crime-free. What the juvenile justice system lacks, however, is a way to consistently define, monitor and measure those positive outcomes in a manner that resonates with the public and legislators. Agencies are beginning to clearly demonstrate which programs and treatments are effective and merit funding.

By knowing which factors help a youth successfully transition into adulthood and thrive in his or her community, states can make informed, evidence-based funding decisions that involve an appropriate array of services. Given the youth development goals and values reflected in the existing practices of many juvenile corrections agencies, it is important that this well-rounded approach to youth development does not carry through to performance measurement at the agency level. Together, recidivism and other outcomes data can paint a more comprehensive picture and supply much needed information for decision-making. Therefore, recidivism and other outcome measures are complementary.

Building the Foundation

Positive youth outcomes generally refer to indicators of protective factors, competence or strengths. The notion of measuring positive outcomes is rooted in a positive youth development (PYD) philosophy. Butts and colleagues note a basic underpinning of PYD is that even youths from the most challenging of circumstances can achieve optimal development if the right mix of resources are present, including opportunities to engage in positive relationships, activities and prosocial experiences with positive role models.[3] By paying attention to the potential positive youth outcomes that can result from the work juvenile justice agencies perform, corrections professionals can begin to answer questions about effectiveness in a more complete way than simply attending to recidivism.

Before corrections professionals can begin to measure positive youth outcomes, they have to consider the intervention that precedes the outcome. Intervention strategies tend to have a built-in theoretical framework that guides the activities and suggests potential outcomes. Therefore, if corrections professionals seek to increase the capacity to measure positive youth outcomes, they must consider the types of interventions used. Traditionally, juvenile justice agencies have followed a deficit-based model—treatment is focused on reducing anger, eliminating drug and alcohol use, or addressing mental health issues. Although these are important treatment interventions, the inherent focus on the problems a youth presents is somewhat inconsistent with measuring the healthy development of a youth through positive youth outcomes.

Positive youth outcomes should address the development of new skills and competencies, establishing a pro-social identity, and other elements essential to transitioning to adulthood for all youths. Since agencies cannot revolutionize their approach to treatment overnight, they need to get creative in discovering elements of existing interventions that lend themselves to positive youth outcomes. For example, if the program is focused on drug and alcohol abuse, is there a way to promote general physical well-being through exercise and self care? If so, the agency can measure health indicators and survey youths on knowledge gains related to maintaining a healthy lifestyle devoid of drugs and alcohol. In an anger-reduction treatment program, are youths being given the opportunity to find alternative methods of expression, such as art, writing or sports? In addition, is there a way to train youths in mediation skills or conflict management?

Many agencies are already engaged in efforts consistent with the measurement of positive youth outcomes. These activities include assessing youths for risk and protective factors upon admission, completing case-planning to provide treatment and opportunities for youths to develop skills, and engaging families and communities in the process. The next step is to quantify these efforts and identify the most relevant positive youth outcomes agencies should track. Ideally, agencies would provide a number of programs or interventions that support positive youth outcomes. Butts and colleagues suggest focusing on six areas, or practice domains, that may be most important in achieving measurable positive youth outcomes: work, education, relationships, community, health and creativity.[4] Currently, agencies may already have the capability to track such outcomes as the number of youths completing vocational training, the number of resumes or job applications submitted, the number of youths earning a high school diploma or GED certificate, or the number of volunteer hours completed.

The goal of connecting recidivism and positive youth outcomes is to paint a more vivid picture of a juvenile justice agency's impact on the youths it serves.

Connecting Recidivism and Positive Youth Outcomes

Agencies should maintain recidivism as a fundamental outcome measure in determining performance. Reducing future criminality is a principal goal of public service agencies. It is an indicator of performance that legislatures and the public are not only used to hearing but also are expecting. The goal of connecting recidivism and positive youth outcomes is to paint a more vivid picture of a juvenile justice agency's impact on the youths it serves. Youths should be returned to their communities with increased skills, gained competence and tools to help them become productive crime-free citizens of their communities. However, the sustainability of measuring and reporting positive youth outcomes is potentially dependent upon correlating those outcomes to recidivism. Presumably, the positive youth outcomes an agency chooses to measure will be inversely correlated with recidivism; in other words, the greater the educational attainment, the lower the recidivism. In an environment that increasingly expects evidence of treatment effectiveness, it is essential to demonstrate to lawmakers and the public that positive youth outcome measures are inversely correlated to recidivism.

For the past year, the Council of Juvenile Correctional Administrators (CJCA) has been examining the issue of measuring positive youth outcomes in a juvenile justice context. The goal of this effort has been to develop a more consistent and comprehensive set of performance measures that address positive youth outcomes that can be implemented in agencies around the country. A theme of the work of this group has been to maintain a nexus back to recidivism while promoting the measurement of positive youth outcomes. A set of guidelines and strategies will result from this effort and should be a resource for agencies to begin to build the foundation of measuring positive youth outcomes.

Measuring Real Success

As CJCA moves forward with development of proposed measures, agencies will be better able to demonstrate the effectiveness of treatments based on achieving positive youth outcomes, and they will be able to retain legislative and public support for those programs. Those measures also will tell a more useful story about whether youths are served well while in the juvenile justice system. It will be apparent when looking at the outcomes achieved by "Aaron" and "Brad" that only one of those youths is succeeding. Through treatment and services provided both within correctional institutions and in communities, it will be clear how to ensure more youths end up like "Aaron."

Notes

1. Names have been changed.
2. Butts, J.A., G. Bazemore, and S.A. Meroe. 2010. *Positive youth justice—Framing justice interventions using the concepts of positive youth development.* Washington, D.C.: Coalition for Juvenile Justice.
3. Catalano, R.F., M.L. Berglund, J.A.M. Ryan, H.S. Lonczak, and J.D. Hawkings. 1998. *Positive youth development in the United States: Research findings on evaluations of positive youth development programs.* Seattle: University of Washington, School of Social Work.
4. Ibid.

Critical Thinking

1. Should taxpayers pay for juvenile delinquents' education while they are in custody?
2. How should juvenile justice agencies measure success?

Create Central

www.mhhe.com/createcentral

Internet References

Bureau of Justice Statistics
www.bjs.gov/index.cfm?ty=tp&tid=17

Humanity in Action
www.humanityinaction.org/knowledgebase/179-an-alternative-approach-to-juvenile-recidivism-harlem-community-justice-center-and-the-juvenile-reentry-program

New York State Division of Criminal Justice Services - Research Report
www.criminaljustice.ny.gov/crimnet/ojsa/dfy/dfy_research_report.pdf

COLLETTE S. PETERS is director of the Oregon Youth Authority and chair of the Council of Juvenile Correctional Administrators Postive Youth Outcomes Committee. **SHANNON MYRICK, PHD**, is a research analyst for the Oregon Youth Authority.

Article

Prepared by: Joanne Naughton

Calculating "Return On Mission": Music as Medicine for Imprisoned Boys

How do we measure a return on human development? Genuine Voices, a non-profit working with detention centers in the US that leverages the determination of volunteers to help adolescent boys, set out to measure their impact. After encountering difficulties, they learned that some things are naturally unquantifiable, and that in lieu of ways to directly report a "return on mission", maybe emotional buzz is enough to support sustainability.

STEPHANIE ORMSTON

Learning Outcomes

After reading this article, you will be able to:

- Describe the effect Genuine Voices has had on some boys in juvenile detention centers.

- Demonstrate how some small non-traditional programs can help kids who have gotten into trouble.

In the Darwinian world of for-profits, only the strongest survive. We have countless ratios like return on investment, return on equity, return on sales, etc., to rate the performance and financial solvency of major companies. However, that isn't the case in the world of non-profits. Measuring success is an open-ended question where everyone has their own answer. In addition, success doesn't guarantee longevity in the life of a non-profit. Organizations with "trendy missions" continue to receive donations, despite gross mismanagement and lack of impact. Countless stories have broken in the last few years about mismanagement of non-profits, including Greg Mortenson's Central Asia Institute. Who could forget the United Way scandal of the early 90s, where CEO William Aramony was sentenced to prison for looting the organization of millions? And still we see countless worthy organizations floundering because they just can't gain momentum. How do we reward those organizations that don't have the political capital or scale to gain notoriety, have no clear way to report impact, but are still successful in executing their mission? How do you measure this "return on mission"?

Take Genuine Voices for example. Founded in 2002, Genuine Voices teaches music to boys committed to juvenile detention centers in the Boston, Massachusetts area. Boys take classes twice a week, and specialize in an area that comes natural to them—drums, guitar, lyric writing, or producing. Once the boys are released, their involvement in the program ends. The boys' identities are kept confidential as they are minors, so it is impossible to reach out and track recidivism rates in alumni of the program. There are success stories of boys who have voluntarily kept in touch with Genuine Voices staff, like Dequan who was featured by Boston.com. But he represents a minority of the over 600 students who participates each year. Especially as an organization with a $14,000 operating budget, resources barely cover program costs, let alone monitoring and evaluation. Artistic director Juri Love has ambitious plans to turn that $14,000 into $50,000 this year and $100,000 in 2014. However, current priorities are paying instructors and increasing the size of the program, not tracking impact. She currently relies on no full-time employees but 30 volunteers who all already know the importance and impact of program. Their priority is to grow the reach of Genuine Voices. Unfortunately, securing funding proves to be a catch-22; to attract donors, Genuine Voices needs to prove it works.

I visited the Casa Isla detention facility with two instructors for a weekly lesson. We drove 15 minutes down a winding road past a security check point, to a remote island just south of Boston. It was fitting, that on this remote island was a population that most of society would rather pretend didn't exist at all. It's no doubt that Genuine Voices is making a difference in the lives of these boys. But like others who have experienced or seen the program firsthand, I cannot quantify the feeling I felt when I observed the lesson. The excitement when we walked into the center was palpable. For once, these boys had something to look forward to in an otherwise monotonous day at the detention center. The instructors adeptly customized the lesson to the needs of the boy that day, from lyric writing to an impromptu jam session. They are not just teachers, but positive role models who commit to the mission, and believe in the power of music to change lives. Love describes their work succinctly, "These boys have been taught that they are a burden on their families and on the system. We let them be something more."

The success of this program is contingent upon consistent and high-quality instructors. I was supposed to meet four teachers, but two were unable to attend because they had to work. It was evident that the two instructors I did meet, Steve Wilkinson and Wills McKenna, both professional musicians, have proven their worth to the boys by showing up and listening week after week. They've gained the trust of the boys—a crucial component in making the program work. But how is this model sustainable? You can't continue to depend on teachers whose only compensation is personal satisfaction. Love's goals for the program are ultimately to compensate her teachers $25 per hour. At two-hour lessons twice a week, this works out to only $5,000 a year to serve approximately 6–8 students. When it costs the Department of Youth Services and taxpayers $100,000 a year to care for one boy, the teacher's salary seems a pittance, especially given the life-long impact it could have on one boy.

There are programs that are beginning to address some of these issues. Non-profits are smaller, more innovative and agile than government programs. Social impact bonds (SIB), which ultimately reward non-profits for reducing the government's costs when dealing with an at risk population, are becoming a way to provide these non-profits the resources to operate on a larger scale. Essentially, the government contracts with an intermediary (like a large bank), who provides a loan to a non-profit. If the non-profit is successful in its initiatives (as rated by a third party rating agency), the state pays back the intermediary. This outsources the risk to for-profit organizations (the bank, in this case), and allows the government to take a chance on an innovative program that it is too sluggish to implement on its own. The first such program in the nation was announced in Massachusetts just last year, with the goal of dealing with juvenile justice and chronic homelessness. However, this initiative is in its infancy; only last year, McKinsey & Company issued a report about the potential of SIBs in the US. It certainly has a long way to go before it can widen its reach to be used with such tiny non-profits like Genuine Voices.

It is a common misconception that these boys have nothing to contribute to society. "These kids work. It's just not socially acceptable," Wilkinson told me, referring to theft, dealings and other unlawful actions that get the boys committed. "They deal to support a parent or younger sibling. We teach them to apply that effort to something positive." The most powerful initiative of Genuine Voices is their involvement with the "Music is Medicine" program. Boys in the centers are commissioned to create original songs for children dealing with terminal illnesses. The song "Believe In You", written by one of the boys I met that night at Casa Isla, will leave the listener with no doubt that these boys have good hearts. Unfortunately, we are still struggling with a system and a society that is reluctant to deal with cases like these and to provide substantial monetary support. Until we can begin to prove that initiatives like these do work, Juri Love and Genuine Voices will have to continue to believe, and do their best to convert others to believe as well.

Critical Thinking

1. What is Wilkinson's theory about the kids he deals with?
2. If Genuine Voices offers success in dealing with kids in trouble, what are the challenges to keeping it going?

Create Central

www.mhhe.com/createcentral

Internet References

Genuine Voices
   www.genuinevoices.com
Idealist
   www.idealist.org/info/Nonprofits/Wrong1

STEPHANIE ORMSTON is a writer for *Student Reporter*. We are a journalism incubator and online media outlet, providing media coverage of events and featuring current topics in management and economics around the world.

Article

Prepared by: Joanne Naughton

Juvenile Confinement in Context

RICHARD A. MENDEL

Learning Outcomes

After reading this article, you will be able to:

- Discuss the research about juvenile confinement.

- Enumerate some of the negative aspects of large, prison-like correctional facilities.

For more than a century, the predominant strategy for the treatment and punishment of serious and sometimes not-so-serious juvenile offenders in the United States has been placement into large juvenile corrections institutions, alternatively known as training schools, reformatories, or youth corrections centers.

Excluding the roughly 21,000 youth held in detention centers daily awaiting their court trials or pending placement in a correctional program, the latest official national count of youth in correctional custody, conducted in 2010, found that roughly 48,000 U.S. youth were confined in correctional facilities or other residential programs each night on the order of a juvenile delinquency court.[1] For perspective, that's about the same number of adolescents that currently reside in midsize American cities like Louisville, Kentucky; Nashville, Tennessee; Baltimore, Maryland; and Portland, Oregon. A high proportion of these confined youth are minorities. According to the most recent national count, 40 percent of confined youth are African Americans and 21 percent are Hispanics; non-Hispanic white youth, who comprise almost 60 percent of the total youth population, were just 34 percent of the confined youth.[2]

America's heavy reliance on juvenile incarceration is unique among the world's developed nations. Though juvenile violent crime arrest rates are only marginally higher in the United States than in many other nations, a recently published international comparison found that America's youth custody rate (including youth in both detention and correctional custody) was 336 of every 100,000 youth in 2002—nearly five times the rate of the next highest nation (69 per 100,000 in South Africa).[3] As the Youth Incarceration Rate figure shows, a number of nations essentially don't incarcerate minors at all. In other words, mass incarceration of troubled and troublemaking adolescents is neither inevitable nor necessary in a modern society.

State juvenile corrections systems in the United States confine youth in many types of facilities, including group homes, residential treatment centers, boot camps, wilderness programs, or county-run youth facilities (some of them locked, others secured only through staff supervision). But the largest share of committed youth—about 36 percent of the total—are held in locked long-term youth correctional facilities operated primarily by state governments or by private firms under contract to states.[4] These facilities are usually large, with many holding 200–300 youth. They typically operate in a regimented (prison-like) fashion and feature correctional hardware such as razor wire, isolation cells, and locked cellblocks.

However, an avalanche of research has emerged over the past three decades about what works and doesn't work in combating juvenile crime. *No Place for Kids: The Case for Reducing Juvenile Incarceration,* the report from which this sidebar is drawn, provides a detailed review of this research and comes to the following conclusion: we now have overwhelming evidence showing that wholesale incarceration of juvenile offenders is a counterproductive public policy. While a small number of youthful offenders pose a serious threat to the public and must be confined, incarcerating a broader swath of the juvenile offender population provides no benefit for public safety. It wastes vast sums of taxpayer dollars. And more often than not, it harms the well-being and dampens the future prospects of the troubled and lawbreaking youth who get locked up. Incarceration is especially ineffective for less-serious youthful offenders. Many studies find that incarceration actually increases recidivism among youth with lower-risk profiles and less-serious offending histories.

Large, prison-like correctional institutions are frequently:

1. Dangerous: America's juvenile corrections institutions subject confined youth to intolerable levels of violence, abuse, and other forms of maltreatment.

2. Ineffective: The outcomes of correctional confinement are poor. Recidivism rates are almost uniformly high, and incarceration in juvenile facilities depresses youths' future success in education and employment.

3. Unnecessary: A substantial percentage of youth confined in youth corrections facilities pose minimal risk to public safety.

4. Obsolete: The most striking finding of recent research is that juvenile rehabilitation programs tend to work if, and only if, they focus on helping youth develop new skills and address personal challenges.

5. Wasteful: Most states are devoting the bulk of their juvenile justice budgets to correctional institutions and other facility placements when nonresidential programming options deliver equal or better results for a fraction of the cost.

6. Inadequate: Despite their exorbitant daily costs, most juvenile correctional facilities are ill-prepared to address the needs of confined youth, many of whom suffer with problems related to mental health, substance abuse, special education needs, and more. Often, these facilities fail to provide even the minimum services appropriate for the care and rehabilitation of youth in confinement.

For the small percentage of juvenile offenders who do need secure facilities, the superiority of small, community-based juvenile corrections facilities over larger, conventional training schools is widely recognized in the juvenile justice field. The advantages of smaller facilities include the chance to keep youth close to home and engage their families, greater opportunity to recruit mentors and other volunteers, and a more hospitable treatment environment.

The primary mission of small secure facilities, as well as group homes and other placement facilities, should be to help youth make lasting behavior changes and build the skills and self-awareness necessary to succeed following release. In pursuing this mission, states will do well to follow the example of Missouri,[5] which closed its long-troubled training schools in the early 1980s. Since then, Missouri's Division of Youth Services (DYS) has divided the state into five regions and built

a continuum of programs in each, ranging from day treatment programs and nonsecure group homes, to moderately secure facilities located in state parks and college campuses, to secure care facilities. None of the facilities holds more than 50 youth, and each of the state's six secure care facilities houses just 30 to 36 youth. In every Missouri facility, youth are placed in small groups that participate together in all education, treatment, meals, recreation, and free time. Throughout their stays in DYS facilities, youth are challenged to discuss their feelings, gain insights into their behaviors, and build their capacity to express their thoughts and emotions clearly, calmly, and respectfully— even when they are upset or angry. DYS staff engage the families of confined youth and work with family members to devise successful reentry plans. DYS assigns a single case manager to oversee each youth from the time of commitment through release and into aftercare, and it provides youth with extensive supervision and support throughout the critical reentry period.

Through this approach, Missouri has achieved reoffending rates that are lower than those of other states. For example, in states other than Missouri, available studies show that 26 to 62 percent of youth released from juvenile custody are reincarcerated on new criminal charges within three years, and 18 to 46 percent within two years. In Missouri, the three-year reincarceration rate is just 16.2 percent.[6]

The time has come for states to embrace a fundamentally different orientation to treating adolescent offenders— an approach grounded in evidence that promises to be far more humane, cost-effective, and protective of public safety than our timeworn and counterproductive reliance on juvenile incarceration. Fortunately, we are seeing an encouraging shift away from juvenile incarceration in many states. From 1997 to 2007, the total population of youth in correctional placements nationwide declined 24 percent, and the total in long-term secure correctional facilities dropped 41 percent. Of the

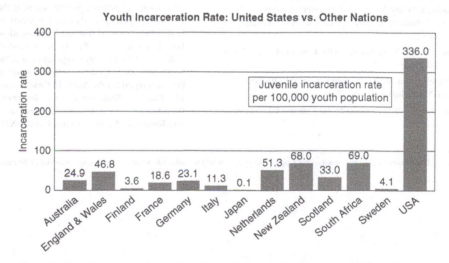

Youth Incarceration Rate: United States vs. Other Nations

Juvenile incarceration rate per 100,000 youth population

Nation	Rate
Australia	24.9
England & Wales	46.8
Finland	3.6
France	18.6
Germany	23.1
Italy	11.3
Japan	0.1
Netherlands	51.3
New Zealand	68.0
Scotland	33.0
South Africa	69.0
Sweden	4.1
USA	336.0

Source: Neal Hazel, *Cross-national Comparison of Youth Justice* (London: Youth Justice Board, 2008), in Richard A. Mendel, *No Place for Kids: The Case for Reducing Juveline Incarceration* (Baltimore: Annie E. Casey Foundation, 2011).

45 states reporting data on the number of youth in correctional custody in both 1997 and 2007, 34 reduced their confinement rates.[7] Since 2007, 52 youth correctional facilities have been shuttered in 18 states nationwide, and several other states have closed units within facilities and reduced bed capacity without shutting down entire facilities.

However, while this wave of facility closures and bed reductions is important and long overdue, it offers little reassurance for the future. In many states, the primary cause for closures has been the short-term fiscal crisis facing state governments. In other states, federal investigations or private class-action lawsuits have been the driving force behind facility closures. The common thread has been that most decisions to shut down facilities have been ad hoc and reactive. The closures have not been based on any new consensus among policy leaders or any new philosophic commitment to reducing reliance on juvenile incarceration, and they have not been informed by evidence-based consideration of how states should best pursue the path toward reduced incarceration.

Looking to the future, we must build a youth corrections system that is rooted in best practice research. Not only do state and local justice systems have to offer a balanced mix of treatment and supervision programs, but they must also calibrate their systems to ensure that each individual youth is directed to the treatments, sanctions, and services best suited to his or her unique needs and circumstances.

For the first time in a generation, America has the opportunity to redesign the deep end of its juvenile justice system. The open question is whether we will seize this opportunity, whether we will not only abandon the long-standing incarceration model but also embrace a more constructive, humane, and cost-effective paradigm for how we treat, educate, and punish youth who break the law.

Endnotes

1. Melissa Sickmund, T. J. Sladky, Wei Kang, and Charles Puzzanchera, "Easy Access to the Census of Juveniles in Residential Placement" (2011), available at www.ojjdp.gov/ojstatbb/ezacjrp.

2. Sickmund et al., "Easy Access to the Census of Juveniles in Residential Placement."

3. Neal Hazel, *Cross-National Comparison of Youth Justice* (London: Youth Justice Board, 2008).

4. Sickmund et al., "Easy Access to the Census of Juveniles in Residential Placement."

5. Richard A. Mendel, *The Missouri Model: Reinventing the Practice of Rehabilitating Youthful Offenders* (Baltimore: Annie E. Casey Foundation, 2010), www.aecf.org/~/media/Pubs/Initiatives/Juvenile%20Detention%20Alternatives%20Initiative/MOModel/MO_Fullreport_webfinal.pdf.

6. Mendel, *The Missouri Model.*

7. 1997 data from Melissa Sickmund, T. J. Sladky, and Wei Kang, "Census of Juveniles in Residential Placement Database," available online at www.ojjdp.gov/ojstatbb/ezacjrp; and 2007 data from Melissa Sickmund, *State Rates of Residential Placement of Juvenile Offenders by Placement Status, Facility Type, and Facility Size: 2007* (Pittsburgh, PA: National Center for Juvenile Justice).

Critical Thinking

1. What does research show about wholesale incarceration of juveniles?

2. What does the evidence show about incarcerating juveniles who have committed serious crimes, instead of taking a more humane approach?

Create Central

www.mhhe.com/createcentral

Internet References

Center for Children's Law and Policy
www.cclp.org/conditions_resources.php
National Council of Juvenile and Family Court Judges
www.ncjfcj.org/our-work/level-4-secure-confinement
The Annie E. Casey Foundation
www.aecf.org/MajorInitiatives/JuvenileDetentionAlternativesInitiative.aspx

RICHARD A. MENDEL is an independent writer and researcher specializing in poverty-related issues in youth, employment, and community economic development. He has written extensively about youth crime prevention and juvenile justice issues, including three nationally disseminated reports published by the American Youth Policy Forum. He is also the author of five major publications for the Annie E. Casey Foundation, including *The Missouri Model: Reinventing the Practice of Rehabilitating Youthful Offenders,* a detailed study of the Missouri youth corrections system. This sidebar is adapted with permission from his latest report for the Annie E. Casey Foundation, *No Place for Kids: The Case for Reducing Juvenile Incarceration,* published in 2011. Both this report and the one on Missouri are available at www.aecf.org/KnowledgeCenter/JuvenileJustice/DetentionReform.aspx.

Article   Prepared by: Joanne Naughton

Whither Young Offenders? The Debate Has Begun

TREY BUNDY

Learning Outcomes

After reading this article, you will be able to:

- Describe some of the problems facing politicians regarding young offenders in California.

- Discuss the effect of state budgets on juvenile justice.

Joaquin E. DiazDeLeon, a former Fresno gang member, spent two years inside California's juvenile prison system. What he found there, he said, was no better than the streets he came from.

Instead of rehabilitating young offenders, he said, correctional officers spent most of their time separating rival gangs. Violence was so pervasive, he said, that he kept his gang affiliation just to protect himself.

"Basically you're being thrown in a box and expected to change," said Mr. DiazDeLeon, 21, now a student at City College of San Francisco.

Gov. Jerry Brown's recent proposal to eliminate California's Division of Juvenile Justice was billed as a way to cut $242 million from the state budget. It was also the culmination of a decade-long effort to shut the state's troubled youth prison system, which for years has been plagued by violence, abuse and decaying facilities.

Much of that effort has been centered in the Bay Area after accusations of abuse and neglect at the institutions surfaced in a 2003 Alameda County lawsuit. In recent years, some local judges often refused to send young offenders to state institutions, preferring to confine them in county facilities regarded as safer and more effective.

Mr. Brown's initiative would take that unofficial policy further. It would scrap the state juvenile justice system and shift responsibility for confining the most violent young offenders to the local level, where they are nearer to family and have more community treatment options. The move would affect the 1,300 youths in state care, down from 10,000 in 1996.

Even among critics of the Division of Juvenile Justice, the proposed shift has set off a new debate over whether counties are equipped to handle an influx of severely troubled young people.

"I'm disgusted with myself to think of defending D.J.J. with all the things that have happened over the years," said Sue Burrell, a lawyer at the Youth Law Center in San Francisco, "but if you ask me right now, I would opt for keeping a very, very small D.J.J. open and not throwing the kids to the wolves."

Ms. Burrell said she was concerned that prosecutors might see counties as unfit to handle serious offenders and thus try many juveniles as adults, forcing teenagers into adult prisons.

Barry Krisberg, a senior fellow at the University of California, Berkeley, School of Law, said that keeping young offenders at the county level might offer them fewer rehabilitation options.

"I would bet that those kids would end up in juvenile hall, in isolation, getting fewer services," Mr. Krisberg said. "I don't think we can shut down the entire state system."

But Dan Macallair, executive director of the Center on Juvenile and Criminal Justice, a nonprofit group in San Francisco, said he believed young offenders could receive better support at the local level. "In county juvenile halls, you don't have the entrenched gang culture and violence you have at the state youth authority," Mr. Macallair said. "The counties can offer a continuum of options—maximum security, minimum security, intensive services in the community—that the state could never come close to matching."

Mr. Macallair, who has called the state institutions "relics of the 19th century," agreed that the proposed state closings presented challenges, but he said too much hand-wringing would keep resources at the state level and prevent needed changes.

"The state system is not set up for major change," he said. "If the money won't be flowing to counties, counties won't get any better, and you'll be left with the status quo."

For years, the Division of Juvenile Justice has been in steady decline. The Preston Youth Correctional Facility, an hour northeast of Stockton, is scheduled to be shut down by June. It will be the ninth state youth detention facility to close since 2002. Only four will remain.

The population of young offenders in state care has plummeted since 1996, to 1,300 from 10,000, because of lower crime rates and laws mandating that only the most serious offenders remain in state custody. The vast majority of young offenders are held at county facilities.

Mr. DiazDeLeon, who was first arrested at 14 on a charge of attempted burglary, agrees with those who say the California youth justice system is obsolete.

"Kids are broken, kids are abused" coming into the state facilities, he said. "I was an abused child growing up into a wounded man."

Mr. DiazDeLeon said the institution's need to constantly quell the threat of violence meant he had essentially been left to rehabilitate himself.

"The correctional officers' job was to keep control of the facility," he said. "When I was there, they were told to do rehabilitation, but they didn't fully engage in that because they didn't really believe rehabilitation was possible for some of the young men there."

If the counties are going to do better than the state, they will need more money and rehabilitation services to deal with young people for whom violence is common, said Donna Hitchens, a retired San Francisco judge who said she was among those who tried to avoid sending young offenders to state institutions.

"On a policy level, it's a great idea," Ms. Hitchens said. "But long-term treatment requires really strong programs in a secure setting, and a campus environment since they're going to be there for so long."

A memo released last week by the Chief Probation Officers of California after the Brown proposal was announced stated that county probation departments were ready to participate in the governor's plan—with one major caveat. "We must be sure we can afford the new responsibilities the state contemplates for local probation," the memo said.

Mr. Brown intends to compensate counties by extending existing sales tax and vehicle license fees, according to the California Department of Finance. The state's 58 county probation departments would split $242 million in state money over the next four years.

In the 2003 Alameda County lawsuit, Judge Jon Tigar of Superior Court found that conditions at state youth institutions were unsafe and not conducive to rehabilitation. The court ordered the Division of Juvenile Justice to provide young offenders with vastly improved facilities, education and treatment programs.

In an interview before the announcement of Mr. Brown's plan, a spokesman for the division, Bill Sessa, said that the state was in 85 percent compliance with the court's mandates and that more changes were in progress.

"What may have been true more than a decade ago totally mischaracterizes the reality of the Division of Juvenile Justice today," Mr. Sessa said.

He said he had no comment on Mr. Brown's proposal to eliminate the Division of Juvenile Justice.

Based on his own experience incarcerated at state and county facilities, Mr. DiazDeLeon said counties should embrace the inevitable.

"I think D.J.J. can be replaced with something better within counties," Mr. DiazDeLeon said. "Their model is outdated. You're already coming from a dysfunctional background and going into dysfunctional system. What do you expect?"

Critical Thinking

1. What are the problems the California juvenile prison faces?
2. How would the state government's proposal to deal with state's youth prison system affect the counties?

Create Central

www.mhhe.com/createcentral

Internet References

PBS Frontline
www.pbs.org/wgbh/pages/frontline/shows/juvenile/stats
The Life of the Law
www.lifeofthelaw.org/10-things-every-juvenile-prison-should-do

Article

Prepared by: Joanne Naughton

Preventing Future Crime with Cognitive Behavioral Therapy

One form of psychotherapy stands out in the criminal justice system.

PATRICK CLARK

Learning Outcomes

After reading this article, you will be able to:

- Define cognitive behavioral therapy and show how it can be applied to criminal offenders.

- Discuss why Americans should be concerned about the way teenagers who commit crimes are treated by the criminal justice system.

ognitive behavioral therapy reduces recidivism in both juveniles and adults.

The therapy assumes that most people can become conscious of their own thoughts and behaviors and then make positive changes to them. A person's thoughts are often the result of experience, and behavior is often influenced and prompted by these thoughts. In addition, thoughts may sometimes become distorted and fail to reflect reality accurately.

Cognitive behavioral therapy has been found to be effective with juvenile and adult offenders; substance abusing and violent offenders; and probationers, prisoners and parolees. It is effective in various criminal justice settings, both in institutions and in the community, and addresses a host of problems associated with criminal behavior. For instance, in most cognitive behavioral therapy programs, offenders improve their social skills, means-ends problem solving, critical reasoning, moral reasoning, cognitive style, self-control, impulse management and self-efficacy.

Recently, Mark Lipsey of Vanderbilt University examined the effectiveness of various approaches to intervention with young offenders.[1] His review analyzed the results of 548 studies from 1958 to 2002 that assessed intervention policies, practices and programs.

Lipsey grouped evaluations into seven categories:

- Counseling
- Deterrence
- Discipline

- Multiple coordinated services
- Restorative programs
- Skill building
- Surveillance

When he combined and compared the effects of these interventions, he found that those based on punishment and deterrence appeared to increase criminal recidivism. On the other hand, therapeutic approaches based on counseling, skill building and multiple services had the greatest impact in reducing further criminal behavior.

Lipsey also examined the effectiveness of various therapeutic interventions. In particular, he compared different counseling and skill-building approaches. He found that cognitive behavioral skill-building approaches were more effective in reducing further criminal behavior than any other intervention.

In a different research review, Nana Landenberger and Lipsey showed that programs based on cognitive behavioral therapy are effective with juvenile and adult criminal offenders in various criminal justice settings, including prison, residential, community probation and parole.[2] They examined research studies published from 1965 through 2005 and found 58 that could be included in their review and analysis. The researchers found that cognitive behavioral therapy significantly reduced recidivism even among high-risk offenders.

Therapeutic approaches based on counseling, skill building and multiple services had the greatest impact in reducing further criminal behavior.

Perceptions Affect Behavior

Beliefs, attitudes and values affect the way people think and how they view problems. These beliefs can distort the way a

What is CBT?

Cognitive behavioral therapy is a treatment that focuses on patterns of thinking and the beliefs, attitudes and values that underlie thinking. CBT has only recently come into prominence as one of the few approaches to psychotherapy that has been, broadly validated with research, although it has been used in psychological therapy for more than 40 years. It is reliably effective with a wide variety of personal problems and behaviors, including those important to criminal justice, such as substance abuse and anti-social, aggressive, delinquent and criminal behavior.

Unlike other approaches to psychotherapy, CBT places responsibility in the hands of clients while supplying them with the tools to solve their problems, focusing on the present rather than the past. People taking part in CBT learn specific skills that can be used to solve the problems they confront all the time as well as skills they can use to achieve legitimate goals and objectives. CBT first concentrates on developing skills to recognize distorted or unrealistic thinking when it happens, and then to changing that thinking or belief to mollify or eliminate problematic behavior.

The programs, often offered in small group settings, incorporate lessons and exercises involving role play, modeling or demonstrations. Individual counseling sessions are often part of CBT. Clients are given homework and conduct experiments between sessions. These components are used to gauge the individual's readiness for change and foster engagement in that change. A willingness to change is necessary for CBT or any other treatment to be effective in reducing further criminal behavior.

Brand name programs often limit clients to 20–30 sessions, lasting over a period of up to 20 weeks. The more treatment provided or the more sessions participants attend over time, the greater the impact on and decrease in recidivism.

The typical CBT program is provided by trained professionals or paraprofessionals. Training for non-therapist group facillitators often involves 40 hours or more of specialized lessons and skill building. Licensed and certified therapists are often part of cognitive programs, especially those involving individual counseling.

Characteristics of the counselor are important to a program's effectiveness. Counselor honesty, empathy and sensitivity are helpful traits. Support and encouragement, partnership or alliance, and acceptance are necessary in establishing effective rapport, which is especially important in CBT because counselors often take on the role of coach. It is important that counselors be consistent in modeling and expressing the prosocial attitudes and behaviors, moral values and reasoning that are often part of CBT with criminal offenders.

Positive findings from research on CBT are common. Over the years, studies have shown the therapy is effective with various problems, including mood disorders, anxiety and personality and behavioral disorders. Unlike other traditional and popular therapies, CBT has been the subject of more than 400 clinical trials involving a broad range of conditions and populations. It has successfully addressed many issues experienced by children, including disruptive or noncompliant behavior, aggressiveness, oppositional defiant disorder and attention deficit hyperactivity disorder. For adults, CBT has been shown to help with marital problems, sexual dysfunction, depression, mood disorders and substance abuse. It has also been shown to be as useful as antidepressant medication for individuals with depression and appears to be superior to medication in preventing relapses.

---

person views reality, interacts with other people and experiences everyday life.

Cognitive behavioral therapy can help restructure distorted thinking and perception, which in turn changes a person's behavior for the better. Characteristics of distorted thinking may include:

- Immature or developmentally arrested thoughts.
- Poor problem solving and decision making.
- An inability to consider the effects of one's behavior.
- An egocentric viewpoint with a negative view or lack of trust in other people.
- A hampered ability to reason and accept blame for wrongdoing.
- A mistaken belief of entitlement, including an inability to delay gratification, confusing wants and needs, and ignoring the rights of other people.
- A tendency to act on impulse, including a lack of self-control and empathy.
- An inability to manage feelings of anger.
- The use of force and violence as a means to achieve goals.

Therapy can help a person address and change these unproductive and detrimental beliefs, views and thoughts.[3]

Cognitive Behavioral Therapy and Criminal Offenders

Landenberger and Lipsey found that even high-risk behavior did not reduce the therapy's effectiveness. For example, some of the greatest effects were among more serious offenders. It may be that the therapy's enabling, self-help approach is more effective in engaging typically resistant clients, that it increases their participation and therefore the benefits of participation. The therapy is more effective in reducing further criminal behavior when clients simultaneously receive other support, such as supervision, employment, education and training, and other mental health counseling.

The cognitive behavioral therapy approach has recently been used in many prepackaged, brand name programs, such as "Reasoning and Rehabilitation," "Aggression Replacement Therapy," "Thinking for Change" and others. The National Institute of Corrections recently published a thorough and comprehensive review of cognitive behavioral therapy, which provides detailed descriptions of these and other programs.[4] Interestingly, although the Landenberger and Lipsey review showed these programs were effective, no single program was superior in reducing recidivism.

More research is needed to determine if it would be effective for offenders to receive cognitive behavioral therapy earlier in their criminal careers or as part of early intervention or parenting training programs.

Notes

1. Lipsey, M.W., "The Primary Factors That Characterize Effective Interventions with Juvenile Offenders: A meta-analytic Overview," *Victims and Offenders* 4 (2009): 124–147.

2. Landenberger, N.A., and M. Lipsey, "The Positive Effects of Cognitive-behavioral Programs for Offenders: A Meta-analysis of Factors Associated with Effective Treatment," *Journal of Experimental Criminology,* 1 (2005): 451–476.

3. Yochelson, S., and S.E. Samenow, *The Criminal Personality, Volume I: A Profile for Change,* New York: Jason Aronson, 1976; and Walters, G., *The Criminal Lifestyle: Patterns of Serious Criminal Conduct,* Newbury Park, Calif.: Sage Publications, 1990.

4. Milkman, H., and K. Wanberg, *Cognitive-Behavioral Treatment: A Review and Discussion for Correction Professionals,* Washington, DC: U.S. Department of Justice, National Institute of Corrections, 2007, http://nicic.gov/Library/021657.

Critical Thinking

1. In what ways can cognitive behavioral therapy reduce recidivism?

2. What do you think about using CBT in parenting programs?

3. Why are counselors' characteristics important?

Create Central

www.mhhe.com/createcentral

Internet References

Department of Corrections - Washington State
   http://offenderchange.org/research/treatment-effectiveness

National Institute of Justice
   www.crimesolutions.gov/PracticeDetails.aspx?ID=16

PATRICK CLARK is a Social Science Analyst with NIJ's Crime Control and Prevention Division.

From *National Institute of Justice Journal,* issue 265, April 2010, pp. 22–25. Published by U.S. Department of Justice.

Article   Prepared by: Joanne Naughton

No Remorse

Should a teenager be given a life sentence?

RACHEL AVIV

Learning Outcomes

After reading this article, you will be able to:

- Show the long-term effects for the public of prosecuting teenagers as adults and confining them in adult facilities.

- Describe the fears felt by a teenager facing confinement in an adult facility.

Shortly after midnight on March 6, 2010, Dakotah Eliason sat in a chair in his bedroom with a .38-calibre pistol in his hands, thinking about what the world would be like if he didn't exist. One of his friends had recently killed himself, and his girlfriend had dumped him. Earlier that night, Dakotah, who was fourteen, had taken his grandfather's loaded gun off the coatrack. The breakup felt like a sign that he would always be a failure, and he figured no one would miss him after a few days. He got a pencil and tried to compose a suicide note, but he didn't know what he should say.

Dakotah wondered if he was ready to die, and contemplated taking someone else's life instead. He thought about how people have good and evil sides, and how the good doesn't always win. It was the theme of an adventure story he was writing. He drank a can of Mountain Dew, then went to the bathroom and looked at himself in the mirror. He was pale and lanky, with sandy bangs swept to the side. "What am I doing?" he said to himself. "Why? Why do I have the gun? I know better than this."

He walked into the living room and stared at his grandfather, Jesse Miles, who was sleeping on the couch. A retired machinist and an avid hunter, Jesse often fell asleep while watching the Discovery Channel, and stayed on the couch all night so his smoker's cough wouldn't wake his wife. For forty-five minutes, Dakotah sat on a wooden chair, three feet from his grandfather, and talked to himself quietly, debating what to do next. If he got hand towels from the bathroom, he could gag his grandpa. If he used a steak knife, the whole thing might be quieter. He figured he'd use the cordless phone on his bed to report the crime. He felt as if he were watching a movie about himself. Finally, at just after three in the morning, he raised the handgun, his arms trembling, and shot his grandfather in the head.

"Man, I shot Papa!" he shouted. He put the gun on the floor and rushed into his grandmother Jean's bedroom. She yelled for Dakotah to call 911, and he followed her orders "like a little puppy," she said later. When officers from the police department in Niles, a rural town in southeast Michigan, arrived, seven minutes later, Dakotah was waiting outside next to his grandmother, who was in her pajamas and frantically waving her hands. Jean explained that Dakotah had shot Jesse. "This is my grandson," she said, placing her hand on his shoulder.

A trooper named Brenda Kiefer handcuffed Dakotah, read him his Miranda rights, and told him that she needed to know what had happened but that she "was not here to judge." She asked if he wanted a parent there and heard him say no. (Dakotah insists that he said "Uh-huh," indicating that he did want a parent present, and that he rarely says "yes" or "no," a habit for which his father scolds him.) Dakotah had always admired police officers, and he responded politely to Kiefer's questions, as his grandfather, unconscious and bleeding heavily, was loaded into an ambulance. Dakotah told Kiefer that he had a loving relationship with his grandparents and often spent the weekends at their home, where he had his own room. He didn't know why he'd picked up the gun, but he guessed that it was "sadness and pent-up anger."

After talking to Kiefer for fifteen minutes, Dakotah was put in a patrol car, which was parked at the bottom of the driveway. The officer who sat up front, Eugene Castro, asked Dakotah his name, and then realized he had gone to high school with Dakotah's father, Steve. "So was he good at sports?" Dakotah asked. Castro said that Steve had played hockey and tried to end the conversation cordially, but Dakotah updated him on his father's path since graduation: after losing his job as a construction worker, he'd begun an associate's-degree program in criminal justice. Dakotah added that it would be nice to be on the police force, because of the job security.

Several times, Castro stepped outside the cruiser to answer phone calls. When Dakotah was alone in the car, which had a video camera running, his breathing became heavy and rapid, and he coughed and made retching noises. Then an Avril Lavigne song, "My Happy Ending," came on the radio. "Ugh, why does this song have to play!" he said. He began singing along with the chorus: "So much for my happy ending / Oh oh, oh oh."

Out the window, Dakotah could see the flash of cameras inside his grandparents' home, a two-story farmhouse that the couple had lived in for thirty-five years. "It looks like forensics is doing their thing," Dakotah said when Castro returned. "So what do you predict will happen to me? I mean, murder charge—that's big. I'm still a minor, but . . ." Castro said he didn't know, and explained that a judge, not the police, would decide. "My life just turned into 'Law & Order,'" Dakotah said. "But with no commercials."

When the officer didn't respond, Dakotah began breathing heavily again. "I wish I could take it back, but now I understand the feeling people get when they do that," he said, drawing out his words slowly. "You feel like nothing could ever hurt you—just for that split second, once you realize what you've done."

Steve Eliason had been asleep for only a few hours when a detective knocked at his door and told him that his stepfather, who had raised him, was in the hospital in critical condition and that his son had been arrested. Still groggy from a night of drinking with his wife, Lisa, and out-of-town guests, Steve expected that there would be some reasonable explanation. Dakotah's only previous encounter with the police involved a missing backpack, and he had quickly been absolved of blame. He was an honor-roll student with a close group of friends who called themselves the Randoms, because, unlike the jocks and the preps who occupied the upper tier of their school's social hierarchy, their hobbies were varied: video games, fan fiction, classic rock, anime.

The detective, Fabian Suarez, drove Steve to the police station and, just before five in the morning, led him into a windowless, fluorescent-lit room with a Formica table and three chairs. Dakotah sat alone at the table, and Steve stared at his son, shook his head, and then pulled up a chair next to him. For the second time that morning, Dakotah heard his Miranda rights—Suarez went through the litany rapidly, in a dispassionate monotone.

"Are you angry with me?" Steve asked Dakotah, his voice shaking. "Is it something I did?" He told Suarez that a family doctor had once suggested that Dakotah see a therapist, because Dakotah was upset that nothing he did could ever please his dad. Dakotah didn't play sports—he preferred singing, drawing, and writing stories—which meant that he didn't have to maintain his grade-point average for a team. "So I try to push him," Steve explained.

Detective Suarez asked if he could have a private conversation with Dakotah, whose focus had drifted; he was shaking his wrists, blowing on the skin where the handcuffs had been. Steve agreed and told Dakotah, "We are trying to get to the bottom of this. Please, please answer."

Alone with the detective, Dakotah was initially sluggish, as if humoring a concerned teacher. But when Suarez asked what made him angriest in life he said that he was mad at his mother, Mary, who had abandoned him when he was a baby and dropped in and out of his life, depending on whether or not she was with a new man.

Dakotah said it had never occurred to him to hurt his grandfather, but "something overcame me." It had been a typically boring Saturday: he played racing and fighting games on his PlayStation console for four hours, and watched part of "Terminator 3" and a few shows on Comedy Central. Then he had a brief, pleasant conversation with his grandmother before she went to sleep. Later that night, he started thinking about how his family and friends were too distant; it felt like everyone he loved was drifting away. For about two hours, the "main argument was homicide or suicide," he told Suarez. "You ever hear people talk about having voices in their head? Well, it's not so much that as multiple personalities. One is like the good guy and the other is essentially the bad guy."

"The thing is when you actually do kill somebody, whether you have an emotional attachment or not, you get about five seconds," Dakotah said. "All the tension goes away." He propped his elbows on the table and rested his head in his hands, rubbing his face. "It's just that initial feeling," he continued. "It's an overwhelming feeling—I'm not really sure how to explain it."

After ten minutes, Steve demanded to be let back into the room. He had spoken with his brother, who was at the hospital, and learned that their father had died. By the time he returned, the interview was over. Steve was aggressive and agitated, and told Dakotah he couldn't make sense of what had happened. "Help me understand," he pleaded. "You always seemed happy."

Dakotah looked up at him blankly, his hands folded on the table.

"You're not showing any remorse, Dakotah. I'm not saying it in a bad way, but is something wrong with your head? Do you have problems with thinking? I mean, because you're a very intelligent young man." Steve told him to imagine what would happen "if you weren't my kid, and I was in this room with the person that shot my dad." He raised his voice: "This is the shit they talk about. Kids get into these goddamn video games and they don't pull their head out of the fucking game. They think they can just go"—he pressed his finger into Dakotah's biceps—"hit the re-start button!" He said he couldn't accept "I don't know" as an answer. "Why would you shoot Papa, D.? Papa loved you."

Dakotah's face had turned deep red, and he hung his head a couple of inches from the table. He wiped his eyes with his sleeve.

"Don't hold it in. Let it out," Steve said. He put his arms around Dakotah, who had begun sobbing, and pulled him toward his chest. Dakotah circled his arms around his father, letting his weight collapse into him. "You've got to be strong for me, O.K.?" Steve whispered, rubbing Dakotah's back and staring at the wall with a bewildered expression. "You're my little boy."

Watching the local news the next day, Steve learned that Dakotah would be tried as an adult for first-degree homicide, which in Michigan carries a mandatory sentence of life imprisonment without the possibility of parole. The county's prosecuting attorney, Arthur Cotter, a towering man with white hair who was elected to office in 2008, had reviewed videotapes of Dakotah's statements to the police and concluded that Dakotah didn't belong in the juvenile justice system, which releases offenders from custody when they turn twenty-one. Cotter said that the decision was easy, because Dakotah had shown "an utter lack of remorse." "Even his father noticed it," he told me.

In Michigan, as in many states, prosecutors can try defendants older than fourteen in adult court without a hearing, a statement of reasons, or an investigation into the adolescent's background. The decision cannot be reviewed or appealed. This allows prosecutors to bypass the juvenile justice system, which was built upon the premise that youths are still malleable, in need of the state's protection, and uniquely capable of rehabilitation.

The first juvenile courts, which emerged at the turn of the twentieth century, aimed to treat criminal behavior, not punish it, by intervening in the domestic lives of children whose parents had failed them. The establishment of a separate court system for youths followed other progressive reforms, like compulsory education and child-labor laws, which extended the boundary of childhood. The psychologist G. Stanley Hall lent scientific legitimacy to the concept of adolescence, describing it, in 1904, as a "genetic period of storm and stress," with a "curve of despondency" that rises at the age of eleven and falls by twenty-three. Juvenile hearings were sealed to the public and focussed on the personal history of the offender rather than on the offense. Judges designed individualized treatment plans to address whatever had thwarted the child's development: neglect, abuse, a poor education, an overcrowded home, unrestricted exposure to books about bandits. In 1910, Benjamin Lindsey, one of the first juvenile-court judges in the country, wrote that "our laws against crime are as inapplicable to children as they would be to idiots."

The juvenile justice system quickly became a model for courts throughout the world—the judicial scholar Francis Allen called it the "greatest legal institution invented in the United States"—but the system's paternalistic outlook often led to capricious rulings. In the sixties, a new generation of children's advocates tried to redefine the "best interests of the child," focussing on liberating rather than protecting youths. In 1967, the Supreme Court reviewed the case of a fifteen-year-old who had been committed to a detention home for six years for making a lewd phone call, and ruled that the "condition of being a boy does not justify a Kangaroo Court." The decision established that juveniles deserve many of the same due-process rights as adults, including the right to a lawyer and the right against self-incrimination.

Once hearings became adversarial (resembling "junior varsity criminal trials," as one court decision put it), the system's original mission was gradually obscured. In the eighties, when youth crime rates began to rise, most visibly in gang-related violence, reformers argued that modern adolescents were more sophisticated than the youths of earlier eras. In 1985, Alfred Regnery, the head of the Justice Department's Office of Juvenile Justice and Delinquency Prevention, accused the juvenile courts of naïvely adopting Rousseau's theory that youths are "incapable of evil unless they are corrupted" and of listening to the "psychobabble of social workers." In the following decade,

juvenile gun homicides more than tripled, leading to widespread hysteria, promoted by sensational news reports, about a rising generation of juvenile "super-predators." They are "doing homicidal violence in 'wolf packs,'" wrote John DiIulio, then a professor of politics and public affairs at Princeton, who helped popularize the idea of a "demographic crime bomb." (He has since expressed regret, acknowledging that the prediction was never fulfilled.) Juvenile courts became increasingly punitive, and by the late nineties nearly half of committed juveniles were behind bars, rather than in community-supervision or treatment programs, and a quarter of them were locked up because of misdemeanors or probation violations. Forty-six states rewrote their laws to make it easier for minors to be tried as adults.

Although judges have long been attuned to the difficulty of trying mentally ill defendants, there is little recognition that people may be incompetent to stand trial because of their age. Each year, more than two hundred thousand offenders younger than eighteen are tried as adults, yet only about half of them understand the Miranda warning. According to studies of delinquent adolescents, they have trouble grasping that a "right" is an absolute privilege that they may exercise without penalty. Defendants fifteen and younger are particularly impaired, and waive their rights much more frequently than do adults. The vast majority misinterpret at least one of the four statements that make up the Miranda warning, stumbling on terms like "consult," "interrogation," "appoint," and "entitled," which may be above their reading level.

At a hearing to determine whether Dakotah's confessions were made voluntarily and could be used at trial, Dakotah maintained that he didn't realize that he was free to stop talking to the police once he had already started. The prosecutor, Arthur Cotter, broke down the Miranda warning and asked Dakotah which sentences he couldn't comprehend. Dakotah conceded that he understood the language ("Yeah, I know what a lawyer is"), but not its implications. He explained, "I just felt I had no choice but to answer the questions."

The judge, Scott Schofield, was not persuaded and ruled that all Dakotah's statements could be admitted as evidence. He pointed out that Dakotah watched "Law & Order," had proofread one of his father's papers for a criminology class, and used big words. (The trooper, Brenda Kiefer, testified that Dakotah, when describing his grandparents' property, had used the word "elevation" and warned that frozen ruts on the driveway were "treacherous.") Schofield dismissed the claim that Dakotah was in a psychotic or altered state of mind. He interpreted Dakotah's reference to hearing voices as an externalization of his own conscience, "a debate that he was having with himself—should I do the right thing, or should I not do the right thing?"

Dakotah often talked of becoming a writer. Throughout his freshman year, he wrote fantasy stories and shared them with his friends, who critiqued the plots and gave him tips for improvement. Tashawn Reese, who collaborated with him, said that Dakotah's stories were about underdogs who faced emotional challenges—the hero falls in love with an irresistible girl who's unavailable, or his parents die, or his school morphs into a crater—and usually the "theme was the eternal struggle between good and evil." The last story Dakotah brought to school was about two boys, one of whom develops demonic powers while the other acquires angelic ones; at the end, both soar into the sky.

Kelsey Crago, who dated Dakotah briefly, couldn't recall his doing anything unusual in the weeks before the murder. She knew that he was disappointed by his recent breakup—his girlfriend had broken things off by text message—but he didn't talk about it, because he didn't like drama. Kelsey described Dakotah as a "great listener, the main person I trusted if I needed advice," but he rarely shared his own problems. In letters to Dakotah, she repeatedly asked him why he had killed his grandfather, but never felt satisfied by his answers. "I wasn't thinking," he told her, and wrote that maybe he had watched too many crime shows.

At the Berrien County Juvenile Center, fifteen miles from his home, Dakotah complained that every time he closed his eyes he saw his grandfather's death, "like a movie." He told a caseworker that he was still trying to figure out what had happened and that he wished he had killed himself instead. He was forced to wear suicide garb, clothes too stiff to be torn, and was unable to sleep. His grandmother Jean, a petite, well-dressed woman with short white hair, wrote him a letter telling him that she forgave him, and visited him at the center after two weeks. "It was hard for him to look at me, with him knowing what he'd done," she told me. "He'd look up and then look away. Mostly, he just held my hand and rubbed it."

Steve berated himself for acting like a "maniac drill instructor" and losing his temper over anything his son did wrong. He also blamed Dakotah's "bio-mom," as he called her. In her statement to the police, Mary explained that she'd never intended to have a child with Steve. "I had a party at my apt.," she wrote. "We got drunk, we got pregnant." (Mary would not talk to me, explaining, "I have nothing to say.") She was rarely involved in Dakotah's life until he was seven; then she went to court to obtain joint custody. When Dakotah was twelve, she changed her mind and relinquished all her rights as a parent. Steve remembers Dakotah coming home from a visit and "brushing his hands like he'd just had crackers and was getting rid of the crumbs. He said, 'Mom finally washed her hands clean of me.'"

For Steve and his wife, the fact that Dakotah had killed his grandfather, a man he had loved, was proof that he'd been temporarily insane. A week after Dakotah was arrested, Steve hired Lanny Fisher, a local attorney who had gone to the same high school, was "great at sports but humble about it," and had been practicing law for three years. (Fisher offered to charge a fraction of his normal fee, since Steve and Lisa were living on her hourly wages from Subway.) Fisher, assuming that the trial would be a battle between mental-health experts, said he was "devastated" when he received the results of Dakotah's psychiatric report. The examiner, who interviewed Dakotah for a little more than three hours, noted that Dakotah preferred his own fantasies to reality, but he did not think his imaginary life had ever reached psychotic proportions.

Two more psychiatric reports were done, and neither found that Dakotah met the criteria for legal insanity, which would

have meant that he could not appreciate the wrongfulness of his crime or conform his behavior to meet the requirements of the law. No history of physical or sexual abuse was uncovered. Fisher and Arthur Cotter had been discussing a possible plea bargain—fourteen years to life for second-degree murder—but after reading the psychiatric reports Cotter chose to go to trial, a decision that several family members endorsed. Jesse Miles's forty-seven-year-old daughter, Vickie Hartz, Steve's stepsister, told me that she was disappointed that Michigan doesn't have the death penalty. "My dad was an easygoing, mellow guy who did everything for that kid," Hartz said. "And Dakotah killed him with as much emotion as if he were moving a chair."

The murder trial began on August 17th, less than six months after Jesse Miles's death. Judge Scott Schofield, who presides over all the criminal trials in Niles, is known for running a "rocket docket" when his cases get local media attention. He set brisk deadlines for motions and hearings, saying, "It's a cliché, I know," but "justice delayed is justice denied." The courtroom was filled to capacity, with reporters from four local TV stations. Schofield referred to the microphone as an ice-cream cone and encouraged jurors to hold it close to their mouths so they wouldn't make a mess.

At the juvenile center, where residents spend six hours a day in school and attend workshops on risk and anger management, Dakotah was "student of the week" three times, and received awards for "social skills," "fabulous achievement and effort," and "making a difference." Still, Cotter requested that Dakotah's legs be shackled during the trial, saying that he might pose a security risk because of "his feelings of power." "When he shot his grandfather, he felt for fifteen seconds that nothing in the world could hurt him," Cotter told the court. Judge Schofield acknowledged that defendants have the right to be free of restraint but concluded that in this case the shackles were warranted, since "the Court has some concerns about Mr. Eliason being psychologically conflicted."

Cotter, in his opening statement, portrayed Dakotah as a sociopath so callous he was capable of "chitchat" and making a "whooey sound" in the patrol car just moments after shooting his grandfather. Dakotah was fascinated by death, he said, and would have killed his grandmother, too, if she hadn't woken up. Cotter cautioned the jury that when they viewed the videotape of Dakotah's interview at the police station they might be moved by the sight of Steve Eliason, "in a true test of the unlimitedness of a parent's love," embracing his son. "Do not confuse the emotions you're going to feel—the empathy that you are going to feel when you watch that point with his father—with any sadness that that young man felt remorse," Cotter said.

Lanny Fisher, unassuming and amiable, opened with a speech that laid bare his own confusion. "Most cases, most stories, they have the who, the what, the where, the when, and the why," he said. "The reason that we're all here today is the why." After months of research, he could find no coherent motive, so he presented the crime's incomprehensibility as proof that it couldn't have been deliberate. Cotter referred to Dakotah as a "young man"; Fisher called him a "boy." He emphasized that in the past year Dakotah had endured a series of losses: his cousin had been in a fatal car crash, his father had told him they were losing their house because he could not pay the mortgage, a friend had committed suicide, and his dog, Bam-Bam, had died of old age.

Fisher's other line of defense was to urge the jury to recall how it felt to be fourteen. "You can't drink," he said. "You have to be twenty-one to do that. You can't smoke, or vote, or join the armed services. You have to be eighteen to do that. Can't even drive a car . . . That's the person that's on trial, ladies and gentlemen."

The trial lasted two and a half days, and much of it focussed on testimony from police officers and forensic technicians who established details about the crime that were not contested by the defense. Fisher chose not to have Dakotah testify, since juveniles tend to make poor witnesses—they are easily misled or intimidated and often give inconsistent, idealized accounts of their own actions. For character witnesses, Fisher called Dakotah's high-school principal, who said that Dakotah was never sent to his office and was "probably not the top student, but pretty good," and a family friend who described him as "very mild-mannered, kind." Since Fisher was not advancing any theory about the crime, his conversations with the witnesses for the defense lacked direction and at times helped the prosecutor's argument as much as his own. When Jean Miles, weeping, took the stand, Fisher helped her paint an image of domestic normalcy:

Fisher: Your house was kind of a getaway for him, wasn't it?

Miles: Yes.

Fisher: It would be you, and Jesse, and Dakotah, and he could kind of play video games, watch movies?

Miles: Yes.

Fisher: And you guys gave him attention?

Miles: Yes.

Fisher: O.K. He had fun over at your house?

Miles: Yes. I hope so.

Cotter concluded the trial by describing Dakotah as a young man incapable of reciprocating his family's love. He argued that the crime exemplified premeditation, since Dakotah "considered the pros and cons of killing" for more than two hours. "It's almost like he was building up the courage to do it," Cotter said, before acting out Dakotah's interior monologue: "Are you going to do it? Do it. Do it! Shoot him." Cotter described Dakotah's reaction to the shooting as "just bizarre": there was "not a tear, not a sob," no "ounce of emotion." He dwelled on Dakotah's remark that the "tension goes away" after murdering someone. "That's when it *starts*, that's when the conscience kicks in," Cotter said. "He's got the emotional curve all wrong."

The expectation that defendants will display remorse either shortly after their crimes or never is generally accepted as common sense. In a *Columbia Law Review* study of cases of juveniles charged with violent crimes, the Emory law

professor Martha Grace Duncan found that youths who failed to express their contrition promptly and appropriately, as adults would, were often penalized for showing "less grief than the system demands." In many cases, she writes, the juveniles appeared to be in shock or in a kind of dissociative state and failed to appreciate the permanence of what they had done. "Less under the sway of the reality principle," they were more prone than adults to engage in forms of denial. But prosecutors and judges interpreted their strange reactions—falling asleep after the crime, giggling, rapping—as signs of irreparable depravity. Duncan found that courts looked for remorse in "psychologically naïve ways, without regard for defense mechanisms, developmental stages, or the ambiguity that inheres in human behavior."

One of Dakotah's closest friends, Christina Wardlaw, who sat through the trial, told me that she had to suppress the urge to laugh as she listened to Dakotah's recorded conversations with the police. "He still saw himself as the same old Dakotah, jabbering and singing and making jokes," she said. "He had no idea what he'd become."

Dakotah's reaction, with its apparent remorselessness, less than three hours after shooting his grandfather, was discussed by three witnesses for the prosecution. It also figured in the jurors' deliberations. They asked to view Dakotah's videotaped conversation with the detective again, and an hour after watching the tape, and just three hours after beginning deliberations, they announced that Dakotah was guilty of first-degree homicide.

One juror told me that several people on the jury were troubled by Dakotah's youth, but they'd been instructed that if the evidence indicated that the offense was premeditated and deliberate the crime was first-degree murder. Age had no place in that calculus. As is required under Michigan law, the jury was not informed that the conviction carried the automatic penalty of life imprisonment without the possibility of parole.

Before the sentencing hearing, Lanny Fisher filed a brief asserting that the punishment violated the Eighth Amendment, which prohibits sentences that are cruel and unusual, based on the "evolving standards of decency in our maturing society." Life imprisonment for juveniles is forbidden by the United Nations Convention on the Rights of the Child, a treaty ratified by every country in the world except the United States and Somalia. In his brief, Fisher relied heavily on two recent Supreme Court cases, which, he maintained, suggest that the U.S. is increasingly recognizing the "distinct emotional, psychological and neurological status of youth."

In a 2005 case, *Roper v. Simmons,* the United States became the last Western country to abolish the death penalty for juveniles. The decision drew on a growing body of scientific research that reaffirmed what, a hundred years earlier, passed for common sense: "the personality traits of juveniles are more transitory, less fixed." Anthony Kennedy, in his opinion, pointed out that the *Diagnostic and Statistical Manual of Mental Disorders* explicitly prohibits psychiatrists from giving people under eighteen a diagnosis of antisocial disorder (a euphemism for sociopathy), since many signs of the disorder—egocentricity, failure to accept responsibility, impulsiveness, proneness to boredom—are natural aspects of adolescence. Kennedy noted that "adolescents are overrepresented statistically in virtually every category of reckless behavior."

The Court extended the reasoning it had used three years earlier when it outlawed capital punishment for defendants with I.Q.s below seventy. But the four dissenting Justices in *Roper* rejected the idea that the same claim of diminished culpability could be made for all juveniles, since the Court's analysis had been based on aggregate differences between youths and adults, which may have little bearing on the sophistication of individual defendants, particularly those at the "margins between adolescence and adulthood." Antonin Scalia criticized the American Psychological Association, which submitted a brief in favor of abolition, for taking a conflicting stance on teen maturity in an earlier case regarding the rights of juveniles to get abortions. The large body of research on adolescent cognition, Scalia wrote, had allowed the Court to "look over the heads of the crowd and pick out its friends," finding empirical support for previously held opinions.

Five years later, in *Graham v. Florida*, the Court again pointed to "developments in psychology and brain science [that] continue to show fundamental differences between juvenile and adult minds," and, for the first time in a quarter century, invalidated a sentence other than capital punishment. Now the Court ruled that for juveniles—but only those whose crimes did not result in death—a sentence that offers "no chance for reconciliation with society, no hope" is cruel and unusual. Life-without-parole sentences have tripled since the early nineties, both because the punishment offers an alternative to death and because of crime policies that emphasize retribution and incapacitation rather than rehabilitation. The ruling did not guarantee young prisoners eventual release, only the possibility of it. In the decision, Justice Kennedy alluded to studies, outlined in a brief submitted by the American Medical Association, showing that the prefrontal cortex, which is associated with behavioral control, does not fully develop until people reach their twenties. Kennedy noted that in many states inmates who are ineligible for parole are denied access to educational programs, leading to the "perverse consequence in which the lack of maturity that led to an offender's crime is reinforced by the prison term."

Judge Schofield gave Cotter a week to submit a written response to Fisher's constitutional challenge and scheduled his own ruling and sentencing for the following week. At the hearing, on October 25th, Schofield gave a rhapsodic speech about how the legislative branch of government makes the law, and how the judicial branch has "nothing to do with that. And that's the way it should be." He called the case a "textbook example of our separation of powers" and denied Fisher's motion. He noted that the punishment wasn't unusual; thirty-nine states allow fourteen-year-olds to be sentenced to life without parole. No appellate or trial court has held that *Graham* applies to those convicted of homicide. Currently, there are some twenty-five hundred American inmates who were given life sentences for killing someone before their eighteenth birthday; for more than half of them, it was their first crime.

During the sentencing, Dakotah, who had just turned fifteen, periodically grasped at his chest and bent over, as if struggling to take in air. He wore a green prison jumpsuit, he had a new military buzz cut, and he showed early signs of a weak beard.

At the end of the hearing, he was given an opportunity to speak before the court for the first time. He stood up and said that his heart was pounding so hard that he thought he was going to die, and he was trying not to pee in his pants. "If I don't regret this every day, then I truly am less than human," he said. "Then I do deserve to die in prison."

He began crying and apologized to his aunt and his cousins, who were sitting on the prosecutor's side of the courtroom and had publicly expressed their wish that he never reenter society. "No matter how much anyone hates me—it doesn't make a difference—I will still love you all because you're my family," Dakotah said. "I never finished that statement at the courthouse or at the station. The tension, it goes away, but it comes back tenfold. You deal with it on a scale that can never be measured."

Nine days after his sentencing, Dakotah was transferred to Thumb Correctional Facility, a medium-security prison on the eastern edge of the state, two hundred miles from his home and sixty miles from Detroit. The forty-acre prison complex, which is a half mile from Interstate 69, is surrounded by three sets of twelve-foot fences, edged with coils of razor-ribbon wire. Although the law mandates that incarcerated juveniles have no contact with adult prisoners, the same protections do not apply to youths who have been prosecuted as adults. The prison has six squat beige brick units, two of which house four hundred and thirty inmates who are under twenty-one years old. They cross paths with the Old Heads, as they are called, during visits to the library, church, and the segregation unit, where prisoners of all ages are punished with solitary confinement.

The prison rarely permits media visits, and, last January, the warden denied my request, citing Dakotah's age and "health-related" concerns. Journalists are subject to the same admission requirements as the general public, so I waited six months, until Dakotah was eligible to update his list of ten visitors who are not immediate family, and visited him for the first time last June, eight months after he had arrived at the prison.

The prison's visiting room has an atmosphere of casual boredom, like the waiting room of a doctor's office. About fifty upholstered metal chairs are arrayed around coffee tables, and inmates and their visitors pass time by playing Uno or checkers, drifting to the vending machines and back, or holding each other subtly enough to escape the guards' scrutiny. Two kisses are permitted, one at the beginning of the visit and one at the end.

I got a Coke for Dakotah, who had been assigned a seat near the guard's podium, and he quietly thanked me, then took a dramatic swig. "If I drink Coke like I'm drinking beer, it's because I've had a few beers before," he said nervously. He admitted that he didn't consider himself cool in other respects. "I was the smiley wannabe emo kid," he said. The only physical activity he excelled at was dodgeball. He had also taken karate, when he was nine, and was grateful to his dad for enrolling him in the class, because "it could definitely be helpful, if I have to protect myself."

At the juvenile center, Dakotah had developed a close relationship with a pastor and been born again. For several months, his mind had been on the afterlife. Since he'd been in prison, though, the spiritual world seemed less relevant. "No two ways about it, I ain't worth shit religiously," he said tentatively, as if testing the sound of the phrase. When I asked why, he explained that he talked like a sailor and was getting to be racist. Black inmates who didn't even know him would tell him to "shut your white ass up," and refer to him as "white bitch," "snow-flake," and "cracker," a term he didn't fully understand until he checked out a book on the Civil War from the prison library.

At the prison's health-care center, Dakotah had received a diagnosis of bipolar disorder, and he now took a heavy daily dose of an antidepressant and a sedative. The drugs had removed "this great weight, this nervous energy pouring off me," but they had also made him less creative. He rarely wrote stories anymore, and even letters to friends felt like an exertion. Though the medications helped, he wasn't convinced that the diagnosis was right; he still wished "someone could pinpoint what's wrong with me." He said that every time he hears a loud noise, like a door slam, "my mind goes right back to the inci-dent, and all I hear is white noise."

Initially, other inmates wanted to know what he was in for (he kept his answer brief: "I shot someone"), but no one asked about his background anymore. Conversations rarely went much deeper than "What's for chow?" He scored well on the G.E.D. exam after taking the prison's prep class, but it was just a review of things he learned freshman year or picked up from the books he used to read secretly when classes were boring. "All I've learned in prison is some better ways to work out," he told me. He earned $1.14 a day mowing the grounds at the prison, and he figured that he would become a professional landscaper. He spoke casually of things he planned to do when he got out of prison, only occasionally catching himself to add "*if* I get out." He cheerily informed me that the prison has a policy whereby "guards will take you cuffed and shackled to your own funeral," before becoming flustered and correcting himself, explaining that he might get to attend the service when his grandmother dies.

Dakotah dreamed of becoming a country or rock singer, though he considered the goal cheesy. His first demo would be called "Generation Millennials." He spent most of his time listening to his MP3 player, purchased from the prison com-missary, and singing along in his eight-by-eleven-foot cell. Depending on how much money his dad put into his account, he could buy about a dozen new songs a month, and he tried to memorize the lyrics to each one. The other day, his crew yard boss had referred to him as "the kid who sings," which he liked, since he'd become accustomed to responding to "white boy."

Dakotah quizzed me on the songs I knew, and each time I failed to recognize a hit he laughed and sang it for me in a whis-pery, high-pitched voice. As soon as he finished one song, he tried to find another, searching for anything I might know. "The only thing I really need is my music," he said, tapping his foot. "If I've got music, I'm straight—I can do my time. You won't hear a peep out of me."

T hree months after the trial, Dakotah's case was assigned to the state appellate defender's office, which represents indigent clients who can't afford private counsel. His lawyer, the office's deputy director, has contested his sentence on the ground that Dakotah received ineffective counsel, in part because Lanny Fisher never brought in an expert to explain why Dakotah failed to show "stereotypical signs of adult-like remorse." A new medical evaluation characterized Dakotah as a "traumatized youth without access to his emotions in the moment." An evidentiary hearing will be held in February to determine whether Dakotah deserves a new trial.

Dakotah's sentence may also be affected by two cases that will be argued before the Supreme Court next term. Both cases, which will be heard in tandem, challenge the constitutional-ity of life-without-parole sentences for juveniles fourteen and younger. The two defendants maintain that early adolescence is a distinct developmental period during which susceptibility to influence reaches its peak. "Relative to the cognition of adults and even older adolescents, young teenage judgment is handi-capped in nearly every conceivable way," one petition reads.

But pegging legal protections to age markers also invites the escalating possibility of further dividing populations. It is well documented, for instance, that girls mature faster than boys, both physically and psychologically. (At a teen-ager's recent murder trial, a University of Pennsylvania neuropsychologist testified that "biology would say" that boys should be held accountable for their crimes at a later age than girls.) Terry Maroney, a Vanderbilt law professor, said that legal arguments based on developmental research, which have become more prevalent since *Roper v. Simmons,* could be used to challenge children's autonomy rights and create an "unduly complicated system with different rules for each potential subgroup." Debo-rah LaBelle, a lawyer and the author of a report on Michigan inmates sentenced to life for crimes they committed before the age of eighteen, said that she doesn't want to redraw a bound-ary that, for more than a century, has reflected the fact that "society has a different kind of responsibility to youth."

In *Roper,* the dissenting Justices argued that judgments about a defendant's maturity and culpability should be left to juries. But, in the new cases before the Supreme Court, both fourteen-year-olds were tried in states with mandatory sentenc-ing for murder, so jurors couldn't take their age into account. One of the petitioners was physically abused by his alcoholic father, had attempted suicide six times, and was drunk and high on the night of the crime. His lawyer has argued that his man-datory penalty is cruel and unusual and violates the Fourteenth Amendment, which protects defendants' rights to due process. In death-penalty cases, trial procedure requires that juries con-sider mitigating factors, such as youth, mental health, and prior record, but there are no parallel safeguards in place for the pen-ultimate punishment.

In Michigan, several judges have described their discomfort with sentencing an adolescent to die in prison, but the state's automatic-sentencing laws leave them no choice. In July, a federal district court ruled that the American Civil Liber-ties Union can proceed with a lawsuit challenging the state's mandatory-sentencing scheme for juveniles. Michigan has the second-highest number of juveniles sentenced to life without parole, and in 2008 the state's House of Representatives voted to abolish the practice, but the bill never passed in the state Senate; the issue is politically unpopular.

Prosecutors, who are elected officials, are also subject to political pressures, yet they have unfettered discretion to set the terms of a juvenile's charge. LaBelle told me, "I can't think of anywhere else in the world where the state can change the legal status of an individual—'Yes, I know you are a child, but now I will make you an adult'—so rapidly and in a factual vacuum." She continued, "We are telling these kids there is no such thing as redemption. They can never make amends."

For many juveniles, it is several years before they grasp the gravity of their crime and the permanence of the penalty. Joshua Miller, a twenty-nine-year-old inmate at the Wilkinson County Correctional Facility, in Mississippi, told me that it wasn't until he reached his mid-twenties that the "'without parole' part of my sentence finally dawned on me." After killing his girlfriend when he was fourteen—she rejected him, and he wanted to stage a "'Romeo and Juliet' kind of thing"—Miller was placed in an adult prison, where older inmates "treated me like the weak coward that I was," he said.

During his first few years of imprisonment, Miller tried to stay abreast of new albums, movies, and fashions, but eventually he realized there was no point in "keeping tabs on a structure I could never be part of." He stopped reading fiction, because it was too painful to "journey into the free world." He said that he has never had sex. He considers his girlfriend, who was thirteen when he murdered her, the love of his life. Although he looks back longingly on his childhood, he doesn't like to hear stories about what became of his peers. "I can't ruin a memory, or I'll lose another attachment to that life," he said. "I refuse to believe that my friends aren't still children."

When I visited the Eliason family in June, Steve, Lisa, and their nine-year-old daughter had moved into Jean Miles's house, in order to save money. They had got a new couch and rearranged the living room, but the rest of the downstairs looked the same as it had in the police photographs. On top of the television was a framed photograph of Dakotah and his family standing in front of a pastoral autumn scene painted on a cinder-block wall in the prison's visiting room. Steve and Jean both told me with pride that Dakotah was learning to be a model inmate. He had called home, upset, the night before because the toilet in his cell had overflowed, and, when the guards wouldn't respond to his calls for help, he stayed composed and mopped up the sewage with his own clothes. "I tell him that if we go through the appeals process and nothing changes, then he can get as wild and crazy as he wants," Steve said. He has noticed Dakotah's language becoming foul, which "eats me up—he was a soft boy."

Steve and I had spoken on the phone several times before, and, in each conversation, he offered new theories about his stepfather's death and the ways it could have been prevented. At the house, he reenacted the crime as his mother sat in a rocking chair beside us. With his thumb and index finger extended like an imaginary handgun, he stood where he assumed Dakotah had been when he pulled the trigger. "If he had just missed by an inch, the bullet would have hit the glass cabinet over there and woken my father, who would have whupped Dakotah's ass," he said. "Then we would have gotten him some help."

Jean cried quietly throughout the demonstration, and added that Dakotah was a "loving grandson up until that moment." "I would bring him home tonight," she said. "I know the person he is." She often thought about what would have happened if she had forced her husband to hide his gun—it was kept by the door in case of intruders—or had sat down with Dakotah for dinner that night. All he ate was three cupcakes. "But I had all kinds of stuff for him in the freezer," she said under her breath.

The family talked about Dakotah's diagnosis of bipolar disorder, though it won't be relevant for the appeal—the legal bar for insanity is higher than simply having a psychiatric diagnosis. Since Dakotah's arrest, Steve had discovered a history of bipolar disorder in his family, and he, too, received a diagnosis of the illness. He often repackages lessons from his own therapy sessions for his son, who calls home every day. The family talks to him on a speakerphone until the prison phone service cuts them off, after fifteen minutes. When Dakotah complains of feeling homesick, Steve jokes with him, "Grow your beard a little thicker, and I'll shave my hair like you. You'll sneak out, and I'll take your place."

By September, Dakotah had spent nearly three months in solitary confinement. In April, 2011, after six months in prison, he got his first ticket for a rule violation, Threatening Behavior, which resulted in the standard punishment: thirty days in segregation. Dakotah had told a boy in his unit that he'd kill him if he kept prying into his case. The boy had been joking around, saying, "Who'd you kill? Who'd you kill?" Two months later, Dakotah received another ticket, for Sexual Misconduct, after a female guard accused him of exposing his penis through the vertical window on his steel door. According to Dakotah, he was sleeping at the time. He told the guard that it must have been his cellmate, but she said the skin she saw looked light, and his cellmate was black. Dakotah confronted his cellmate, a fifteen-year-old convicted of sexual assault, "but he just laughs about it," he said. "He giggles about all sorts of childish shit."

Two weeks after his punishment ended, he and his cellmate got into a fistfight, and, at the end of August, both boys were transferred to the segregation unit. His cinder-block cell had one barred window, a bed, a stainless-steel desk and stool that were attached to the floor, a toilet, a sink, and a mirror. All his meals were delivered to him through a metal flap on his door, starting with breakfast, at 4 A.M. The only time he could leave his cell was to shower, three times a week; he was handcuffed on the way there and locked into the shower stall.

When I visited Dakotah in September, it was the first time in nearly three weeks that he'd had an extended conversation with another person. We sat in a narrow cinder-block room, divided in half by shatterproof glass, and spoke to each other using rotary telephones whose dial pads had been removed. Dakotah had been animated in our previous conversations, but now he spoke in a dull, listless tone and sat slouched in his chair, his head resting against the wall of the cubicle. His eyes were dilated, and his lips were so chapped they looked bruised.

He told me that he was disgusted with himself for ruining his chance to see his family, who, for more than a month, had planned to visit on the second Sunday in September. It was the second time they'd had to cancel their plans at the last minute because he'd been placed in seclusion. (After a week without calls or letters from Dakotah, Steve had called the prison, and a phone operator told him that Dakotah was in the segregation unit, where visiting hours are restricted to Friday mornings.) Dakotah spent his first few nights in the segregation cell lying underneath his steel-framed bed, on the concrete floor, wearing nothing but shorts. "Oh, man, I was going off the deep end, like, living below the water," he said, jiggling the phone cord. "The little flame lighting my candle of sanity just blew out."

The effects of the sedative he'd been prescribed seemed to have worn off, and he struggled to sleep through the night. He woke up in cold sweats, with such vivid, violent dreams that he examined his body to see if he'd somehow been injured. "I don't understand sleep anymore," he told me. He had developed a theory, adapted from "The Matrix," which he had watched countless times, that maybe life is an illusion, a kind of thought experiment, and dreams are the true reality.

Dakotah began talking to himself in his cell, little comments and reminders at first, and then, as the days passed, full conversations. "I go into this other mode," he said, blowing air out of his mouth. "I can have all these conversations crisscrossing the room; there's a version of me on the bed, at the desk, at the sink."

At the end of my previous visits, Dakotah had chattered rapidly, nearly free-associating, occasionally singing, as if he would lose his visitor as soon as he paused. I had found myself coming to visiting hours later, to avoid prolonging the drama of separating. He would pick lint or stray hairs off my shirt or touch a scab on my hand, assuring me that it would fall off soon—any excuse for physical contact. But this time, our first visit with glass between us, he was the one to end the conversation. "I'm worn out," he told me. "My mind is kind of dead."

His sixteenth birthday was the next week, and I wished him happy birthday. "Yeah, I'm alive," he said, rolling his eyes. "Whoopdefuckingwhoo."

The day before Dakotah's birthday, September 23rd, Steve drove four hours to the prison to surprise him. Dakotah had recently been transferred to the Behavioral Modification Unit, where he had contact with other prisoners, but most of his privileges, including use of the phone, were still suspended. In the partitioned cubicle, Steve and Dakotah pressed their knuckles against the glass, as if they were touching. It had been three months since they'd seen each other. "You look pasty, son," Steve said tenderly. Dakotah, smiling broadly, smoothed the collar of his prison jumpsuit and confessed, "I don't feel like I look so good."

Steve updated Dakotah on developments in the lives of neighbors, relatives, and their pets, and then spoke at length about the mood-stabilizing medication he'd been taking. He

said that he no longer acted like a tyrant at home, high-strung and aggressive. "That's one of our traits—not knowing how to express our emotions," he told Dakotah. The more Steve talked about their matching diagnoses, the more he seemed to convince himself that he was complicit in Dakotah's crime. He couldn't forgive himself for yelling at his children, which he now saw as a form of abuse. Dakotah, quiet and deferential, deflected his father's comments with reassuring jokes. (At an earlier visit, he described his dad as his role model, except for his domineering manner: "He was Sgt. Pepper, and I was the Lonely Heart Band.")

Steve wore an oversized tank top, which revealed a tattoo on his right shoulder in memory of his stepfather: "J.E.M., 1940–2010." Dakotah had wept when he first saw the tattoo, more than a year earlier, and now he intended to get one, too. He also wanted the name of his dead dog tattooed on his biceps, his dead cat on his forearm, and his great-grandmother's initials on his chest. At his father's request, he planned to wait until he got to the adult side of the prison, since the Old Heads were more likely to clean their needles.

Both father and son vaguely hoped that other problems, too, would be resolved on the adult side of prison: the units might be less chaotic and noisy, the inmates calmer and more responsible. Steve had reconciled himself to the possibility that Dakotah would eventually get affiliated—with the Aryan Brotherhood, he guessed—because he would need that protection. At the end of the visit, Steve reassured Dakotah that he would find mentors when he moved to the adult population. "Not someone who will take advantage of you but a man who was locked away from his own kids," Steve said. "I want a father in there watching over you."

Critical Thinking

1. Do you think a teenager who commits murder should receive a life sentence?

2. Should a teenager who commits murder be tried as if he were an adult?

3. If Dakotah Eliason should ever be released from prison, do you believe he will be a danger to society?

4. What do you think of the arguments made in the two cases that will soon go to the U.S. Supreme Court?

Create Central

www.mhhe.com/createcentral

Internet References

National Criminal Justice Reference Service
www.ncjrs.gov/pdffiles1/ojjdp/232434.pdf

Teen Advocates USA
http://teenadvocatesusa.homestead.com/innocencebetrayed_commentary.html

Article   Prepared by: Joanne Naughton

Why Jonathan McClard Still Matters

Excerpted from a speech given by Gabrielle Horowitz-Prisco, director of the CA's Juvenile Justice Project, during the Raise the Age – NY! campaign launch press conference on July 11, 2013.

Learning Outcomes

After reading this article, you will be able to:

- Explain the fears a parent might have whose child is incarcerated.

- Show the harmful effects of putting teenagers in adult facilities.

About a year ago, I was writing a piece on youth in adult jails and prisons and I wanted to write about Jonathan McClard, a seventeen year old boy in Missouri who committed suicide by hanging in an adult facility as he was awaiting transfer to a notoriously abusive adult prison.

I had met Jonathan's mother, Tracy, at a youth justice event—after Jonathan's death, she quit her job as a school teacher to devote herself to getting kids out of adult jails and prisons. Over dinner, Tracy described to me the marked changes she observed in Jonathan's appearance as he spent time in adult facilities—the hardening and shutting down, the fighting he was forced to do, and his fear. She described her powerlessness as a mother to get her son out of what she knew was a life-threatening situation. How Jonathan had been placed in solitary confinement as punishment for putting his hands in his lap during their visit. The impact of solitary on his mind and spirit.

How she believed that it was his fear of being raped in prison that led him to take his own life.

I wanted to make sure that Tracy was okay with me writing these details down, with their potential publication. So I called her at home one night and asked.

I remember this moment—she said "let me check something with my husband" and she put the phone down and I could hear through the distance. She said: "Do you think it is accurate to say that it seems like Jonathan killed himself because he was afraid of being raped?" Her husband said yes. She got back on the phone and said: "if it helps another parent not go through what we have gone through, you can talk about that—you can share whatever part of his life will help."

Do you know those moments where the world sort of stops, time slows down, and you feel things deep, deep in your belly? It was one of those moments. I felt the presence of my own partner one room away from me. We were newly engaged and our whole lives together seemed spread out before us—full of joy and promise.

I remembered that Tracy's husband and son both tried to commit suicide themselves as they grappled with the pain of losing Jonathan. Her daughter had been hospitalized with severe anxiety. And I thought about how when our conversation was over, I would go into the living room and have a light-hearted normal night at home with the person I love so much, but Tracy and her husband may never again have that kind of night.

I thought about what I want you to know: Jonathan's death is not unique—children in adult jails are 36 times more likely to commit suicide than children in adult detention facilities, and the National Prison Rape Elimination Commission stated that "more than any other group of incarcerated persons, youth incarcerated with adults are probably at the highest risk for sexual abuse."

And children in adult jails and prisons are often placed in solitary confinement for up to 23 hours a day—where they are fed through a small slot in the door so that the only contact they have is a hand coming through a slot in the door. Can you imagine that: just an arm coming through a slot to push food in to a child. Children in solitary do not leave their cells to go to school or programs, and can stay for months and even years at a time.

This all happens in New York State, and it happens because we prosecute 16- and 17-year olds as adults and confine them in adult jails and prisons. This practice causes children immeasurable physical, emotional and sexual trauma.

And it is bad for public safety—children prosecuted as adults are far more likely to commit crime and violence in the future than youth prosecuted in the youth justice system.

Finally, it is bad for taxpayers. Not only does prosecuting children as adults keep many young people from lifelong education and employment opportunities—nearby Connecticut is spending approximately 2 million dollars less on youth justice than it was 10 years ago—despite having raised the age and adding millions of dollars to community services.

Most importantly, now is the time to act, so that the next time we are here at a press conference, you do not hear from another mother who lost her son or daughter while we were waiting for the law to change.

Critical Thinking

1. Do you believe teenagers should be considered adults in the criminal justice system?
2. Is it a good idea to prosecute children as adults when they commit very violent crimes?
3. Should the violence an inmate faces in prison be part of the punishment, or do inmates have a right to be incarcerated in a safe environment?

Create Central

www.mhhe.com/createcentral

Internet References

Correctional Association of New York
www.correctionalassociation.org/campaigns/raise-the-age
Justice Policy Institute
www.justicepolicy.org/images/upload/97-02_rep_riskjuvenilesface_jj.pdf

Unit 6

UNIT

Prepared by: Joanne Naughton

Punishment and Corrections

In the American system of criminal justice, the term "corrections" has a special meaning. It designates programs and agencies that have legal authority over the custody or supervision of people who have been convicted of a criminal act by the courts. The correctional process begins with the sentencing of the convicted offender. The predominant sentencing pattern in the United States encourages maximum judicial discretion and offers a range of alternatives, from probation (supervised, conditional freedom within the community) through imprisonment, to the death penalty.

This unit focuses on the current condition of the U.S. penal system and the effects that sentencing, probation, imprisonment, and parole have on the rehabilitation of criminals.

Article   Prepared by: Joanne Naughton

Bring Back the Lash
Why Flogging Is More Humane than Prison

PETER MOSKOS

Learning Outcomes

After reading this article, you will be able to:

- Argue that the lash instead of prison might not be so preposterous after all.

- Explain how the punishment of flogging is not torture.

You're about to get whipped. Mentally more than physically. It's going to hurt—but it's supposed to.

I write in defense of flogging, something most people consider too radical for debate and even unworthy of intellectual discussion. But please, don't turn the page, upset I dared to broach the subject.

My defense of flogging—whipping, caning, lashing, call it what you will—is meant to be provocative, but only because something extreme is needed to shatter the status quo. There are 2.3 million Americans in our prisons and jails. That is too many. I want to reduce cruelty, and corporal punishment, once common in America and still practiced in places like Singapore, may be the answer.

So first let me begin with a simple question: Given the choice between five years in prison and ten brutal lashes, which would you choose?

Yes, flogging is a severe and even brutal form of punishment. Under the lash, skin is literally ripped from the body. But prison means losing a part of your life and everything you care for. Compared to this, flogging is just a few very painful strokes on the behind. And it's over in a few minutes.

If you had the choice, if you were given the option of staying out of jail, wouldn't you choose to be flogged and released?

Consider your answer to that question. Then consider the fact that the United States now has more prisoners than any other country in the world. Ever. In sheer numbers and as a percentage of the population. Our rate of incarceration is roughly seven times that of Canada or any Western European country. Despite our "land of the free" rhetoric, we deem it necessary to incarcerate more of our people than the world's most draconian regimes. We have more prisoners than China, and they have *a billion* more people than we do. We have more prisoners than soldiers; prison guards outnumber Marines.

It wasn't always this way. In 1970, just 338,000 Americans were behind bars. There was even talk of abolishing prison altogether. That didn't happen. Instead, fear of crime led to "tough-on-crime" politics and the war on drugs. Crime has gone up and down since then, but the incarceration rate has only increased, a whopping 500 percent in the past forty years.

In truth, there is very little correlation between incarceration and the crime rate. From 1970 to 1991 crime rose while we locked up a million more people. Since then we've locked up another million and crime has gone down. Is there something so special about that *second* million? Were they the only ones who were "real criminals"? Did we simply get it wrong with the first 1.3 million people we put behind bars?

Today's prison reformers—and I wish them well—tinker at the edges of a massive failed system. We need much more drastic action. To bring our incarceration back to a civilized level—one we used to have, and one much more befitting a rich, modern nation—we would have to reduce the number of prisoners by 85 percent. Without alternative punishments, this will not happen anytime soon. Even the most optimistically progressive opponent of prison has no plan to release two million prisoners.

Perhaps, as a law-abiding citizen, with all there is to worry about in the world today, you don't have the fate of convicted criminals in our prison system at the top of your list of concerns. But who hasn't, at some point, committed a crime? Perhaps you've taken illegal drugs. Maybe you once got into a fight with a friend, stranger, or lover that came to blows. Or you drove back from a bar drunk. Or you clicked on an online picture of somebody who turned out to be a bit young. Perhaps you accepted a "gift" from a family member and told the IRS it was a loan. Or did you go for the white-collar big leagues and embezzle millions of dollars? If your luck runs out, you can end up in jail for almost anything, big or small. Even if you have done nothing wrong, imagine that in a horrific twist of fate you are convicted of a crime you did not commit. It's not inconceivable; it happens all the time.

As you sit in court on sentencing day, you begin to wonder what prison will be like. Are there drugs, gangs, and long times in solitary? Will you come out stronger—or broken? Will you be raped? Will it be like the brutal TV show *Oz*? God, you hope not. But you don't know. And that's the rub. Prison is a mystery to all but the millions of people forced to live and work in this gigantic government-run system of containment. And as long as we don't look at what happens on the inside, as long as we refuse to consider alternatives, nothing will change.

Is flogging still too cruel to contemplate? If so, given the hypothetical choice between prison and flogging, why did you choose flogging? Perhaps it's not as crazy as you thought. And even if you're adamant that flogging is a barbaric, inhumane form of punishment, how can offering criminals the choice of the lash in lieu of incarceration be so bad? If flogging were really worse than prison, nobody would choose it. Of course most people would choose to be caned over incarceration. And that's my point. Faced with the choice between hard time and the lash, the lash is better. What does that say about prison?

Sometime in the past few decades we seem to have lost the concept of justice in a free society. Now we settle for simple efficiency of process. We tried rehabilitation and ended up with supermax and solitary confinement. Crime, violence, and drug prohibition help explain why so *many* people are behind bars. But they don't explain why so many people are *behind bars*.

I am not proposing to completely end confinement or shut down every prison. Some inmates are, of course, too violent and hazardous to simply flog and release. Pedophiles, terrorists, serial rapists, and murderers, for example, need to remain behind bars—but they are relatively few in number. They are being kept in prison not only to punish them, but also because we don't want them to hurt us. We're afraid of them. But for the millions of other prisoners—particularly those caught up in the war on drugs (which I for one would end tomorrow if I could)—the lash is better than a prison cell. Why not at least offer the choice?

Is flogging still too cruel to contemplate? If so, given the hypothetical choice between prison and flogging, why did you choose flogging? Perhaps it's not as crazy as you thought.

That prisons have failed in such a spectacular manner should matter more than it does. But it should come as no surprise, since prisons were designed not to punish, but to "cure." Just as hospitals were for the physically sick, penitentiaries were created—mostly by Quakers in the late eighteenth century—to heal the criminally ill. A stated goal of the early prison advocates was nothing less than the complete elimination of punishment. The penitentiary would be a kinder and gentler sentence, one geared to personal salvation, less crime, and a better life for all. Like so many utopian fairy tales, the movement to cure criminals failed. Early prison reforms may have had the best of intentions, but today we should know better.

The disastrous consequences of prison became clear as soon as the first one was built, in Philadelphia in 1790: inmates began

to go crazy. When Charles Dickens toured this prison, he noted with despair, "I hold this slow and daily tampering with the mysteries of the brain, to be immeasurably worse than any torture of the body."

Today violent offenders are mixed with immigrants who may have committed no crime other than crossing our border. Lifers are thrown in the same cellblock as people who serve twelve months. Kids get raped. The mentally ill are left to fend for themselves in some antipsychotic-medicine haze. And given the impossible task of total control, some guards inevitably abuse their authority.

Because one stint in prison so often leads to another, millions of criminals have come to alternate between incarceration and freedom while their families and communities suffer the economic and social consequences of their absence. When I was a police officer in Baltimore's rough Eastern District, I don't think I ever arrested anybody for the first time. Even the juveniles I arrested all had a record. Because not only does incarceration not "cure" criminality, in many ways in makes it worse. From behind bars a prisoner can't be a parent, hold a job, maintain a relationship, or take care of their elders. Their spouse suffers. Their children suffer. And because of this, in the long run, we all suffer.

But maybe you still have your doubts about flogging. Perhaps you are concerned that the practice is torture. It is not. Torture is meant to achieve a goal, and until that goal is achieved, it continues. Punishment is finite and is prescribed in accordance with clear rules of law. And certainly offering criminals the option of flogging cannot be viewed as more torturous than the status quo.

Indeed it is our current system of imprisonment that most resembles torture. Overwhelming evidence suggests that by locking people in cells and denying them meaningful human contact, as is the case with solitary confinement, we cause irreparable damage; when prisoners are held in group living quarters, they often form criminal associations and reinforce aggressive antisocial norms; and through parole boards' decisions, we hold the power to continue such punishment for extended periods of time. In addition, it's terribly expensive. And for what? What do we gain? Why incapacitate criminals in a non-rehabilitative environment never meant for punishment? It is like being entombed alive, something more torturous than flogging could ever be.

And worse, given that life inside the concertina wire is so well hidden from those of us on the outside, prison is a dishonest way of dealing with the problem of punishment. Flogging, on the other hand, is different. Physical violence has the advantage of being honest, transparent, inexpensive, and easy to understand. What you see is what you get. If you want someone to receive more punishment, you give more lashes. If you want them to receive less punishment, you give fewer.

As ugly as it may seem, corporal punishment would be an effective and comparatively humane way to bring our prison population back in line with world standards. To those in prison (after the approval of some parole board designed to keep the truly dangerous behind bars) we could offer the lash in exchange for sentence years. I propose that each six months of incarceration be exchanged for one lash. As a result, our prison population would plummet. This would not only save money, it would also save prisons for those who truly deserve to be there. And if you think that flogging isn't punishment enough, that prisons are necessary precisely because they torture so cruelly and horribly—then we've entered a truly bizarre world of unparalleled cruelty. Flogging may be too harsh or too lenient, but it can't be both.

As ugly as it may seem, corporal punishment would be an effective and comparatively humane way to bring our prison population back in line with world standards.

Make no mistake: this is punishment, and punishment must by definition hurt. Even under controlled conditions, with doctors present and the convict choosing a lashing over a prison sentence, the details of flogging are enough to make most people queasy. Those receiving lashes have described the cane cutting through layers of flesh and tissue, leaving "furrows that were . . . bloody pulp." Even if these wounds were attended to immediately, a full recovery could take weeks or months. In some cases, the scars would remain as permanent reminders of the ordeal.

The lash, which metes out punishment without falsely promising betterment, is an unequivocal expression of society's condemnation. For better or for worse, flogging would air the dirty laundry of race and punishment in America in a way that prisons—which, by their very design, are removed from society—can never do. To highlight an injustice is in no way to condone it. Quite the opposite.

Without a radical defense of flogging, changes to our current defective system of justice are hard to imagine. The glacial pace of reform promises only the most minor adjustments to the massive machinery of incarceration. Bringing back the lash is one way to destroy it—if not completely, then at least for the millions of Americans for whom the punishment of prison is far, far worse than the crime they have committed. Yes, flogging may seem brutal and retrograde, but only because we are in mass denial about the greater brutality of our supposedly civilized and progressive prisons.

Critical Thinking

1. What were prisons designed to do?
2. Do they accomplish their goals?
3. Are today's American prisons places of torture?
4. Should corporal punishment ever be an option in the American criminal justice system?

Create Central

www.mhhe.com/createcentral

Internet References

Harper's Magazine
    harpers.org/blog/2011/07/in-defense-of-flogging-six-questions-for-peter-moskos
TIME U.S.
    http://content.time.com/time/nation/article/0,8599,2079933,00.html

---

PETER MOSKOS is a sociologist at John Jay College of Criminal Justice and the Graduate Center of the City University of New York. He is a former Baltimore police officer and the author of *Cop in the Hood.* This article is adapted with permission from the author's forthcoming book *In Defense of Flogging,* available in May from Basic Books. Copyright © 2011.

From *Washington Monthly,* May/June 2011, pp. 12–14. Copyright © 2011 by Washington Monthly Publishing, LLC, 1319 F St. NW, Suite 710, Washington, DC 20004. (202)393-5155. Reprinted by permission. www.washingtonmonthly.com.

Article   Prepared by: Joanne Naughton

The Torture of Solitary

Solitary confinement, once regarded as a humane method of rehabilitation, unravels the mind. Yet today, more than 25,000 U.S. prisoners languish in isolated cells.

STEPHANIE ELIZONDO GRIEST

Learning Outcomes

After reading this article, you will be able to:

- Describe how solitary confinement came to be used in prisons.
- Show how evidence of failure at Eastern State Penitentiary didn't stop other prisons from implementing solitary confinement in the 19th century.
- Demonstrate how increased penalties for drug crimes saw the birth of "Supermax" prisons—a modern version of solitary confinement.

Here is what I knew about Joe Loya before stepping into his car: During a 14-month stretch in the late 1980s, he stole a quarter-million dollars from 30 Southern California banks by donning a tailored suit and, occasionally, a fedora, striding up to bank tellers, and, in a low and smoky voice, demanding all their money. His panache earned him the nickname "The Beirut Bandit" because, he said, "no one could believe a Mexican from East L.A. could be so smooth." He was finally bum-rushed by undercover agents while reading the newspaper at a UCLA campus café. (His girlfriend had tipped them off.) As he served out a seven-year prison sentence, he grew increasingly violent, once chomping a chunk off the ear of an inmate who had snaked his copy of *Playboy*. When his former cellmate was slaughtered in their old cell, Loya was pegged as a primary suspect and consigned to Security Housing Unit—otherwise known as solitary confinement—for two years, until cleared of the charges. He was released in 1996, at age 35.

All of this I could handle. But when he started careening 77 miles per hour down a Northern Californian freeway, slicing in and out of traffic, I began to worry. Tall and husky with mocha-colored skin, Loya was wearing Ray-Bans and a pinstriped shirt untucked over jeans. His temples were flecked with gray.

"There is something seductive about solitary confinement," he mused. "It is the myth of the American male: I walk alone. There is a sense that solitary is a kind of adventure, and men love adventure."

We narrowly avoided sideswiping an SUV, which blared its horn.

"It sounds like you already had a lot of adventure," I offered.

Maybe too much. Loya's mother died of cancer when he was nine, leaving him with a little brother and a Bible-thumping father for emotional support. He sought comfort in an older female neighbor, who repeatedly molested him. Meanwhile, his father tried to beat the demons out of him. After an especially brutal pummeling at age 16, Loya plunged a steak knife into his father's neck. The old man survived, but Loya landed in county custody, embarking from there on a decade-long crime spree that included auto theft, larceny, fraud, and, finally, the bank robberies that landed him in prison.

"No adventure is like solitary," he said, gliding into another lane. "It's almost erotic, like—like masturbation. You don't rely on anyone else to pleasure you. You just do it yourself. Solitary is just you creating your own universe with you at the center of it, to sleep, to read, to jack off, to think, to be with yourself."

He glanced at me and grinned. "When you come out of solitary, you know that you've taken stock of yourself. You know who you are."

In his case, that meant discovering a knack for the pen. Halfway through his prison sentence, Loya struck up a correspondence with the writer Richard Rodriguez, who emboldened him to pursue his literary tendencies. Six years after his release, Loya starred in a one-man show he'd written about his past called *The Man Who Outgrew His Prison Cell*, which HarperCollins later published as a memoir.

The exit for San Leandro loomed ahead. Loya zipped across three lanes, pivoted east, then doglegged through an upscale neighborhood. "Pretentious bullshit," he muttered at a sign featuring the word "estates" in floral script. We pulled up to a cream-colored house with rust-brown trim. Inside, the living room radiated newness. Black-and-white photographs of sidewalk cafés in foreign lands were propped against the walls, waiting to be hung. Teddy bears, blankets, and teething toys were scattered on the floor. Just a few months earlier, Loya and his wife had been nesting in East Oakland, but they decamped after five shootings occurred within a few blocks of their home. The safety of their 16-month-old daughter trumped their desire to help "foster community."

Loya motioned for me to sit. We stared at each other for a long moment.

"So, solitary," I said.

"So, solitary," he repeated, combing his fingers through his gel-spiked hair. "Rule number one is, you make your bunk in the morning and you don't lie on it again. Not until lunch, and even then, just for a nap. Your bunk is like quicksand. Spend too much time on it, and your mind will grow sloppy. You have to be vigilant. You have to take control of your thoughts before they grip hold of you. Mind games help, because they keep you sharp.

"First, you sit on the edge of your bunk. Don't lie on it. SIT. Find a spot on the wall. OK, now—stare. That's it. Stare. Don't look away. Just keep staring at it, staring at it, at that same little spot, for a whole entire minute. Once you got that, stare at it for five minutes. Then 10. Then 20.

"That's when things start to happen. Things like light. Panels of light will slowly open as your peripheral vision recedes into darkness. And then that spot on the wall, it will dance. It will become a dog or a horse, and after a while it will become a man, and that man, he will start to walk. If you concentrate hard enough, deep enough, long enough, a little movie will flicker.

"Eventually, this will happen without you even trying. Faces will appear, but without you concentrating. You just open your eyes, and a scene appears right in front of you. But then those faces, they start to morph, like in that Michael Jackson video. Only, they morph into people you don't want to see. People you f****d over. People suffering. People in pain.

"And then you start hearing things."

When Philadelphia Quakers conceived of solitary confinement in the late 18th century, the punishment was regarded as humanitarian. At the time, convicts were typically hanged, flogged, or tossed into wretchedly overcrowded dungeons. What these prisoners needed, Quakers argued, was a spiritual renovation. Give a man ample time and quiet space to reflect upon his misdeeds, and he will recover his bond with God. He will grieve. He will repent. He will walk away a rehabilitated man.

And so, after conducting a few test runs at local jailhouses, Philadelphia, a city infused with the theology of the Quakers who had helped to found it, sank a record $800,000 into building a prison on an elevated piece of farmland just north of the city limits (known today as the Fairmount District). The structure consisted entirely of isolation cellblocks. In 1829, Eastern State Penitentiary opened its iron-studded doors. Its high stone walls and castellated towers suggested a fortress, yet its Gothic façade was redolent of a monastery. For 142 years, it tried to be both.

"If reform is possible, it will happen here," proclaimed a sign in the modern-day visitor's center. When I visited a few years ago, I walked down a corridor draped with cobwebs, gripping a map. Every few feet, I passed another cell. Some were whitewashed and barren; others were refurbished with rusty cots and wobbly workbenches. Entering a cell required ducking your head, an act of supplication. The room measured eight feet by 12 feet, with a barrel ceiling that reached 10 feet at the crown. A tiny round skylight-known as "the Eye of God"—cast a circle of sunshine on the floor. I stepped inside it as legions of inmates had done before me, following the light as it slowly revolved around the cell, the sole indicator of time's passage. As the soft glow warmed my face, I imagined the horrors that had once transpired here.

First, you were hooded. A black woolen sheath covered your head, clung to your shoulders, clouded your vision. Supposedly, this kept you from discerning the prison's layout (and thus concocting an escape), but it also disabled you. Guards shoved you forward, warning when to duck, when to turn.

Next, you were assigned a number corresponding to your spot in the admissions log. For the duration of your sentence, you'd be known only by this number. It was written above your cell door, stitched on your shirt, shouted when you were needed.

In quick succession, you were examined by a physician, shorn by a barber, and shown to a shower. By the time you emerged, dripping wet, your belongings had been confiscated: your socks, your shirt, your underwear, the contents of your pockets. In exchange, you received woolen trousers, a close-fitting jacket, a shirt, two handkerchiefs, two pairs of stockings, and coarse leather shoes—all of which itched.

Then you were led (or, if you resisted, dragged or carried) to your cell. At last, you could pull off the mask. Aside from a cot, a stool, and a whale-oil lamp, the cell was empty. No paper, no ink, no reading material. Nothing whatsoever to occupy your time, at least those first weeks. (Eventually, you'd be permitted to cobble shoes or roll cigars for the prison's profit.) A side door led to a small yard where—if you behaved—you'd be allowed to exercise for an hour a day. Baths were offered every two to three weeks. Aside from that, you'd spend your entire sentence between those white walls, visited only by the warden, a clergyman, and your own mounting regret.

All seven cellblocks connected to a central surveillance hub, like the spokes of a wheel. The walls were 18 inches thick. But architecture wasn't the only cause of the silence that engulfed the place. In the early days, the guards pulled woolen stockings over their boots to muffle their footsteps and wrapped the wheels of the food cart in leather to quiet its creaking. Yet the inmates were inventive with their noisemaking. They shouted down the toilet every time they flushed it. They banged on the water pipes, each clang corresponding to a different letter of the alphabet. The guards retaliated by covering the skylights, eclipsing the prisoners even from God. If the noise persisted, they stormed the cells. In wintertime, they stripped the offending inmates, chained them to the wall, and tossed buckets of cold water on them until icicles hung from their limbs. In summertime, they strapped inmates into chairs for days at a stretch, until their legs ballooned. If the inmates *still* kept talking, the guards put them in the "iron gag," a five-inch metal brace that was clamped over their tongues and attached by chains to their wrists, which were handcuffed behind their backs.

Yet the physical pain of these tortures—common in many prisons at the time—paled beside the mental anguish of solitude. Charles Dickens spent an afternoon visiting Eastern State inmates in 1842, and wrote an account of the experience in his travelogue *American Notes:* "On the haggard face of every man among these prisoners, the same expression sat. I know not what to liken it to. It had something of that strained attention which we see upon the faces of the blind and deaf, mingled with a kind of horror, as though they had all been secretly terrified." At another point in the book, Dickens wrote:

> I hold this slow and daily tampering with the mysteries of the brain, to be immeasurably worse than any torture of the body: and because its ghastly signs and tokens are not so palpable to the eye and sense of touch as scars upon the flesh; because its wounds are not upon the surface, and it extorts few cries that human ears can hear; therefore I the more denounce it, as a secret punishment which slumbering humanity is not roused up to stay.

The prison's annual reports listed scores of suicides, and while loneliness was never cited as a factor, a certain side effect was. One report described a "white male, aged 17" who died of "debility. . . . Persistent masturbation was the sole cause of his death." Another mentioned a prisoner who set his cell ablaze and snuffed up all the smoke. Cause of death: "excessive masturbation." In fact, the 1838 report ascribed 12 cases of insanity to this "solitary vice."

Eastern State gradually abandoned the practice of solitary confinement. There were simply too many bodies—with too few minds—to keep. As early as 1841, the warden was doubling up the inmates, and by the turn of the century, cells bunked as many as four apiece. Solitary confinement also grew costly. Whereas inmates at other penitentiaries could toil together in chain gangs, quarrying marble or tending crops, Eastern State inmates could only labor within the confines of their cells, and the piecemeal tasks they performed didn't turn enough profit. The "crucible of good intentions," as the authors of a history of Eastern State call it, finally shuttered in 1971, reopening a quarter-century later as a museum and, during the Halloween season, as "the scariest haunted house in America!" (according to television talk-show host Rachael Ray).

Eastern State Penitentiary was widely considered a failure, but that didn't stop other prisons from implementing its "separate system"—with equally disastrous results. In the second half of the 19th century, German researchers published 37 studies documenting the psychotic illnesses suffered by their country's isolated inmates, including hallucinations, delusions, and "psychomotor excitation." In England, guards at Pentonville Prison had to cart so many inmates off to the insane asylum each year that the warden finally ruled that no one be isolated longer than 12 months.

In 1890, the U.S. Supreme Court nearly declared the punishment unconstitutional. Writing for the majority, Justice Samuel Miller argued,

> A considerable number of the prisoners fell, after even a short confinement, into a semi-fatuous condition, from which it was next to impossible to arouse them, and

others became violently insane; others, still, committed suicide; while those who stood the ordeal better were not generally reformed, and in most cases did not recover sufficient mental activity to be of any subsequent service to the community.

Solitary confinement largely fell out of practice in the century that followed, save as a short-term punishment for exceedingly bad behavior.

Fast-forward to the 1970s. Increased penalties for drug crimes swelled the nation's prison population. Ronald Reagan's "war on drugs" sent the number yet higher. Meanwhile, lawmakers wishing to seem tough on crime dissolved the bulk of prison educational and occupational programs, leaving inmates with an infinity of hours and no way to fill them. When two correctional officers were shanked to death in a single day at Marion Federal Prison in Illinois in 1983, the warden ordered the entire facility put on "permanent lockdown," forbidding inmates to leave their cells to work, take classes, eat in the cafeteria, or do anything but shower. Heralded as a success, the Marion lockdown spawned a new breed of prison called the "Supermax," which cooped all inmates in solitary cells for no less than 23 hours a day. More than 60 such prisons have sprung up across the nation, housing up to 25,000 inmates. Tens of thousands of other men and women—nobody knows the exact number—are languishing in what are essentially concrete cages at other facilities. And they aren't all just staying for days or weeks or months or even years. Some Americans are enduring solitary confinement for decades.

Robert Hillary King is a star in certain circles. He is the subject of a British documentary narrated by Samuel L. Jackson, and has published an autobiography and touted it to hundreds of groups around the world. He has mingled with members of Congress, gabbed with historian Howard Zinn, and befriended the cofounders of the Body Shop. The cause behind his célèbre isn't so glittering: He survived one of the longest known stints in solitary confinement. For 29 years, King passed all but perhaps an hour a day inside a six-by-nine-foot concrete cell at Louisiana State Penitentiary at Angola. Since his release in 2001, he has launched a one-man campaign to end this form of punishment.

"I saw men so desperate, they ripped prison doors apart," King told me in a slow Cajun drawl when we met at a café in Austin. "They starved themselves. They cut themselves. My soul still mourns for them."

King, in his late sixties, walks with a noble gait. That day in Austin, he was wearing sunglasses, a black ankh necklace, and an ivy cap turned backward. Tattoos of daggers and spiders covered his arms, and his face was pockmarked, yet he exuded yogic tranquility. The tops of his knuckles were tattooed with the word L-O-V-E, while the bottoms read H-A-T-E.

King was born in 1942 to a mother who drank and a father who split. Although his grandmother was still rearing some of her own nine children, she added him to her brood. One of his earliest memories is of watching an uncle strangle a rat and stew it for the family's supper. After living in a smattering of

Louisiana towns, including New Orleans, King ditched home at 15 to ride the rails with a couple of hoboes. A brief stint in reform school followed, and at 18 he received the first of several prison sentences for armed robberies he claims not to have committed (though he acknowledges other crimes), landing at Angola, known as the nation's bloodiest prison. A former plantation so massive that the entire island of Manhattan could fit on its grounds, Angola was named after the African nation where the bulk of its slaves originated.

The first thing King noticed upon his arrival was that the majority of the inmates were black and the guards were uniformly white. Known as "Freemen," the guards lived with their families on the prison grounds, served by inmates called "houseboys." Before the light of dawn, the Freemen marched the inmates down to the fields and watched on horseback as they cut, bladed, ditched, and quarter-drained sugarcane in a work line for up to 16 hours a day. In 1951 more than 30 inmates slashed their own Achilles tendons with razorblades to protest these working conditions. The Freemen called them the "Heel String Gang" after that.

King thus spent the 1960s in a time warp. While serving out his sentences at Angola, he was trapped in the pages of *Uncle Tom's Cabin*. During his intermittent stretches of freedom, however, he lived in the spirit of the nation's flourishing civil rights movement. "By 1969, everybody who was black, even those with just a trace of black blood, wanted to be Black and Proud. It was a time of consciousness. I loved it," he said.

He didn't have long to revel in it: By 1970 he had racked up yet another conviction, for robbery, which carried a 35-year sentence. While awaiting transfer to Angola, he shared a cell with some Black Panthers who had just been arrested in a police shootout. Their ideology enthralled him. "Through our discussions, I grasped the historical plight of blacks and other poor people in America. I saw that, for these people, America is one great big prison, a perpetuation and continuation of slavery."

Back in Angola, he befriended two inmates also serving time for robbery, Herman Wallace and Albert Woodfox. They had recently founded the nation's first prison chapter of the Black Panther Party, and invited him to join. Under their tutelage, King started cracking books—the Bible, philosophy, and especially law—and leading political discussions and hunger strikes.

Angola was a war zone in the 1970s. Roving gangs raped vulnerable inmates and forced them into prostitution. Stabbings occurred on an almost daily basis. When a young white Freeman joined the list of fatalities, after being knifed 32 times, Wallace and Woodfox were pinned with the blame—despite dubious testimony from a witness who was legally blind, another who was on antipsychotic medication, and a third whom the warden had bribed with a carton of cigarettes a week for life. Wallace and Woodfox were exiled to Closed Cell Restriction, Angola's isolated chamber. King soon shared their fate, after he was falsely accused of murdering a fellow inmate. In time, these Panthers would be christened "the Angola Three" by activists and championed by human rights groups such as Amnesty International. Back then, however, they felt as though they'd just been sucked down a hellhole, never to resurface.

The first years of solitary were the hardest. Denied even exercise privileges, King did crunches, jumping jacks, and pushups in the skinny plot between his toilet and cot. He read. He wrote. He paced. Most of his family had either died or wandered away, so letters were scant and visitors nonexistent. Other inmates lived on his cellblock, but he could only communicate with them by passing notes or shouting—and if caught, he'd be thrown in the "dungeon," a darkened room without a mattress or even a blanket, for weeks at a time. Black Pantherism became King's touchstone. He meditated on its tenets like a lotused monk.

A sweet tooth inspired a risky hobby: candy making. Having learned a few culinary tricks from Angola's chief cook years earlier, King fashioned a stove out of scraps of metal and wire, transformed Coke cans into a pot, and, using toilet paper for fuel, started cooking confections atop his toilet seat (so he could quickly conceal the contraption inside the bowl to avoid detection, if need be). Before long, inmates were sneaking him pats of butter and packets of sugar stashed at breakfast, while Freemen smuggled in bags of pecans. King's pralines grew famous; requests streamed in all the way from Angola's death row.

The bulk of King's time, however, was devoted to a thick stack of law books, in hopes that the contents might free him. Eventually, in 1975, he was able to win a retrial for the murder. Another man testified to doing the killing solo, but an all-white jury convicted King again anyway. Back in solitary, King wrote a flurry of letters—signed "the Angola 3"—that landed in capable hands. Human rights groups began to champion the trio's cause, while top lawyers adopted their cases pro bono. After a great deal of legal wrangling, in 2001 King's advocates won him a reprieve of sorts: He could walk if he promised not to sue for wrongful conviction. He agreed—though as he stalked out the gate, he paused to shout, "I may be free of Angola, but Angola will never be free of me!"

The cases of Wallace and Woodfox have proven more difficult. Angola's warden has repeatedly accused the two of "still trying to practice Black Pantherism," which he has likened to the doctrines of the Ku Klux Klan. The men briefly rejoined the general prison population after a 2008 visit from Representative John Conyers (D-Mich.), but have since been returned to isolation. Wallace and Woodfox have now endured more time in solitary confinement than anyone in U.S. penal history: 40 years each, as of April.

Angola Three lead counsel George Kendall and his team are currently pursuing two legal cases in the Louisiana courts, one of which argues that indefinite solitary confinement violates the constitutional guarantee against cruel and unusual punishment. His clients hope to live to see the outcome, but the odds are formidable: Approximately 85 percent of Angola's inmates die in captivity. Wallace turned 70 in October. Woodfox has blood pressure so high that once a nurse who was administering a medical exam checked her machine to make sure it wasn't broken. But according to Kendall, the two men are still mentally sharp. "I really braced myself for our first meeting," he admitted to me in an interview. "I thought that after so many years in solitary, they'd be lying on the floor sucking their thumbs. But no: You are still able to have a conversation with them about what is happening in the Middle East. By sheer determination, they have not let this confinement crush them."

After he was released with nothing but a one-way bus ticket and a few rumpled bills in his pocket, King moved to New Orleans to forge a new life—only to lose everything he'd cobbled together in the floodwaters of Hurricane Katrina. "I cried more during those first two weeks after Katrina than I did the whole time I was in Angola," he said, shaking his head.

Texan friends rescued him in a boat and helped him relocate to Austin. He travels at least two weeks a month campaigning for the release of Woodfox and Wallace. Speaking engagements cover most of his bills, as do profits from the pralines he perfected in prison and now sells over the Internet. They arrive in a package stamped with a sleek black panther and labeled "King's Freelines."

Four years have passed since my car ride with Joe Loya. Curious how he was faring, I called him in January. His daughter is a vivacious kindergartener now; he has been happily married for 13 years. Several of his television and movie scripts are being shopped around Hollywood.

Yet Loya still feels solitary's grip now and then. In 2003, hallucinations so haunted him that he checked into a hospital for eight days. He has developed a case of tinnitus and sometimes hears sounds like the rumbling of a crowd, a reminder of those long days in solitary he had recalled the day he drove me through Oakland.

"At first, you think it is only blood rushing in your head, but then the silence just gets sucked out your ear. Literally. There is a suction sound. Eventually, you start hearing radio static, and it grows louder and louder. Before long, you can't eat. You can't sleep. You're f***ing drowning in sound. After a few months of that, you realize there's no such thing as silence anymore."

Critical Thinking

1. Do you believe long-term solitary confinement has a legitimate place in the prison system?

2. Should a sentencing court have anything to say about whether a person serves his sentence of incarceration in solitary confinement?

Create Central

www.mhhe.com/createcentral

Internet References

American Psychological Association
www.apa.org/monitor/2012/05/solitary.aspx

Crime Museum
www.crimemuseum.org/solitary_confinement

Physicians for Human Rights
http://physiciansforhumanrights.org/blog/un-advisor-says-solitary-confinement-in-us-is-torture.html

STEPHANIE ELIZONDO GRIEST is the author of *Mexican Enough: My Life Between the Borderlines* (2008) and *Around the Bloc: My Life in Moscow, Beijing, and Havana* (2004). She splits her time between Corpus Christi, Texas, and Iowa City, Iowa.

Article   Prepared by: Joanne Naughton

The F.B.I. Deemed Agents Faultless in 150 Shootings

CHARLIE SAVAGE AND MICHAEL SCHMIDT

Learning Outcomes

After reading this article, you will be able to:

- Discuss the process that takes place whenever an F.B.I. agent fires his weapon.
- Compare the F.B.I.'s internal review of the shooting of Joseph Schultz with independent evaluations.

After contradictory stories emerged about an F.B.I. agent's killing last month of a Chechen man in Orlando, Fla., who was being questioned over ties to the Boston Marathon bombing suspects, the bureau reassured the public that it would clear up the murky episode.

"The F.B.I. takes very seriously any shooting incidents involving our agents, and as such we have an effective, time-tested process for addressing them internally," a bureau spokesman said.

But if such internal investigations are time-tested, their outcomes are also predictable: from 1993 to early 2011, F.B.I. agents fatally shot about 70 "subjects" and wounded about 80 others—and every one of those episodes was deemed justified, according to interviews and internal F.B.I. records obtained by *The New York Times* through a Freedom of Information Act lawsuit.

The last two years have followed the same pattern: an F.B.I. spokesman said that since 2011, there had been no findings of improper intentional shootings.

In most of the shootings, the F.B.I.'s internal investigation was the only official inquiry. In the Orlando case, for example, there have been conflicting accounts about basic facts like whether the Chechen man, Ibragim Todashev, attacked an agent with a knife, was unarmed or was brandishing a metal pole. But Orlando homicide detectives are not independently investigating what happened.

"We had nothing to do with it," said Sgt. Jim Young, an Orlando police spokesman. "It's a federal matter, and we're deferring everything to the F.B.I."

Occasionally, the F.B.I. does discipline an agent. Out of 289 deliberate shootings covered by the documents, many of which left no one wounded, five were deemed to be "bad shoots," in agents' parlance—encounters that did not comply with the bureau's policy, which allows deadly force if agents fear that their lives or those of fellow agents are in danger. A typical punishment involved adding letters of censure to agents' files. But in none of the five cases did a bullet hit anyone.

Critics say the fact that for at least two decades no agent has been disciplined for any instance of deliberately shooting someone raises questions about the credibility of the bureau's internal investigations. Samuel Walker, a professor of criminal justice at the University of Nebraska Omaha who studies internal law enforcement investigations, called the bureau's conclusions about cases of improper shootings "suspiciously low."

Current and former F.B.I. officials defended the bureau's handling of shootings, arguing that the scant findings of improper behavior were attributable to several factors. Agents tend to be older, more experienced and better trained than city police officers. And they generally are involved only in planned operations and tend to go in with "overwhelming presence," minimizing the chaos that can lead to shooting the wrong people, said Tim Murphy, a former deputy director of the F.B.I. who conducted some investigations of shootings over his 23-year career.

The F.B.I.'s shootings range from episodes so obscure that they attract no news media attention to high-profile cases like the 2009 killing of an imam in a Detroit-area warehouse that is the subject of a lawsuit alleging a cover-up, and a 2002 shooting in Maryland in which the bureau paid $1.3 million to a victim and yet, the records show, deemed the shooting to have been justified.

With rare exceptions—like suicides—whenever an agent fires his weapon outside of training, a team of agents from the F.B.I.'s Inspection Division, sometimes with a liaison from the local police, compiles a report reconstructing what happened. This "shooting incident review team" interviews witnesses and studies medical, ballistics and autopsy reports, eventually producing a narrative. Such reports typically do not include whether an agent had been involved in any previous shootings, because they focus only on the episode in question, officials said.

That narrative, along with binders of supporting information, is then submitted to a "shooting incident review group"—a panel of high-level F.B.I. officials in Washington. The panel produces its own narrative as part of a report saying whether the shooting complied with bureau policy—and recommends what discipline to mete out if it did not—along with any broader observations about "lessons learned" to change training or procedures.

F.B.I. officials stressed that their shooting reviews were carried out under the oversight of both the Justice Department's inspector general and the Civil Rights Division, and that local prosecutors have the authority to bring charges.

The 2,200 pages of records obtained by *The Times* include an internal F.B.I. study that compiled shooting episode statistics over a 17-year period, as well as a collection of individual narratives of intentional shootings from 1993 to early 2011. Gunfire was exchanged in 58 such episodes; 9 law enforcement officials died, and 38 were wounded.

The five "bad shoots" included cases in which an agent fired a warning shot after feeling threatened by a group of men, an agent fired at a weapon lying on the ground to disable it during an arrest, and two agents fired their weapons while chasing fugitives but hit no one. In another case, an agent fired at a safe during a demonstration, and ricocheting material caused minor cuts in a crowd of onlookers.

Four of the cases were in the mid-1990s, and the fifth was in 2003.

In many cases, the accuracy of the F.B.I. narrative is difficult to evaluate because no independent alternative report has been produced. As part of the reporting for this article, the F.B.I. voluntarily made available a list of shootings since 2007 that gave rise to lawsuits, but it was rare for any such case to have led to a full report by an independent authority.

Occasionally, however, there were alternative reviews. One, involving a March 2002 episode in which an agent shot an innocent Maryland man in the head after mistaking him for a bank robbery suspect, offers a case study in how the nuances of an F.B.I. official narrative can come under scrutiny.

In that episode, agents thought that the suspect would be riding in a car driven by his sister and wearing a white baseball cap. An innocent man, Joseph Schultz, then 20, happened to cross their path, wearing a white cap and being driven by his girlfriend. Moments after F.B.I. agents carrying rifles pulled their car over and surrounded it, Agent Christopher Braga shot Mr. Schultz in the jaw. He later underwent facial reconstruction surgery, and in 2007 the bureau paid $1.3 million to settle a lawsuit.

The internal review, however, deemed it a good shoot. In the F.B.I.'s narrative, Agent Braga says that he shouted "show me your hands," but that Mr. Schultz instead reached toward his waist, so Agent Braga fired "to eliminate the threat." While one member of the review group said that "after reading the materials provided, he could not visualize the presence of 'imminent danger' to law enforcement officers," the rest of the group voted to find the shooting justified, citing the "totality of the circumstances surrounding the incident," including that it involved a "high-risk stop."

But an Anne Arundel County police detective prepared an independent report about the episode, and a lawyer for Mr. Schultz, Arnold Weiner, conducted a further investigation for the lawsuit. Both raised several subtle but important differences.

For example, the F.B.I. narrative describes a lengthy chase of Mr. Schultz's car after agents turned on their siren at an intersection, bolstering an impression that it was reasonable for Agent Braga to fear that Mr. Schultz was a dangerous fugitive. The narrative spends a full page describing this moment in great detail, saying that the car "rapidly accelerated" and that one agent shouted for it to stop "over and over again." It cites another agent as estimating that the car stopped "approximately 100 yards" from the intersection.

By contrast, the police report describes this moment in a short, skeptical paragraph. Noting that agents said they had thought the car was fleeing, it points out that the car "was, however, in a merge lane and would need to accelerate to enter traffic." Moreover, a crash reconstruction specialist hired for the lawsuit estimated that the car had reached a maximum speed of 12 miles per hour, and an F.B.I. sketch, obtained in the lawsuit, put broken glass from a car window 142 feet 8 inches from the intersection.

The F.B.I. narrative does not cite Mr. Schultz's statement and omits that a crucial fact was disputed: how Mr. Schultz had moved in the car. In a 2003 sworn statement, Agent Braga said that Mr. Schultz "turned to his left, towards the middle of the car, and reached down." But Mr. Schultz insisted that he had instead reached toward the car door on his right because he had been listening to another agent who was simultaneously shouting "open the door."

A former F.B.I. agent, hired to write a report analyzing the episode for the plaintiffs, concluded that "no reasonable F.B.I. agent in Braga's position would reasonably have believed that deadly force was justified." He also noted pointedly that Agent Braga had been involved in a previous shooting episode in 2000 that he portrayed as questionable, although it had been found to be justified by the F.B.I.'s internal review process.

Asked to comment on the case, a lawyer for Agent Braga, Andrew White, noted last week that a grand jury had declined to indict his client in the shooting.

In some cases, alternative official accounts for several other shootings dovetailed with internal F.B.I. narratives.

One involved the October 2009 death of Luqman Ameen Abdullah, a prayer leader at a Detroit-area mosque who was suspected of conspiring to sell stolen goods and was shot during a raid on a warehouse. The F.B.I. report says that Mr. Abdullah got down on the ground but kept his hands hidden, so a dog was unleashed to pull his arms into view. He then pulled out a gun and shot the dog, the report says, and he was in turn shot by four agents.

The Michigan chapter of the Council on American-Islamic Relations filed a lawsuit against the F.B.I. The group was concerned in part because the handgun had no recoverable fingerprints and because of facial injuries to Mr. Abdullah. It also contends that the dog may have been shot instead by the F.B.I. agents and the gun thrown down in a cover-up.

A report by the Michigan attorney general's office, however, detailed an array of evidence that it says "corroborates the statements of the agents as to the sequence of events," including that bullet fragments in the dog's corpse were consistent with the handgun, not the rifles used by the F.B.I. agents. Such an independent account of an F.B.I. shooting is rare. After the recent killing of Mr. Todashev in Orlando, both the Florida chapter of the same group and his father have called for investigators outside the F.B.I. to scrutinize the episode.

James J. Wedick, who spent 34 years at the bureau, said the F.B.I. should change its procedures for its own good.

"At the least, it is a perception issue, and over the years the bureau has had a deaf ear to it," he said. "But if you have a shooting that has a few more complicated factors and an ethnic issue, the bureau's image goes down the toilet if it doesn't investigate itself properly."

Critical Thinking

1. Do you believe that the F.B.I.'s internal investigation should be the only official inquiry into questionable shootings by F.B.I. personnel?

2. If the F.B.I. deems a shooting to have been justified, is paying $1.3 million to the victim also justified?

Create Central

www.mhhe.com/createcentral

Internet References

Democracy Now
   www.democracynow.org/2013/6/21/the_fbis_license_to_kill_agents

Federal Bureau of Investigation (F.B.I.)
   www.fbi.gov/news/updates-on-investigation-into-multiple-explosions-in-boston

Article

Prepared by: Joanne Naughton

Gaming the System: How the Political Strategies of Private Prison Companies Promote Ineffective Incarceration Policies

Learning Outcomes

After reading this article, you will be able to:

- Show the effect of drug laws on the high incarceration rates of the United States.

- Explain some of the factors that contribute to the high incarceration rate in the United States.

- Argue that private prisons contribute to the high American incarceration rate.

Introduction

Approximately 129,000 people were held in privately managed correctional facilities in the United States as of December 31, 2009;[1] 16.4 percent of federal and 6.8 percent of state populations were held in private facilities. Since 2000, private prisons have increased their share of the "market" substantially: the number of people held in private federal facilities increased approximately 120 percent, while the number held in private state facilities increased approximately 33 percent. During this same period, the total number of people in prison increased less than 16 percent. Meanwhile, spending on corrections has increased 72 percent since 1997, to $74 billion in 2007.[2] The two largest private prison companies, Corrections Corporation of America (CCA) and GEO Group, combined had over $2.9 billion in revenue in 2010.[3]

As revenues of private prison companies have grown over the past decade, the companies have had more resources with which to build political power, and they have used this power to promote policies that lead to higher rates of incarceration.

The following are some of the main findings in the Justice Policy Institute's June 2011 report, *Gaming the System: How the Political Strategies of Private Prison Companies Promote Ineffective Incarceration Policies.*

The Players

Today, two companies own and/or operate the majority of for-profit private prisons, with a number of smaller companies running facilities across the country.

Corrections Corporation of America

Founded in 1983, the Corrections Corporation of America (CCA) is the first and largest private prison company in the U.S.[4] In 2010, CCA operated 66 correctional and detention facilities, 45 of which they owned with contracts in 19 states, the District of Columbia and with the three federal detention agencies.[5]

In 2010, CCA saw record revenue of $1.67 billion, up $46 million from 2009.[6] The majority of that revenue (50 percent or $838.5 million) came from state contracts, with 13 percent ($214 million) from the state of California;[7] approximately 10,250 people from the state of California are held in prisons run by CCA.[8] The other significant portion of their revenue was from federal contracts, which accounted for 43 percent of revenue in 2010.

The GEO Group (Formerly Wackenhut Corrections Corporation)

Currently, GEO operates 118 correctional, detention, and residential treatment facilities encompassing approximately 80,600 beds around the world.[9] The U.S. Corrections Business Unit is the company's founding operating unit and accounts for over 60 percent of GEO's total annual revenue.[10] Founded in 1984 under the name Wackenhut Corrections Corporation, the company solidified its first contract with the Bureau of Immigration and Custody Enforcement, in 1987.[11]

As of 2010, GEO contracts with 13 states, the Federal Bureau of Prison, the U.S. Marshals Service, and U.S. Immigration and Customs Enforcement.[12] In 2010, 66 percent ($842 million) of GEO's $1.27 billion in revenue was from U.S. corrections contracts.[13] Of the $842 million in revenue, 47 percent came from corrections contracts with 11 states.[14]

On August 12, 2010 the GEO Group acquired Cornell Companies—a for-profit private prison company with revenues of over $400 million in 2009[15]—in a merger estimated at $730 million.[16] With the acquisition of Cornell by GEO, the majority of private prisons are now under the management of either GEO or CCA.

The Stakes

Over the past 15 years, while the incarceration rate in the U.S. has grown, it has been outpaced by the growth in the number of people placed in private prisons. Due to ineffective criminal justice policies that promote incarceration over more effective alternatives, an increasing need for prison beds has resulted in more private prison contracts and subsequently more revenue for private prison companies as states have less money to pay for the construction of their own prison beds.

However, between 2008 and 2009 the number of people in state prisons declined for the first time in 40 years.[17] While the number of people in federal prisons continues to rise, the decline in the state prison population—private prison companies' largest revenue stream—sets the stage for private prison companies to implement an aggressive, multipronged strategy to ensure their growing revenues.

The Strategy: The Triangle of Private Prison Political Influence

Since private prison contracts are written by state and federal policymakers and overseen by state and federal agency administrators, it is in the best interest of private prison companies to build the connections needed to influence policies related to incarceration. For-profit private prison companies primarily use three strategies to influence policy: lobbying, direct campaign contributions, and building relationships, networks, and associations.[18]

Campaign Donations

By maintaining contacts and favorable ties with policymakers, private prison companies can attempt to shape the debate around the privatization of prisons and criminal justice policy. One way to do that is to make direct, monetary contributions to political campaigns for elected officials and specific policies. These updated figures have emerged in the fall of 2011:

- Since 2000, private prison companies have contributed over $7.2 million to state candidates and political parties.[19]
- Between the 2002 and 2012 election cycles, CCA and GEO's Political Action Committees (PACs) have doled out $1,212,889[20] and $1,010,002[21] respectively to federal parties, candidates and committees.

- Since 2000, private prison companies (CCA, GEO and Cornell Corrections) have given $867,010 —to federal candidates alone.[22]

Lobbying

Similar to other industries, private prison companies employ lobbying firms and lobbyists to advocate for their business interests in Congress and state legislatures. Since private prisons make money from putting people behind bars, their lobbying efforts focus on bills that affect incarceration and law enforcement, such as appropriations for corrections and detention.

Over the last decade, CCA, GEO and Cornell Corrections spent, on average, hundreds of thousands of dollars to employ lobbyists to represent their business interests to federal policymakers. Since 2003, CCA has spent upwards of $900,000 annually on federal lobbying.[23]

- Since 2000, private prison companies (CCA, GEO and Cornell Corrections) have spent over $21 million on federal lobbying efforts with the majority,[24] over $17 million being spent by CCA alone.[25]

Relationships and Associations

Organizational theories about relationships and leadership indicate that individual people influence the operations and behavior of an organization through prior relationships, associations, experiences, and networks.[26] In other words, people bring with them the lens of previous affiliations, and a sense of obligation to represent their world view; they may also be subject to pressure from previous professional relations to act in ways that benefit these relations.

Private prison companies have benefited from their relationships with government officials as evidenced by appointments of former employees to key state and federal positions. The pervasiveness of these connections is evidenced with the recent example from the Kasich Administration in Ohio.

After serving 18 years in the U.S. House of Representatives John Kasich retired in 2000 and took a managing director position in Ohio with Lehman Brothers.[27] Lehman Brothers has a long standing history with private prison companies, spending most of the late 1990s and 2000s before their collapse underwriting bonds and managing credit for both CCA and Cornell.[28] After winning the governorship of Ohio in 2010, Kasich laid out his plans for privatizing state prison operations along with appointing a former CCA employee to head the Ohio Department of Rehabilitation and Correction.[29] Rounding out Kasich's connections to CCA is his close friend and former Congressional chief of staff whose lobbying firm was hired to represent CCA in January 2011.[30]

Losing the Game

When private prison companies are successful at the game of political influence, their profits rise, benefitting their stockholders and top management. However, growing evidence shows that many people lose in this political game at the individual and community levels. The policies that private prison companies promote negatively impact communities in terms of costs and public safety. And the increasing use of private prisons due to rising incarceration rates negatively impacts private prison employees. But the biggest losers in this political game are the people who are taken away from their families and communities due to the policies private prison companies promote to increase the number of people going into prisons and the length of time they spend behind bars.

Recommendations

- States and the federal government should look for real solutions to the problem of growing jail and prison populations.
- Invest in front-end treatment and services in the community, whether private or public.
- Additional research is needed to effectively evaluate the cost and recidivism reduction claims of the private prison industry.

Notes

1. Heather C. West, William J. Sabol, and Sarah J. Greenman, *Prisoners in 2009* (Bureau of Justice Statistics, Washington, DC: 2010). http://bjs.ojp.usdoj.gov/content/pub/pdf/p09.pdf.

2. Camille Graham Camp and George M. Camp, *The Corrections Yearbook, 1997* (South Salem, NY: The Criminal Justice Institute, 1997); Tracey Kyckelhahn, *Justice Expenditure and Employment Extracts 2007,* Table 1 (Washington, DC: Bureau of Justice Statistics, 2010).

3. Corrections Corporation of America, *2010 Annual Report,* 2011; The GEO Group, *2010 Annual Report* (Boca Raton, FL: The GEO Group, 2011). www.geogroup.com/AR_2010/images/Geo_Group-AR2010.pdf.

4. Corrections Corporation of America, "About CCA," November 2010. www.cca.com/about.

5. Corrections Corporation of America, *2010 Annual Report,* 2011.

6. Corrections Corporation of America, *2010 Annual Report,* 2011.

7. Corrections Corporation of America, *2010 Annual Report,* 2011.

8. Corrections Corporation of America, *2010 Annual Report,* 2011.

9. The GEO Group, Inc., "Who We Are," December 2010.

10. The GEO Group, Inc., "Who We Are," December 2010; The GEO Group Inc., *2009 Annual Report* (Boca Raton, FL: The GEO Group, 2010). www.geogroup.com/AR_2009_ClientDL/images/GEO_Group-AR2009.pdf.

11. The GEO Group, Inc., "Historic Milestones," December 2010. www.geogroup.com/history.asp.

12. The GEO Group, Inc., "Federal, State, and Local Partnerships," December 2010. www.geogroup.com/federal-state-local.asp.

13. The GEO Group, *2010 Annual Report,* 2011.

14. Alaska, Louisiana, Virginia, Indiana, Texas, Oklahoma, Mississippi, California, Arizona, New Mexico and Florida; The GEO Group, *2010 Annual Report,* 2011.

15. Cornell Companies, Inc., *2009 Annual Report—Form 10-K* (Washington, DC: U.S. Securities and Exchange Commission, 2010). www.sec.gov/Archives/edgar/data/1016152/000110465910010293/a09-36304_110k.htm#Item15_ExhibitsAndFinancialStatem_125526.

16. The GEO Group, Inc., *The GEO Group Completes Transformational Merger with Cornell Companies* (Boca Raton, FL: 2010). www.thegeogroupinc.com/documents/Merger.pdf.

17. Heather C. West and others, *Prisoners in 2009,* 2010.

18. Brigette Sarabi and Edwin Bender, *The Prison Payoff: The Role of Politics and Private Prisons in the Incarceration Boom* (Portland, OR: Western States Center and the Western Prison Project, 2000).

19. National Institute on Money in State Politics, "Correctional facilities construction & management/for-profit Contributions to All Candidates and Committees," accessed September 28, 2011.

20. Center for Responsive Politics, "CCA 2002–2012 Election Cycle PAC Giving — to Parties, Candidates, and Committees," accessed September 28, 2011. www.opensecrets.org/pacs/lookup2.php?cycle=2012&strID=C00366468.

21. Center for Responsive Politics, "The GEO Group 2002–2012 Election Cycle PAC Giving - to Parties, Candidates, and Committees," accessed September 28, 2011. www.opensecrets.org/pacs/lookup2.php?strID=C00382150.

22. Center for Responsive Politics, "Miscellaneous Business: PAC Contributions to Federal Candidates," accessed September 28, 2011. www.opensecrets.org/pacs/industry.php?txt=N12&cycle=2012.

23. Center for Responsive Politics, "Lobbying Corrections Corp of America—Summary 2010," June 2011. www.opensecrets.org/lobby/clientsum.php?lname=Corrections+Corp+of+America&year=2010.

24. Center for Responsive Politics, "Wackenhut Corp 2000–2003 Annual Federal Lobbying," accessed September 28, 2011. www.opensecrets.org/lobby/clientsum.php?id=D000026342&year=2003; Center for Responsive Politics, "The GEO Group 2004–2011 Annual Federal Lobbying," accessed September 28, 2011. www.opensecrets.org/lobby/clientsum.php?id=D000022003&year=2011; Center for Responsive Politics, "CCA 2000–2011 Annual Federal Lobbying," accessed September 28, 2011. www.opensecrets.org/lobby/clientsum.php?id=D000021940&year=2011; Center for Responsive Politics, "Cornell Companies 2000 and 2006–2010 Annual Federal Lobbying," accessed September 28, 2011. www.opensecrets.org/lobby/clientsum.php?id=D000025148&year=2010.

25. Center for Responsive Politics, "CCA 2000–2011 Annual Federal Lobbying," accessed September 28, 2011. www.opensecrets.org/lobby/clientsum.php?id=D000021940&year=2011.

26. Christine Oliver, "Determinants of Interorganizational Relationships: Integration and Future Directions," *The Academy of Management Review* 15, no. 2 (1990): 241–265.

27. *The New York Times,* "Lehman Hires Kasich," January 11, 2001. www.nytimes.com/2001/01/11/business/lehman-hires-kasich.html.

28. Public Services International Research Unit, *Prison Privatization Report International* (London, England: University of Greenwich, 2001). www.psiru.org/justice/ppri44.asp.

29. Mark Niquette, "Private-prison Consultant Chosen to Run ODRC," *Columbus Dispatch,* January 4, 2011. www.dispatch

Gaming the System: How the Political Strategies of Private Prison Companies Promote Ineffective Incarceration Policies by Unknown

145

.com/live/content/local_news/stories/2011/01/04/
private-prison-consultant-chosen-to-run-ODRC.html.

30. Joe Hallett, "Kasich: Ex-advisers Won't Get Lobbying Favors," *Columbus Dispatch*, February 2, 2011. www.dispatchpolitics .com/live/content/local_news/stories/2011/02/02/copy/ kasich-ex-advisers-wont-get-lobbying-favors.html?adsec= politics&sid=101.

Critical Thinking

1. What effect has the increased political influence of private prison companies had on stockholders top management? On communities?

2. Do you believe there are any alternatives to incarcerating lawbreakers?

Create Central

www.mhhe.com/createcentral

Internet References

American Civil Liberties Union
www.aclu.org/prisoners-rights/private-prisons
Corrections
www.corrections.com/news/article/34534-unprotected-private-prison-personnel-and-civil-liability

Article
Prepared by: Joanne Naughton

Prison Re-entry Programs Help Inmates Leave the Criminal Mindset Behind, but Few Have Access to the Classes

CINDY CHANG

Learning Outcomes

After reading this article, you will be able to:

- Show why inmates should have access to education.
- Discuss some of the re-entry challenges faced by former inmates.

The rats, the roaches, the stabbings and the suicides have never stopped J.C. Alford from coming back. Out of prison for a year or two, then back on a drug charge here, a burglary there—it's a cycle he's been repeating since 1977. More than three decades since his first arrest, he is now 52, sitting in a classroom full of other inmates at Orleans Parish Prison, learning how to leave his criminal ways behind.

"What you been doing while locked up?" Leo Hayden, director of the prison's new re-entry program, asked the class one afternoon in December. "Nuttin'," "Sleep all day," came the answers.

So it has gone for Alford during his stints at the prison, notorious for its poor living conditions. Each time his release date arrived, he was let out on the street, no better than when he entered, perhaps worse for the company he kept—until now.

"All these years I've been coming back here, nobody give a damn about nobody back here," said Alford, a gray knit cap pulled over his head, his beaded necklace and tattoo-covered legs distinguishing him in a sea of orange jumpsuits.

"You know what's different now? You're going back out there with me in your corner," Hayden replied, to applause. One inmate, then another, came up to shake Hayden's hand. No more idleness. Their days are now occupied with coursework: anger management, character-building, job interviewing, computer training, money management, resume writing.

Hayden is like a rock star with this audience of convicted felons, singing of the troubles they've known and how to be a better man. A former NFL running back whose drug habit landed him behind bars for five years, he speaks from hard experience. Sheriff Marlin Gusman brought Hayden down from Chicago to run a 10-week curriculum for prisoners nearing release. For the first time, the hundreds of men serving state time at OPP are targets of a concerted effort to prevent them from ever losing their freedom again.

On Family Night, relatives bring their loved ones' favorite foods and listen to guest speakers. If someone needs an outfit for an interview, Hayden has been known to pull a shirt from his own closet. There are the Hayden-invented mantras that some graduates will repeat to themselves over and over as they face the trials and temptations of life on the outside.

Two months at the tail end of their sentences might be too little, too late. Still, it is something, and many of the men are hungry for second chances. Until Gusman launched the re-entry program a year ago with Hayden and a staff of four, an Orleans Parish Prison inmate was simply shown the door on his release date, after months or years of sitting around with nothing to do. Statewide, 50 percent of ex-cons end up back in prison within five years.

"We're helping people reconnect with their humanity," Hayden said. "If we do that, the killings will stop. People will realize that losing their freedom is not a rite of passage but a sentence to death."

Re-entry Programs Scarce

Louisiana's prison system has a unique and damaging wrinkle. Fewer than half of inmates are housed in state prisons like Angola, Dixon or Hunt. The rest serve out their time in the custody of a sheriff, whether in their home parish or somewhere in rural north Louisiana's prison belt—often so the sheriff can make a profit.

These are the very people who will soon be back on the streets because they are serving less time for less serious crimes. Of the 15,000 prisoners released each year, 11,000 come from local prisons.

All inmates leaving state prisons receive a version of the 10-week re-entry program. While behind bars, they can learn trades such as auto mechanics and welding. Lifers at Angola state penitentiary have ample opportunities to better themselves.

But most in local prisons are not even getting the basic re-entry curriculum, let alone new skills that could help them land a decent job. Louisiana's world-leading incarceration rate—one in 86 adults is behind bars—makes the question of re-entry especially crucial. In New Orleans, the nation's murder capital, one in 14 black men is in state custody, with many more having served time at some point in their lives. At any given time, about 6,600 people in the city are on probation or parole.

Jimmy LeBlanc, head of the Department of Corrections, is a believer in re-entry. He started the re-entry program at Dixon Correctional Center when he was the warden there, and he has made re-entry a centerpiece of his systemwide reform efforts.

Under LeBlanc's plan, the pilot program in Orleans Parish, along with a similar one in Shreveport, will eventually develop into regional re-entry centers, hosting all soon-to-be released inmates from those areas. LeBlanc hopes that, someday, all local prison inmates will graduate from re-entry. But with budget cutbacks, as well as the need for buy-in from every sheriff, the goal remains elusive.

Re-entry has also become a buzz word among New Orleans city officials, who are making room for it in their anti-violence initiatives. More business owners are ready to offer ex-cons what they need most: jobs.

The average education level among Louisiana prison inmates is seventh grade, limiting many to menial, low-paying jobs. In addition to whatever got them in trouble in the first place, they now have the stigma of a criminal record. Usually, the path to success requires avoiding old friends and old haunts.

The obstacles are daunting. But there is increasing recognition that turning miscreants into productive citizens could someday make the city safer.

"They're at this place, 60 miles from nowhere, and we're giving them a timeout," said Arthur Hunter, an Orleans Parish Criminal Court judge who co-founded a re-entry program at the Louisiana State Penitentiary at Angola. "Are they just sitting in a chair and looking at the wall, or is something constructive being done so they won't have to get that timeout again? It goes back to not only being tough and giving them punishment but also being smart as well. Re-entry is being smart. Smart is also cheaper for taxpayers."

'You Can Make a Dent'

Almost two years in, the OPP program is too young to have generated hard statistics. Hayden estimates that about half have found jobs, but it is too soon to tell how many will end up back in prison. There are some who can't be helped, like the four graduates who were murdered in their short time back on the streets.

"When we lose one, it's always a gut check, because the work becomes life and death," Hayden said.

Hunter's Angola program, which he started with another Orleans Parish judge, Laurie White, could be described as the Cadillac of re-entry. About 60 young men who would otherwise be doing their time at OPP have been sent to Angola to learn from reformed lifers who serve as mentors. Participants receive instruction in a trade, such as auto mechanics, plumbing or air-conditioning repair, from fellow inmates.

They are also assigned "social mentors" who know the criminal mindset and counsel the younger men on how to leave it behind. The program may eventually expand, but because of the resources required, its reach is limited.

Lafayette Parish Sheriff Mike Neustrom is one of the few Louisiana sheriffs who has made rehabilitating inmates a priority. He devotes about $2.5 million of his annual budget to an array of educational, substance abuse and mental-health services that begin as soon as a person is sentenced. Neustrom said he believes the investment is worth it because it will ultimately result in less crime.

"The bottom line is, most of them are going to come back to Lafayette—it's where they grew up," he said. "If they're better when they come back, that's good. That's the hope. That's the intent."

Gusman, the Orleans Parish sheriff, sees Lafayette as a model, but one that may be out of reach. More than money, he needs space. His annual re-entry budget of $500,000 could accommodate more students, but the makeshift classrooms can only hold so many at a time. The current plan for a new FEMA-funded prison calls for a drastically downsized facility that may not have much space for education programs such as re-entry. A recent move to temporary quarters doubled re-entry from 90 to 200 inmates. Others, such as violent offenders, do not qualify for the program at all, even though they, too, will soon be back on the streets of New Orleans.

"We're doing the right thing. I think we need to do more, offer more and invest more resources," Gusman said. "Real evil people? I don't see them here."

For those who work with parolees and are used to seeing the same names reappear on their rolls, the positive impact of re-entry is a given. After LeBlanc started the Dixon program, parole officers noticed a difference: A person released from Dixon was more likely to beat the odds and turn his life around.

Many of those who end up incarcerated again have not committed new crimes but have merely violated the conditions of their parole. Staying out of trouble also includes keeping appointments, cutting ties with other convicted felons and not going near drugs or alcohol—some of the same "soft skills" emphasized in the re-entry curriculum.

"You can make a dent," Frank Palestina, head of probation and parole for the New Orleans district, said of re-entry. "Focus on not having anything—like I said, inmate in, inmate out. I'm telling you, my first 10 years, '91 to '01, these people didn't change. . . . How can you change when you're not adding any new ingredients?"

Getting a Chance

"How many of you guys truly think that you are a bad person?" Hayden asked the class.

"In other's eyesight, there's always going to be judgment," one inmate responded. "The things you've done are always going to be there. You this, you that, you going to be there forever. I don't feel like I'm a bad person myself, but the rest of the world is going to feel that way."

It was the perfect lead-in to one of Hayden's favorite maxims: "Living justly in an unjust world." You may have been dealt a bad hand, but you need to stop blaming others and make the best of it.

"When they view us as felons, that's when we need to be our most gracious, our most intelligent, our most committed, to dispel all those myths about us, to be the most human," Hayden said. "They'll give you a chance."

Victor McGill, 42, serving time for forgery, was not content with making do. He seized on Hayden's use of the word "chance." Why aren't there vocational programs in prison, so we can learn a trade and have a better chance of becoming productive members of society? he asked.

The class applauded. Hayden explained that he is doing the best he can with limited resources. He described the bulletin board in his office, which is covered with the business cards he requests from every single person he meets—his doctor, a visiting journalist—on the off chance of procuring a job for an ex-con. Then he laid out the challenges, without sugar coating.

"The problem is, the economy is at rock bottom. I know there are college students looking for the same jobs," Hayden said. "We've got to be real creative. What's going to keep me from hiring the college student? I don't know. We've got to figure it out and make you competitive, gentlemen, make you somebody that somebody wants to hire."

One man asked about work release—with the limited slots in the city, could they be shipped up north to gain a foothold in the workforce there? Hayden noted that most of the guys in the room were not even eligible for work release.

A morale boost arrived a few minutes later. Hayden pulled out a turquoise jumpsuit emblazoned on the back with the word "Re-entry." He had finagled a few hundred dollars so the students could take pride in their uniforms, a cut above the usual prison orange.

"Don't forget us, Mr. Leo!" several called as Hayden left.

'Don't Stop, Don't Give Up'

As Hayden pointed out, it is a tough world for ex-cons, made even tougher by the slow economy. At the Community Service Center in Uptown, tales of woe from former prisoners are common, despite the help with housing and job placement they receive from the small nonprofit. Several said they were homeless.

Elbert Best, 45, served two years for theft and aggravated flight from a police officer, actions he says were brought on by a substance-abuse problem. He started at LaSalle Correctional, a privately run prison near Jena, before being transferred to the custody of the Madison Parish sheriff. He says the move cost him a chance at a work-release job, which could have gotten him back on his feet. He was willing to consider relocating up north if that job had led to a permanent offer.

In seven months living with his mother and young daughter in Gentilly, Best sent out numerous job applications. Despite two decades of experience in the hospitality industry, he did not get a single interview, a failure he attributes in part to his criminal record. Patience and perseverance are a must. In January,

he moved to Connecticut to try his luck there, and he is now employed as a restaurant cook.

"Don't stop, don't give up," he said. "Even if you may have several doors closed and you're on the brink of giving up, one of those doors might open."

As part of a growing citywide re-entry initiative, the New Orleans Business Council is recruiting companies willing to employ ex-offenders. But the solution is not as simple as providing jobs, said Dwayne Bernal, president of Royal Engineering, who is coordinating the Business Council effort. The thousands of former prisoners living in New Orleans also need help with housing, transportation and mental health issues, or they will revert to their old ways.

"You can't distance yourself from them. They're not on an island and you can expect them not to exist," Bernal said. "If you don't provide that opportunity, you will see recidivism."

Success Story

Kevin Payton is one success story to come out of Orleans Parish Prison re-entry. At 44, he has racked up six convictions on burglary, theft and drug charges.

His re-entry instructors advised him to make a detailed game plan for his first days on the outside, and he followed it to the letter. Mock job interviews gave him confidence to face real employers. Within days, he had secured a position at a restaurant on the Riverwalk from a manager willing to give him a chance. On weekends, he waited tables. During the week, he loaded a chicken boat. He recently started a new job at a concrete plant in eastern New Orleans.

He is slowly earning back the trust he lost with his relatives, who used to hide their wallets and car keys from him. Now, he shares a car with his mother and mows her lawn in his spare time. He has a steady girlfriend, instead of splitting his time among "three or five" women.

He often recites one of Hayden's mantras: To stay out of trouble, he must change "people, places and things." He still keeps the journal he started while in re-entry. Recently, he returned to the prison on Broad Street, neatly dressed in a button-down shirt and jeans, not as a convict, but as an inspirational speaker for the class.

"Look at me, I'm a big old boy, I'm going to work in the morning and coming back tired," Payton told his former cohorts. "I'm not running from the police. There ain't nobody kicked my momma's door in looking for me."

Critical Thinking

1. Since most people who are incarcerated are eventually released, what purposes should incarceration serve?
2. What makes the question of re-entry especially crucial in Louisiana?

Create Central

www.mhhe.com/createcentral

Internet References

PBS

www.pbs.org/wnet/religionandethics/2013/01/11/january-11-2013-prisons-for-profit/14485

United States Department of Justice

www.justice.gov/archive/fbci/progmenu_reentry.html

CINDY CHANG can be reached at cchang@timespicayune.com or 504.826.3386.

Article   Prepared by: Joanne Naughton

War on Drugs Failure Gives Way to Treatment in States, Cities

SAKI KNAFO

Learning Outcomes

After reading this article, you will be able to:

- Discuss some of the new alternative ways of dealing with drug law offenders.
- Describe what has happened in Texas as a result of reforms enacted by lawmakers.

Four years ago, police officers and prosecutors in Seattle decided they'd had enough of the usual ways of fighting the war on drugs.

The police were tired of arresting the same drug users and prostitutes again and again, and the prosecutors had run out of money to keep putting people in jail. So the police department, the prosecutor's office, and the city's elected leaders decided to try something radically different.

With the approval of Seattle prosecutors and politicians, the police began directing repeat drug offenders to social-service workers who offered to help them pay for rent and school and referred them to business owners who were willing to hire people with criminal backgrounds.

The police weren't entirely hopeful that the strategy would pan out. But with a growing number of neighborhood leaders and business owners demanding safer, quieter streets, they had little choice but to try something new.

Today, their doubts are giving way to a growing confidence that they're onto something significant. "People we've dealt with over and over and over again are getting treatment and getting into housing and getting jobs," said Lt. Deanna Nollette, a supervisor in the police department. "It's a pretty big surprise."

"Law Enforcement Assisted Diversion," or LEAD, as the public-safety strategy is known in Seattle, is just one of a fast-growing number of alternatives to the traditional "tough on crime" approach that has defined America's drug war for four decades. Lawmakers throughout the country have increasingly turned to these strategies to deflect the steep costs of incarcerating the soaring population of drug offenders.

Some of these alternatives are more punitive than others, and policy experts and prison-reform advocates disagree on the best way to treat drug offenders. But taken as a whole, these alternatives represent a major shift in America's response to illegal drug use.

"As someone who has been in this now for 25 years, and thought that change was glacial, never mind incremental, what has happened recently is extraordinary," said Howard Josepher, the founder of Exponents, a 25-year-old drug-abuse treatment program in New York City.

In Texas, legislators have sharply increased investments in treatment programs and in drug courts—specialized judicial systems whose judges can order drug offenders to undergo treatment as an alternative to jail. In California, where the prisons are so crowded that the state has been ordered by a federal court to reduce the prison population by thousands of inmates, counties have been granted an expanded role in deciding whether to lock up low-level offenders or connect them with drug counselors. From New York to Arkansas to Florida, states have seen their prison populations decline after years of growth.

The burgeoning availability of these alternatives is largely born out of necessity. Since the mid-1970s, when lawmakers first began enacting tough anti-drug policies that have collectively come to be known as the "war on drugs," the number of people behind bars has increased fivefold, peaking at 2.2 million in 2010. Drug offenses accounted for much of the surge. From 1980 to 2010, the number of those incarcerated on drug charges shot up from 41,000 to more than a half-million.

Criminal justice advocates have long decried the punitive laws behind this trend, stressing the disproportionately heavy toll exacted on racial and ethnic minorities, who make up more than 60 percent of the prison population, despite using drugs and committing crimes at a rate similar to whites.

But only in recent years have lawmakers thrown their weight behind serious reform efforts. And while most of these calls for changes have come from statehouses and county headquarters, federal government officials have begun adding their voices to the chorus of reformers. In recent months, members of Congress from both parties have teamed up to introduce legislation that would reduce penalties for nonviolent drug offenders. And last week, in what has widely been hailed as a historic announcement, Attorney General Eric Holder declared that the Justice Department would do its part to cut down on severe sentences for those convicted of nonviolent drug crimes.

Some of the most striking changes have unfolded in places not always associated with progressive reforms. In Texas, for example, lawmakers have cut billions of dollars from the prison system, while investing hundreds of millions in drug courts and in counseling programs that aim to help people recover from drug addictions and get their lives under control. Proponents point out that the changes haven't reversed the state's decades of declining crime rates:

From 2007, the first year of the shift, to 2011, the most recent year for which detailed data is available, the number of violent crimes in Texas dropped by nearly 20,000, and property crimes fell by five times as much. The state authorized the closing of one prison in 2011 and two more this year.

In Georgia, meanwhile, where 1 out of every 13 adults are either on probation, parole, or behind bars, lawmakers have passed a reform package that expands the state's treatment programs, drug courts, and the use of electronic monitoring as an substitute for prison time. States that include South Carolina and Kansas have adopted similar measures.

Not everyone is on board with these changes, however. "Probably the biggest obstacle to these reforms is what I would call establishment politicians and officeholders, and this really means on the left or on the right," said Vikrant Reddy, a policy analyst with the conservative Texas Public Policy Foundation in Austin. "I think there are still politicians who haven't broken free of the thinking of the past. They don't seem to understand that there has been a sea change among American voters, who don't always feel that incarceration is the best tack when it comes to what we do about low-level nonviolent crime."

Another obstacle to the universal adoption of these reforms is the continued scarcity of funding for programs that treat addiction. "There aren't a lot of open slots," said Doug McVay, a drug policy expert and the editor of the online book *Drug War Facts.* "And we've chosen to put money into cleaning up the mess, rather than trying to make things better so that there isn't a mess in the first place."

Yet, for those in the growing ranks of reformers—a loose alliance that spans the political spectrum from former House Speaker Newt Gingrich (R) to California Lt. Gov. Gavin Newsom (D)—the debate is no longer over whether to change the country's drug policies, but how. At the center of the conversation is the proliferation of drug courts. While conservatives and many liberals see the expansion of these courts as key to reform, libertarians and some on the left say society's response to drug abuse should take place outside the courthouse altogether.

Seattle's LEAD program, some reformers say, could prove to be a pioneering example of how police departments can help accomplish this goal. Although results from a study of the program aren't finished, cities from San Francisco to New York have already reached out to the program's supervisors for guidance.

Lisa Daugaard, a longtime public defender and one of the program's coordinators, likened LEAD to a drug court "without the stigma and costs of court involvement." Unlike most drug courts, she said, the program doesn't require participants to stay off drugs or even seek treatment. "LEAD is not only for people who are involved in drug activities because of addiction," she noted. "Some are involved for a wage."

About half the program's participants end up accepting some form of treatment, but they do so voluntarily, Daugaard said, without facing any pressure from judges or prosecutors. "It's not that we're indifferent about people moving toward sobriety," she said. "It's that requiring that is not the best way to engage people."

Levi Hoagland, a 34-year-old former high school football star who is preparing to end his year-long stay at a California rehabilitation center, can see the advantages of both the drug court system and the less punitive approach championed by the likes of Daugaard. Several years ago, while suffering from mental breakdown brought on by a methamphetamine binge, he deliberately rammed his car into a parked van and ended up in jail, where he agreed to enter a substance-abuse treatment program under the supervision of a drug court judge.

Some of the more hardened criminals in the jail scoffed at the idea, Hoagland said. But he was ready for a change.

"I couldn't listen to a guy who's got the word 'guilty' tattooed across his back," Hoagland said.

Now, as he gets ready to assimilate back into the outside world, he is wary of the obstacles faced by those who have run afoul of the criminal justice system. Like many other Californians, Hoagland is ineligible for food stamps because of the state's lifetime ban on applicants with past felony convictions, and he's concerned about how his past may look to prospective employers.

Still, it was his brush with the criminal justice system that caused him to seek treatment. And getting sober, he said, has been the "miracle of my life."

"I have two beautiful children and they used to be the most important thing in the world to me, but that's changed," Hoagland said. "The most important thing for me today is to stay clean and sober, and that allows me to be a dad to somebody."

Critical Thinking

1. What has been the experience of Seattle with their new policy?
2. Does incarcerating drug law violators work?

Create Central

www.mhhe.com/createcentral

Internet References

Drug War Facts
  http://drugwarfacts.org/cms/Drug_Courts#sthash.1OivuGaF.dpbs
National Association of Drug Court Professionals
  www.nadcp.org/Drug%20Courts%20Are%20the%20Most%20
  Sensible%20and%20Proven%20Alternative%20to%20Incarceration
National Institute of Justice
  www.crimesolutions.gov/ProgramDetails.aspx?ID=89

Article Prepared by: Joanne Naughton

Addressing Gender Issues among Staff in Community Corrections

KELLI D. STEVENS

Learning Outcomes

After reading this article, you will be able to:

- Indicate the kinds of problems facing women in the workforce.
- Explain the difference between sexual harassment and gender discrimination.

Gender-responsiveness research in the criminal justice field has increased during the past decade as professionals learn more about differences between male and female offenders: their unique pathways to crime, their varying needs and gender-specific strategies to reduce crime. Gender responsiveness is also relevant to female professionals in community corrections because organizations need to recognize and address the needs of women in the workplace. While community corrections organizations are actively addressing the needs of female offenders, they are still struggling to meet the needs of female professionals working in the field.

Female Offenders in the System

The number of women under correctional supervision has increased significantly during the past several decades, but the policies addressing the criminality of women and how they are treated in the criminal justice system have not kept pace. Researchers have explored "gendered justice" and found most women in the criminal justice system are charged with nonviolent offenses and do not pose a serious risk to public safety.[1] The increase in the incarceration rate of women has been influenced by structural and social causes of crime that have been largely ignored, while focusing on risk models based on male characteristics and male criminality.[2]

Meda Chesney-Lind found that women have a high rate of technical violations while under community supervision, but strategies for dealing with technical violators are based on male criminality and do not generally take into account the needs of women.[3] Ann Jacobs proposes a matrix model of addressing the needs of women under community supervision

that includes recognizing challenges women face (poverty, substance abuse, homelessness, at-risk children and chronic physical and mental illness); developing a life plan within the domains of subsistence, residence, children and family, health, mental health and sobriety, and criminal justice compliance; and taking into consideration the degree of functionality of the individual.[4]

Prominent researchers in the field of gender issues in the criminal justice system developed six guiding principles to help organizations effectively supervise female offenders:

- Acknowledge that gender makes a difference;
- Create an environment based on safety, respect and dignity;
- Develop policies, practices and programs that are relational and promote healthy connections to children, family, significant others and the community;
- Address substance abuse, trauma and mental health issues through comprehensive, integrated and culturally relevant services, and appropriate supervision;
- Provide women with opportunities to improve their socioeconomic conditions; and
- Establish a system of community supervision and reentry with comprehensive, collaborative services.[5]

Gender issues, however, do not only apply to the inmates; community corrections agencies also need to consider the gender issues that may be affecting their staff.

Women in the Work Force

Women continue to face sexual harassment and gender discrimination, including disparity in pay—a phenomenon known as the "motherhood penalty"—and lack of promotional opportunities.

Sexual Harassment

Sexual harassment is defined as "unwelcome sexual advances, requests for sexual favors, and other verbal or physical conduct of a sexual nature."[6] Examination of gender proportions on sexual harassment situations in the workplace has shown sexual harassment is more common in workgroups where males are the majority because these contexts reinforce traditional sex roles.[7] The sex-role spillover theory explains that men are more likely to behave in a manner consistent with their social roles of being aggressive when they are in male-skewed workgroups than when they are in female-skewed workgroups.[8] As more women have entered the field of community corrections and provided a balance in the workgroup composition, sexual harassment complaints have decreased and working conditions seem to have improved during the past several decades. However, problems still exist.

Gender Discrimination

Women continue to experience gender discrimination in the modern workplace. According to the U.S. Department of Labor, the average weekly salary of women in 2008 was only 81 percent of that of men.[9] Despite the fact that 43.6 percent of women comprised the full-time work force in 2005, women made up only 31 percent of workers in the highest earnings category. Scholarly research supports the "motherhood penalty," which posits mothers earn less than their male counterparts. Having two to four children can decrease a woman's wages from 4 percent to 8 percent.[10] The opposite—the "fatherhood premium"[11]—has been shown to be true for males. In light of the U.S. Department of Labor statistics regarding the disparity in pay between men and women in similar positions, and a plethora of empirical research supporting gender discrimination regarding pay scales and promotional opportunities, community corrections organizations need to examine their current compensation structures and promotional processes to bring those in line with current gender-responsive strategies.

Commitment

Gender biases are manifested in a variety of contexts within organizations. Research has shown that gender bias is present in perceptions of commitment to the organization.[12] Commitment has been associated with lower absenteeism, lower turnover rates and increased intention to stay with the agency.[13] However, when examining these issues as they pertain to women employed in community corrections organizations, problems become evident. Women may often be the primary caregiver for their children, parents or other family members, which can explain absenteeism, but does not mean they are less committed to their jobs than their male counterparts. Because of the nature of community corrections and requirements for supervising offenders, when an employee is absent, the absence impacts his or her co-workers more so than a traditional office job. Turnover rates and perceived lack of intention to remain at one community corrections agency throughout their entire career does not translate into women being less valuable to the organization. Rather, an array of other social and structural factors could be at play. The increase in the number of single parents, increase in costs for child care, lack of child care options, and lack of equal pay and opportunities for women are explanations largely ignored.

The Glass Ceiling

The glass ceiling effect refers to a form of inequality where artificial obstacles hinder the advancement of women and minorities, and where the obstacles are more severe at higher occupational levels.[14] Women may be in positions close enough to the top levels of administration in community corrections organizations, but still more men than women are in top-ranking positions. Advancement opportunities have improved for women in community corrections, but organizations should continue to strive toward global gender-responsiveness strategies.

Organizational Politics

Organizational politics play a key role in power structures and even in informal interactions. Women in community corrections organizations can, and do, experience gendered organizational politics. Although not always overt, these politics can be masculine in nature, which can act as a barrier to their careers due to political activity being "linked to the performance, achievement and maintenance of power."[15] Formal internal policies, procedures and practices of an organization can create separations along gender lines, vertically and horizontally, whereby men hold the majority of top positions of power; the language used within the organization can promote gendered divisions (men as actors, women as supporters); and employees might accept these divisions as part of the organizational culture.[16]

These divisions become useful for men in the arena of promotions and career advancement, as there tends to be more informal and formal mentorship for male employees through the organizational politics of some community corrections organizations.

Improving Institutional Practices

The term "evidence-based practices" is used quite frequently today by community corrections professionals, but how many organizations are actually implementing and breathing life into this concept? Community corrections agencies at all levels—federal, state and local—have provided and continue to provide training to staff regarding evidence-based practices in relation to supervising the offender population. Additionally, community corrections organizations have recognized the importance of implementing programs and services grounded in empirical research to improve offender outcomes. However, it is yet to be determined how this principle has migrated into other aspects of operating a community corrections organization: hierarchical structures, communication practices, organizational culture, recruitment practices, training and on-boarding of new staff, retention of current staff, management and leadership practices, and gender responsivity.

Community corrections has placed importance on evidence-based practices and understanding what motivates offenders. The empirical research discussed throughout this article and the proposed guiding principles for implementing gender-responsive strategies for female offenders also can be applied to address gender issues for female professionals in community corrections.

Gender Matters

Agencies need to analyze their recruitment and hiring procedures, written policies and procedures, informal policies and practices, mentoring programs for staff and promotional opportunities as they relate to women. For example, do written policies default to using gender-specific descriptors (e.g., he or his), where the majority of employees are women? Or are job descriptions gender-neutral, excluding overall gender biases and gender-biased language? Staff retention and succession planning are critical issues in recruiting, developing and retaining experienced employees, so it is time to address gender issues in the community corrections work force.

Gender and Organizational Environment

Create an environment based on safety, respect and dignity. Are policies relating to the safety of female officers gender biased? Does the agency's policy relating to field work only allow for female officers to conduct home visits on female offenders, and male officers to conduct home visits on male offenders? Or do women have to take a field partner with them while doing field work? In some situations this is appropriate, but blanket policies such as this are discriminatory. A less discriminatory policy would be to account for the safety issues through self-defense training, nonlethal weapons training and ethics policies rather than limiting the jobs based on gender.

Another recommendation in this area is to provide all employees with clear sexual harassment policies and take appropriate action when such complaints are made. Considering that one out of four girls will suffer from sexual violence during their lifetime,[17] this means that a portion of the female community corrections professionals have suffered sexual abuse. Employers have a responsibility to ensure they are providing appropriate work environments for all employees and understand sexual harassment in the workplace could further traumatize victims of sexual abuse.

Relationships

The organizational culture should be inclusive of informal networking opportunities and formal mentoring programs for women wanting to advance in the organization—absent of masculine-oriented organizational politics. The "relational principles women bring to the environment can have mutually beneficial consequences for multiple stakeholders"[18] (including probationers, victims, judges and the community). Because women place high importance on relationships, community corrections organizations should allow for flexibility to maintain important relationships so as not to penalize staff for maintaining these relationships. This will maximize benefits for employees and the organization.

A System of Community and Collaboration

Does the organization have a fair representation of women on important committees tasked with making important decisions or recommending substantial changes within the organization? "Because women in the workplace help build connections rather than hierarchies,"[19] fostering collaborative relationships will improve organizational functioning.

Community corrections organizations that truly embrace evidence-based practices should turn to the research available on gender responsivity not only regarding effectively managing their female offender populations, but also to glean ideas for how to appropriately respond to the needs of women in the workplace. Some strides have already been made in this area. For example, there has been an increase in the number of special trainings regarding gender-responsiveness strategies for female offenders, professional organizations sponsoring focus groups and publications dedicated to women's issues, and leadership training for women.

Notes

1. Greenfeld, L.A. and T.L. Snell. 1999. *Women offenders.* Washington, D.C.: Bureau of Justice Statistics.

2. Covington, S.S. and B.E. Bloom. 2003. *Gendered justice: Women in the criminal justice system.* Durham, N.C.: Carolina Academic Press.

3. Chesney-Lind, M. 1998. The forgotten offender, women in prison: From partial justice to vengeful equity. *Corrections Today,* 60(7):66–73. Alexandria, Va.: American Correctional Association.

4. Jacobs, A.L. 2005. Improving the odds: Women in community corrections. *Women, Girls & Criminal Justice,* 6(5):65–80. New York: Women's Prison Association.

5. Bloom, B., B. Owen and S. Covington. 2003. *Gender-responsive strategies: Research, practice, and guiding principles for women offenders.* Washington, D.C.: U.S. Department of Justice, National Institute of Corrections.

6. Equal Employment Opportunity Commission. 1980. Guidelines on discrimination because of sex. *Federal Register,* 45:74676–74677. Washington, D.C.: U.S. Equal Employment Opportunity Commission.

7. Burian, B.K., B.J. Yanico and C.R. Martinez. 1998. Group gender composition effects on judgments of sexual harassment. *Psychology of Women Quarterly,* 22(3):465–480. Hoboken, N.J.: John Wiley & Sons Inc.

   Fitzgerald, L.F., F. Drasgow, C.L. Hulin, M.J. Gelfand and V.J. Magley. 1997. Antecedents and consequences of sexual harassment in organizations: A test of an integrated model. *Journal of Applied Psychology,* 82(4):578–589. Washington, D.C.: American Psychological Association.

   Gutek, B.A. 1985. *Sex and the workplace.* San Francisco: Jossey Bass.

   Gutek, B.A., A.G. Cohen and A.M. Konrad. 1990. Predicting social-sexual behavior at work: A contact hypothesis. *Academy of Management Journal,* 33(3):560–577. Briarcliff Manor, N.Y.: Academy of Management.

8. Goldberg, C.B. 2001. The impact of the proportion of women in one's workgroup, profession, and friendship circle on males' and females' responses to sexual harassment. *Sex Roles,* 45(5–6):359–374. New York: Springer.

9. U.S. Department of Labor. 2009. *Highlights of women's earnings in 2008.* Washington, D.C.: U.S. Bureau of Labor Statistics.

10. Glauber, R. 2007. Marriage and the motherhood wage penalty among African Americans, Hispanics, and whites. *Journal of*

Marriage and Family, 69:951–961. Malden, Mass.: Blackwell Publishing.

11. Glauber, R. 2008. Race and gender in families and at work: The fatherhood wage premium. *Gender and Society,* 22:8–30. Kingston, R.I.: Sociologists for Women in Society.

12. Bailyn, L. 1993. *Breaking the mold: Women, men and time in the new corporate world.* New York: The Free Press.

   Voydanoff, P. 1987. *Work and family life.* Newbury Park, Calif.: Sage.

13. Angle, H. and J. Perry. 1981. An empirical assessment of organizational commitment and organizational effectiveness. *Administrative Science Quarterly,* 26(1):1–14. Ithaca, N.Y.: Johnson Graduate School of Management at Cornell University.

   Mowday, R.T., L.W. Porter and R.M. Steers. 1979. *Employee-organization linkages: The psychology of commitment, absenteeism, and turnover.* New York: Academic Press.

14. Maume, D.J. 2004. Is the glass ceiling a unique form of inequality?: Evidence from a random-effects model of managerial attainment. *Work and Occupations,* 31(2):250–274. Thousand Oaks, Calif.: Sage Publications.

15. Davey, Kate Mackenzie. 2008. Women's accounts of organizational politics as a gendering process. *Gender, Work and Organization,* 15(6):650–671. Malden, Mass.: Wiley-Blackwell.

16. Acker, J. 1998. The future of "gender and organizations": Connections and boundaries. *Gender, Work and Organization,* 5(4):195–206. Staffordshire, United Kingdom: Wiley-Blackwell.

17. Centers for Disease Control and Prevention. 2007. *Understanding sexual violence fact sheet.* Retrieved from www.cdc.gov/ncipc/pub-res/images/SV%20Factsheet.pdf.

18. Fletcher, J.K. 1999. *Disappearing acts: Gender, race and relational practice at work.* Cambridge, Mass.: Massachusetts Institute of Technology.

19. Ibid.

Critical Thinking

1. When supervising female offenders in the community, how does their gender make a difference?
2. How does gender affect women who work in corrections?

Create Central

www.mhhe.com/createcentral

Internet References

National Center for Biotechnolgy Information
   www.ncbi.nlm.nih.gov/books/NBK64123
Western Criminolgy Review
   http://wcr.sonoma.edu/v08n1/16.lambert/lambert.pdf